Girljock

Also by Roxxie

Co-editor:

Dagger: On Butch Women

Girljock

the book

edited by
Roxxie

St. Martin's Press
New York

Design by: Junie Lee

Visit the Stonewall Inn website at *http://www.stonewallinn.com*

Library of Congress Cataloging-in-Publication Data
Girljock : the book / edited by Roxxie.
p.   cm.
Anthology of articles originally published in Girljock magazine.
ISBN 0-312-15134-9
1. Lesbian athletes. I. Roxxie. II. Girljock.
GV708.6.G574   1998
796'.086'643—DC21   96-47871
CIP

First Stonewall Inn Edition: July 1998
10 9 8 7 6 5 4 3 2 1

This book is dedicated to Leah Marglous Thein,
whose bowling trophies were too numerous to count
and who always kept a special drawer of pens and paper waiting for me.

"Jog on, Jog on, the foot-path way,
and merrily hent the stile-a,
a merry heart goes all the day,
your sad tires in a mile-a."
—William Shakespeare

"Fuck *The Well of Loneliness.*
Good-bye to all that.
We're here to have fun."
—*Girjock* Magazine's Motto

CONTENTS

ACKNOWLEDGMENTS

This book could not have been composed without the assistance of the following people, so, thank you: Rachel Reily, Bonnie Rosen, Doris and Bud Nugent, Amy Cheney, Alexis Gannon, Ben Brody, Kathleen Bonnet, Peggy Sue Teising, Zane Tlapek, Keith Kahla, Mikel Wadewitz, and Susan Fox Rogers. Special thanks to photographer Phyllis Christopher for her help in selecting the photographs and illustrations for this book.

Also, special thanks to the inspiration from memories of my grandmother Leah Marglous Thein, and also the memories of my dear friends Jason Lazzeri, Tom Shearer, Sara Deerheart Woolery, and Nat Pearson.

Special thanks to the following Girljock supporters: Maria Vetrano, Lisa Garcia, Michelle Rau, Stacey Foss, Daniel Bao, Jennie Van Heuit, Joan Hilty, Nigel French, Shar Rednour, Angela Bocage, The men from DPN, Andy Hsiao, Jeff Z. Klein, Suzanne Reid, Elissa Perry, Cassie Coleman, Nancy Boutilier, Ted Soqui, Susie McCormick, Rodney Dunican, Canterbury Press, Lauren Eliot and Jane White, Lyanne Lyanderthal Monique Oblivia Chopin Miller, Marilyn Carino, Sofia Ramos, Lorraine Artinger, Trina Robbins, Cristi Delgado, Donna Z., Kevin Sawad Brooks, Christina Smith, Robin Stevens, Sharon Cho, Tracy Dean, Harumi Kubo, Diana Jacobs, Linnea Due, Anne Butigan, Karen Bowen, Joyce Gianera, Angie Denis, Alison Gallant, Laura Miller, Daphne Gottlieb, Caitlin Groom, Mo Phalon, Emily Chang, Maryanne Carter, Page, Romy Kozak, Stephanie Rosenbaum, Gina Fields, Susan Fox Rogers, Cherie Bombardier, Pam Russell, Doug Schmidt, Lisa Brown, Jayne Keene, Leisa Fearing, Terry Sapp, Daniel Rosen, Jackie Weltman, Sunah Cherwin, Cheela Smith, Zeke Paradock, Stafford, Lucija Kordic, Marguerite Lutton, Vicki Randle, Downtown Donna, Susie Bright, Lea Delaria, Gretchen Phillips, Alexa Wilke, Lily Burana, Robin Simmons, Norma Ramos, Joan Lipkin, Michelle Tea and Sini Anderson, Liz Zivic, Kate Sorensen, Sabrino Alonso, Louis Rosen, Sternie Kissin-Rosen, and everyone else who has contributed time and effort to this publication.

SIGNS OF BEING A GIRLJOCK

There is a line you cross over. The rest of the world ceases to exist and the only thing left is an event, an action. The fly ball to catch, the open goal waiting for the ball at your feet, or the tennis ball suspended in air the second before you smack into it.

If your diary, like mine at age seventeen, has ever had a note: *Every damn day I play volleyball for two hours.* (Fill in the sport of your choice, but the sentiment remains the same.)

If you know the word "peak" doesn't just mean the top of a mountain but the top of a mountain of training.

If the word interval has a stopwatch attached to it.

If you can remember finding a rhythm, like a clockwork rhythm of fielding, in a sport.

If your sports uniform feels like a normal part of your skin.

If someone asks you to identify yourself on their pager by your jersey number.

If you ever wished to be taller, just so you'd be a better_____ player.

If, no matter your age, you wish you still had recess every afternoon and could head to the playground to move about, stretch, and play sports.

If any of the above describes you, then you may be a Girljock. But these are only *some* of the signs.

What is [a] Girljock?

THE GIRLJOCK STATE OF MIND

jock (jok) n. (slang) an athlete.

girl (gurl) n. 1. a female child. 2. a young woman 3. (informal) a woman of any age, a woman assistant or employee. (> considered offensive by many people in this definition).

"What is a Girljock? Or who?" wrote Amy Cheney in *Girljock's* second issue, in the initial essay establishing herself as Dear Femme Jock, *Girljock's* answerwoman.

I knew the girl who asked me to write something about lesbians and sports was a girljock. She was butch. She had dark curly hair. Her jeans fit perfectly across her solid thighs. She could have been wearing a jockstrap. But I don't think she was. So where did that leave me? It left me wondering.

I have a black lace Jogbra. I've got black Lycra that clings to my curves with a hot pink slash from my knee to my ass. I've got a bathing suit with a cap to match. My biking shorts are zebra-striped. I'm happy. I have accessories. I'm a Femme Jock, not a Femme bot. My idea of exercise used to be a brisk chat (as JoAnne Loulan says, much as I'd like to have said it myself). But now, with all these accessories . . . I have places to go, butches to meet. There's nothing quite so intimate as sweating together, breathing hard, in a public place. There's nothing quite so satisfying as a hot shower, sauna, and terry towel rub afterward. And food tastes better when you are a girljock. Haven't you noticed?

MYTHICAL ATTRIBUTES OF WOMEN (LESBIAN AND STRAIGHT) IN SPORTS

Our society has cooked up a bunch of myths about sportswomen, and sportswomen face them every day. One common misconception about women in sports is that sports breed lesbians. If so, then the modern lesbian

  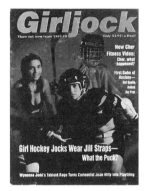

movement would have descended out of women's field hockey. Nice thought, right? Radical lesbian activists with hockey sticks and big muscles. While that might describe some activists, women's field hockey has only given birth to more women's field hockey.

Another classic myth is that softball is full of lesbians—an idea that emerged from one of the great pillars of intelligence, the U.S. Army, which historically conducted its witchhunts for lesbians by heading for the softball games. It is true that lesbians play softball, even lots of lesbians; but many straight women play softball too. In total softball gear, it is hard to tell who is this, that, or the other thing: *They all look like softball players.*

Some people will swear that softball is *the* lesbian game; some will swear soccer is *the* lesbian game; still others insist that it is rugby, or tennis, or golf. Why do people think we are all in one sport or another? We are in every game under the sun.

From deep in the land of leisure-time theory, there are demographics showing lesbians having more leisure time (to put into sports) than their straight and married counterparts,

but what about single straight women? Under that reasoning, it would give them lots of free time too. Would this mean that single women play sports more than nonsingle women? Getting down past the meat of the question to the bone—pardon my nonvegetarian analogy—nobody exactly knows what or why so many lesbians enjoy sports, but lots of women enjoy sports, period. If you like women, and you want to meet new sporting female friends, sports can help you do it, especially if you like women who like sports.

To sum up: The real relationship of lesbians to sports is there are lots of lesbian jocks, and you really can't tell who the lesbians are. There are many more lesbians in sports than will or ever can come out, and then there are the women who aren't lesbians but who are bisexual. There are the women who are friends with lesbians, there are women who will be lesbians next year, or the women who are not sexual at all because they are too tired from training so much. There are all types in all kinds of sports.

There has also been a distinct lesbian sports movement. It is the product of the old time gay/lesbian bar leagues for softball, bowling, pool, or the like, and the newer Gay Games movement; both coupled with the gay/lesbian visibility/rights movements. This climate has given rise to many lesbian-identified teams, tournaments, or leagues. There's Seattle's multisport Lesbian and Gay Sport Festival. There's a lesbian golf tournament in Texas called the "Bad Girls Golf Tournament," and there is San Francisco's soccer tournament, "The Festival of the Babes," which is "open to all lesbians and women willing to be mistaken for lesbians." Different types of women play in this tournament, and you can't tell who is what, but the tournament has the reputation for being extremely fun.

There is one more myth floating around out there—that lesbians who play sports are better lovers. Of course, dear reader, that one is true, true, true; and I would never let all my sports friends down by letting you think otherwise.

HOW GIRLJOCK STARTED

When I was approaching my Saturn return (i.e., when all the planets realign in the same configuration as when you were born—you reexamine your life, putting everything back in a new order) in my late twenties, I started to get a little nervous. When I'd read the classic eighties manual of how-to-really-find-yourself-and-thrive, *What Color is Your Parachute?*, the only favorite thing I learned about myself was that I remembered from high school how much I loved to make all the girls in my classes laugh.

The age of thirty was looming on my horizon, and I still wasn't sure exactly what I wanted to . . . be. I took a few journalism classes, but what is a writer without a subject? Besides the day job, the comic collection, the journalism classes, I played sports.

So I wrote my first sports article. It was an interview with a fifty-one-year-old woman who played on her college's tennis team.

Exactly how did a fifty-one-year-old create a tennis game that was competitive with younger, faster, stronger players? I had to know. Her secret was off-speed shots and "fluff" shots that would catch her opponents off guard. I was fascinated.

In my day job, I was in charge of a magazine section at a big public library. I kept imagining silly variations on magazines we kept. I drew cartoons of the titles: "American Demographics" became "American Demongraphics," complete with a silly devil on the cover. I imagined "Geek Out," the magazine for the modern uncomfortable.

Then one day, I imagined a magazine that would discuss a mixture of questions about sports, questions about being a lesbian athlete, questions about being female in the masculine sporting universe, crushes on the field, and more. My main dilemma that summer, 1990, was: Should I go to the Gay Games or not? There were so many ways to participate in political statements, and would the price of the Gay Games be worth it, or was there a better, cost-effective, more useful way to make a political statement? Who knew? I imagined

that there would be a discussion in a magazine somewhere I'd like to read, so I dreamed up a magazine with interviews of many leading women athletes discussing whether or not to go to the Gay Games.

"To Go to the Gay Games or Not to Go?" was my composition for the first issue of *Girljock,* and I made the small folio called *Girljock: The magazine for the athletic lesbian with a political consciousness.* It was a small photocopied fanzine of drawings from all my cartooning women friends who accepted the challenge of making a sports cartoon, a manifesto about art that announced, "Fuck the *Well of Loneliness,* Good-bye to all that. We're here to have fun," and the first ever issue had a print run of thirty.

I took them to a friend's birthday party in July, 1990, and almost every woman at the party looked at *Girljock* and laughed. "What Real *Girljocks* Talk About," the cover promised, and "Oh no, what do we put on the back?" asked the back cover. My friends all wanted copies. I had to photocopy more of them, and took them to a couple of local bookstores. They were a hit.

It had started out as a joke, something to amuse my friends, but it hit a nerve. That October, I was breakfasting at a friend's house when suddenly she looked at the newspaper and shrieked. Brian Bouldrey had an article on fanzines in *San Francisco Weekly,* and he said *Girljock* was his "personal favorite." People from all over began sending me submissions and stories, and the next issue was made up of entirely new material. It won "Publisher's Choice" of *Factsheet Five #41,* the guide to small magazines and fanzines. We grew from a digest-sized folio to a full-size printed publication with a two-color cover and, one Thursday after soccer practice, there was a letter waiting for me from a large distribution company that wanted to carry *Girljock.* After a few more issues, we advanced to a four-color cover, and today we hear from advertising agencies, subscribers, distributors, and book-stores around the world. We are probably the most untraditional group to ever have received votes for "Team of the Year, 1994" from the *Village Voice.* We even have a web site (http://www.girljock.com), and a section of America Online (Keyword: Girljock).

When I originally imagined *Girljock* magazine as a forum on the lesbian sporting experience, the bits of mainstream media coverage of women in sports either ignored lesbians or would merely report the fact that so-and-so was accused of being a lesbian, or all too rarely, so-and-so came out of the closet. The reality of the lesbian experience differs from what the mainstream of media will report. In *Girljock* magazine we are describing our own sporting lives, without the mainstream media's bias. Good-bye to all that mainstream mush.

Since there aren't a lot of women's sports writings (yet), many times we have published

the pioneer article on a particular aspect of a particular sport.

Not all the women we have interviewed, or the contributors, or the *Girljock* staff are lesbians. But all of them believe in the value of being part of a new lesbian-positive athletic female universe. We are all disgusted with the butchphobia and lesbophobia which has held back the women's sports world.

We've come a long way baby, but some have certainly gone the other way. Condé Nast Publications took a swing at us as they launched their new *Sports for Women* magazine. In their first direct mail piece, they tried to disclaim any association with the girljock universe:

"Sexy, splashy beauty secrets of the new glam-jocks. They're not the "girl-jocks" of the past. *No. Not by a long shot. They're chic."*

Chic: See, last year I was sure that wearing a few-sizes-too-large pair of shiny blue soccer shorts was chic. And maybe you, dear reader, did too since it was all the rage. I'm sure that you, like me, discovered that the double XL shorts had complications we never expected. They distracted the very group I tried so carefully to work and succeed with. My very own soccer teammates worried about whether or not my extra big shorts would stay up. So much for chic.

Back to *Girljock: The Magazine.* My original small photocopied booklet of drawings has become something bigger, more than just my wondering about whether or not to go the Gay Games. *Girljock: The Book* contains many of the best stories, cartoons, and photographs from our early issues onward.

Welcome to the world of the girljock, and remember to drink lots of water.

—*Roxxi*

The Sporting Way

PART ONE

1

In Search of the Rugby Goddess

by Maria Vetrano

They came bearing mouth guards. They came wearing boots. They arrived with their big blue-and-red striped shirts with specially-made noninjurious buttons and little, but durable, rugby shorts with double seams and drawstrings. There wasn't a designer label in sight. These women had come to play one of the most demanding and least understood sports in the world, the inimitable game of women's rugby.

When I walked onto the pitch which

Beantown Women's Rugby call home, a much-used field on the banks of the Charles River, I was overcome by a sense of nostalgia for the game I have known and loved for years.

It took me back to my freshman year of college when I stumbled onto one of the rowdiest, tightest-knit, and most iconoclastic groups of women I had ever encountered. On the backs of their team jackets, they wore skulls and crossbones. They took me in as one

Photo © Leisa Fearing

of the uninitiated and told me the rules: "No jewelry, no barrettes, and no fingernails. Passing, kicking, running, and tackling are okay; high tackling is not. Choose between the pack (or the scrum) and the backs (the runners). Play by the rules, don't talk to the ref, and party with the other team after the game. By the way, there are about 150 rugby songs for you to learn and one question: Can you chug?" It was a far cry from the tennis team (I threw my Chrissie Everts to the wind) —and after just one game, I knew I was in love.

THE RUCK WITHIN

The novice sunny-(or rainy-) day rugby spectator is in for a real treat when she ventures to see her first rugby game. A world in and of itself, rugby has its own outfits, rules, protocols, and vocabulary. Here's a little run down of some of the rugby words with which you should acquaint yourself. You may meet a special rugby someone one day and need to understand the language.

Pitch: The field on which you play, which may be covered with grass, snow, or mud during the various seasons of the year.

Mouth guard: A rugby player's only piece of protective equipment.

Glamour Position: Fullbacks tend to be pretty glamorous. Like goalies, they are the last person on the pitch to stop an opponent from scoring. With positional requirements such as speed, moves tackling, and kicking, they are often the best athletes on their teams. Of course, they still sweat and work really hard. Glamour, in rugby, is a matter of scale.

Forward: AKA scrummie. These tenacious sorts travel in a pack, supporting their backs and making plenty of plays of their own.

The Pack: The scrum.

Back: Speed and moves required. Backs are a forward-moving line of players who run and pass like mad and do plenty of scoring.

Prop: Sturdy types who enjoy the clashing of firm objects.

Hooker: Small is fine here. Good feet required. The hooker "hooks" the ball back into her scrum during scrum-downs.

Scrum-down: When two opposing interlocked groups of players come together like puzzle pieces moving with maximum power. Each scrum is a tight unit that tries to push the other scrum off the ball, which is rolled between them at the hookers' feet.

Scrum-half: Similar to a quarter-back, the scrum-half calls the plays. She is also the primary link between the scrum and the backs.

Wing-forward: AKA Flanker. An outer position in the scrum, requiring good tacking skills and speed.

Second-row: A woman who is willing to sacrifice her ears (and her glamour) for the good of the game. "Who's that woman running around with a bandage on her head?" It's the second-row, who tapes her ears to protect them from the rubbing of other peoples' bodies. No kidding.

Rugger: Affectionate term for rugby player.

Ruck: In rugby, you must release the ball when you are tackled. A ruck occurs when one player goes down with the ball and her sister scrummies create a supportive body bridge over her so that she can crawl away to safety.

Hands in the ruck: Something you're not allowed to do. Opposing players step over you and "toe" the ball back to their team. Since they're wearing boots, you may end up with cleat marks about which you can boast at the post-game party. It's a good idea to get out of the ruck if you can.

Boots (cleats): No, I don't know why they're called boots, but I think it started in England, where the game of rugby was born. Soon they'll be saying "colour" and "analyse" and you'll have to feign an English accent just to play.

Maul: Like it sounds. A player traveling with the ball often encounters an opponent, who will try to tackle her. When a player turns her back to her opponent and presents the ball back to her own scrum, it's called a maul. Opponents are also trying to get control of the ball. That's where "maul" comes in.

Shoot-the-Boot: When a lucky player is selected to drink out of another player's boot. A dubious award, sometimes bestowed on rookie players.

Drink-up: The post-game festivities, usually held at bars that favor robust and muddy women who drink beer and sing songs 'til the wee hours. It's a traditional bonding thing with your team and your opponents.

Rugby is all about love. For the women of Beantown Rugby, Boston's winningest team in history at any professional or amateur level, rugby is a labor of love. You can see it in their faces—at practices, during warm-ups and games, and when they talk about their sport with a member of the outside world. "Rugby is the ultimate team sport," they say.

Is rugby a paradigm for larger women's issues? Mary Jo Kane, who played Beantown rugby for twelve years as a second row, comments, "Right now they're politicizing women's health issues. They're politicizing self-esteem in young girls. One of the things they've talked about is the benefit that boys and men have from playing team sports. I think that there's a kind of nontraditional leadership that women experience from doing things like playing rugby that can be brought into other environments."

Boston women's rugby was born in 1976. Rugby lore has it (and there's always plenty of rugby lore) that a young woman named K. O. Onufried was so keen to play rugby that she began playing on the men's rugby team at the University of Massachusetts and later became one of Beantown's formative players. What kind of woman could play men's rugby, you might wonder? Surely, she must have been six-foot-three with bulging muscles and a neck of steel. Don't let the stereotypes fool you. The beauty of rugby is that there's a position for every body type—short, tall, stocky, powerful, sinewy, and fast, with different needs for every position. And with long blond hair, great hands, and a runner's build, K. O. Onufried defied any stereotype of a woman who would play a contact sport with men. What she did

have, like all the historically great women ruggers of past and present, was a driven, never-say-die mentality and a total understanding of the game. K. O. played rugby for seventeen years. Even after "retirement" (you **don't** quit rugby, you retire—and sometimes players go in and out of retirement from season to season), K. O. is still part of the very fabric of the game. Her name is passed down from rugby generation to generation. You can still hear the older players telling the younger players about her as they stand by the sidelines of the pitch: "Ever hear about K. O., the rugby goddess?"

FROM THE SIDELINES

On a warm fall day, I watched the Beantown women power-over and outfinesse their competitors. With a record like theirs, it's something to which you think they must have grown accustomed. Surely, they don't have to work that hard to defeat a less talented competitor. But when you look a little closer, you can see fly-half Mary Dixey running sophisticated plays with the rest of the backs, looping in and out, dodging, passing, tackling. The scrum runs behind in support, like some integral strand of DNA, they weave in and out of the backs, setting up mauls and rucks, corkscrew passing so adroitly, it looks like they've been playing together forever. And some of them have come close. Props Betsy Kimball and Annie (Gina) Flavin, and Eight Jan Rutkowski, have played Beantown rugby for more than sixteen years apiece. That's longer than most players in any competitive team sport. It's also longer than most jobs and most relationships. Experience and continuity bring their benefits to the playing field. They

FUN RUGBY FACTS

Hot Spots for Women's Rugby
In the U.S.—San Francisco (three teams—Bay Area She-hawks, Berkeley, and Chaos); Boston (two teams—Beantown and Boston Women's Rugby); Atlanta; Florida (Florida State of Tallahassee); Minnesota; New York; Washington; Maryland.
Internationally—England, New Zealand, Wales, Canada.

Big Tournaments
Saranac Lake Tournament in Upstate New York every August.

National Championships
Location varies every year. Last year's nationals were held in Long Beach, California. It was Beantown versus San Francisco's Bay Area She-hawks, who won by one point.

World Championships
First held in 1991 in Cardiff, Wales, this year's world championships will be held in Holland in April of 1994. Playing for the U.S. World Cup [Eagles] women's rugby team is akin to being an Olympian—you're the best in your country and you're facing international competitors.

Countries Who Fielded Teams at the Last World Championships
The U.S., Canada, England, Sweden, Holland, Spain, Russia, Japan, Wales, Italy, France, New Zealand.

Mary Jo Kane on the Physicality of Women's Rugby
"I have a different sense of my body out in the world and a sense of my own power because of the experience of being in a very physical environment, playing a contact sport. . . . I feel safer as a women than I think a lot of other women do."

Why Do So Many Lawyers Play Rugby?
"It's one of the great unsolved mysteries." (Betsy Kimball, lawyer and 18-year Beantown veteran.)

Memorable Rugby Weather Conditions
"We played in about six inches of water on the field, driving rain, thirty-five degrees, and windy as hell." (Patty Connell, Beantown scrum-half and U.S. Eagle.)

A Tough Scrum-down
"When the scrums came together, it sounded like bone on bone, instead of flesh on flesh." (Patty Connell on the U.S. Eagles 1991 game versus New Zealand.)

also bring great war stories. It's always a pleasure when you go out for a beer with these gals and one exclaims, "Hey, remember back in '82 at nationals when . . . !" And the dialogue becomes so lively and interesting that two hours later you know enough about Beantown women's rugby to play Truth or Dare with them and be a real threat.

With a team record of 367 wins, 23 losses, an annual presence at women's nationals, and many players on the U.S. Eagles team (the elite American team that plays in world rugby championships), Beantown women's rugby is a force to be reckoned with. They've even got imported talent. Scrum-half and team captain Patty Connell, stellar full-back Mary (Sully) Sullivan, Christie Stevens, and Brett Newton all emigrated to the Boston area to join the Beantown roster. (Beantown has a way of attracting some of the best players anywhere. According to rumor, it is because of "those stories they tell.")

It's tough to watch Beantown play and believe that they're just out for a bit of a workout on a sunny day. Beantown rugby is the most professional amateur team this *Girljock* reporter has ever encountered. These women train hard to stay in shape. Their practices are efficient, well-designed training sessions, full of rugby drills, aerobic conditioning, and wind sprints. They practice and play in mud, snow, rain, and wind, and they tackle with no more equipment than a mouth guard.

You would think that they'd have sponsors, big sponsors, and fans. Yet on the afternoon I watched Beantown score the afternoon away, there were only a few dozen fans on the sidelines—mostly former players and significant others, AKA rugby widows—wives or rugby husbands, as the case may be. The lack of big sponsors seems terribly unfair. The other New England teams choke in the clutch, but not Beantown. They have dominated New England rugby for many years and have been a major player on the national scene since the birth of the women's sport.

SCENES FROM A MAUL

To get a true insider's view of rugby, you really have to play the game—feel the boots at the bottom of the ruck, the sweat, the pain, the collision of forces, the exhilaration. That's why I attended an authentic Beantown practice, I told myself, to be the George Plimptonette of the women's rugby world. Sometimes noble aspirations should be quashed by the indelible stamp of reality. Well, heck, I used to play the game—four years in college and a few years upon graduation, even a spring season on Beantown's "B" team. I had once loved the game, the ferocity of competition, the camaraderie, the songs (and the parties). But I'm a little older now and I love my neck. I remembered the joy and also the sacrifice.

There I was. Players sitting on the sidelines, removing their sneakers and putting on their boots. No Mr. Rogers to warm my heart during this little episode. I blithely did the same, greeting players as they walked by and telling them that I was there to write a story (so they wouldn't expect me to be a real player).

Rugby Goddess power is so strong that even Barbara Bush, the Barbara Bush, was caught in this tributary rugby pose. Barbara demonstrated this rugby worshipping in front of the USA Eagles National Rugby team at the White House.

Photo © The USA Eagles photo Archives

The warm-up circle began—thirty-some players spread out on a field, focusing attention on Sully, the warm-up leader. I couldn't remember what it was that made me feel like ever leaving.

Somehow I survived long enough to join the team for passing and tackling drills, expertly led by Coach Joan Morrissey, a former Beantown standout. Joan's practice is one of the best organized I've attended for any sport—ice hockey, soccer, you name it. She knows what she is doing and so do the players, running patterns on the pitch, encouraging each other, and focusing on the drill of the moment.

And then there was scrum, my personal point-of-no-return. The Beantown gals remembered that I'd been a prop, which is just like it sounds, a person who holds another person up. Actually, two props hold up one hooker, who is suspended between them. When two opposing scrums come together, the props are the first to "hit" or make contact. Tough on the hairdo, this is a position for the strong of neck.

As I opposed the ever-sturdy Christie Stevens, I knew I was in big trouble. She tried to be gentle with me, but I had played this game before, and thought that on some level, I could step right back into it. Famous last thoughts. About two scrum downs from the end of practice, I was beginning to get some position back, but my neck was already killing me and I was thinking of Advil and hot baths.

After some interval running led by the always cheerful Sully, practice was finally over. Actually, it was over after a meeting on an upcoming rugby tournament that Beantown

had organized for collegiate women's teams, and at which they'd be spending their Saturday managing everything from refereeing to the concession stand. The practice had taken over two hours. For the Beantown players, that means two two-plus-hour practices a week, a Saturday of games with travel time thrown in here and there, and their own personal training, which is an unspoken requirement at their level of play. From their dedication and expertise, you would think they'd be playing for salaries. From the looks on their faces, you can see that they play because they love the sport.

I half winced when I saw a recent Lands' End catalog glorifying the U.S. Men's Eagles [Rugby] team. What's their record? A few wins and a bunch of losses? Mainstream corporate sponsors are accustomed to aggrandizing rugged competitors who exhibit unabashed physicality on the field, court, or ice—as long as they're a bunch of guys! I keep having visions of corporate sponsors embracing modern Amazonian athletes, beautiful or not, lesbian or straight, holding them up as icons to be admired, not feared, denigrated, or misunderstood. Sports should be empowering for women. It's time that American culture empowered women by admitting them to the world of sport without caveats.

Many of the Beantown players with whom I spoke talk about how rugby gets into your blood. I had to wonder when Mary Jo Kane told me that Beantown women have given birth to a total of fifteen girls over the past few years. That's enough for one side of a rugby team. Better look out in about 2005: Beantown, The Second Generation, may be coming your way.

Wave Obsession & Surfgirl Revelations

by Chela Zabin

It's Monday, 4:45 A.M., and I've been awake for some time, waiting for the alarm, calculating the quickest way to get my gear together and get out the door. Coffee? Forget it, my body is filled with adrenaline. I guiltily kiss my girlfriend good-bye and slip out the door. I've got a hot date.

At least I think I do. I have a strong feeling that a southwest swell has come in overnight, and with a minus tide at 3:30 A.M., the west side of Santa Cruz is going to be kicking. I may be wrong, but what the heck, I can always go out to breakfast and get to work early.

It's dark and foggy, but as I round the cliff near Cowell's Beach, I can see white water. Yes, there are waves, and lots of them. I pull up to the cliff. The waves are breaking out by the point, they're three to five feet high, long and glassy. It looks like the best swell of the summer, and best of all, I see only one other surfer.

In minutes, I'm slipping into my other skin, transforming myself into something black, sleek, and marine, and then slithering into the water. It's cold and still so dark that the two of us can barely see the waves coming until they're almost on us. For the next hour, we take long, luscious rides, dropping, turning, cutting back, squeezing every last drop of juice from each wave, and paddling back out for more. Too soon, it's ten to seven, time for me to go. I catch a wave and ride it to the stair-way. Standing by my car, I get dressed for work, but this is really where I'll be all day.

My coworkers don't get it. "You got up at what time?" "You're crazy!"

But my surfing friends understand. Forsaking a warm morning in bed is really a small sacrifice. Surfing is a demanding sport, especially for women, who are still fighting for respect out in the waves. Everyone has to learn how to read waves and how to ride them, figure out what size and shape board is best and how to pay for it, fight the crowds and the elements, and look like a fool on numerous occasions. But women also have to learn to deal with the attitude in the line-up and our own beliefs about ourselves. Why do we bother with it? Because catching a great wave can keep you pumped up for weeks and teach you a lot about life.

"I don't give up as easily," said J. J. Nevius, who has been surfing since she was ten—sixteen years ago. She is a shortboarder with a hot, aggressive style: "Surfing has totally taught me that. I've been trashed so many times, I should have given up a long time ago . . . It helps me with my depression . . . it's a very spiritual kind of thing . . . I've learned how to conquer fear, to push myself."

"My ability to assert myself has completely changed," said Blu Forman, a carpenter and a longboarder who has been surfing regularly

FAVORITE SPOTS, ETC.

Dee Ann Cecil:
Spot: The Path at Byron's Bay in Australia, between Sydney and Brisbane.
Shaper: Johnny Rice, in Santa Cruz.

Cynthia Landes:
Spot: Cowell's Beach.
Shop: Heat Wave, Beach 'n Bikini, Freeline, in that order, all in Santa Cruz. Dislikes: Arrow Surf Shop.

J. J. Nevius:
Spot: Everywhere in Mexico.
SC: Steamer's, middle peak.
LA: Zuma and Zeros, in Malibu area. Bad spots-Stockton (in S.C.), Topanga. Santa Cruz generally is better for women than Southern California. *"When I first came to Santa Cruz I had never seen so many women. In LA it was a special treat to see another woman in the water. In Santa Cruz you see one every day."*
Shop: Fluid Drive in LA.

Juanita Ortiz:
Spot: Hawaii: She liked everywhere she went, and hit all the major places except The Pipeline. *"I would never go to The Pipeline"* (It's a huge, barreling, left-breaking wave, only for experts). Ortiz liked Hawaii the best and said she got no shit there because people thought she was a native. "I look like I belong there." In Santa Cruz she likes Cowell's. Turtle Bay in Trinidad is also a favorite.
Shaper: Jeffrey Scott.
Thinks all the Santa Cruz shops are cool.

Blu Forman:
Favorite S.C. spot: When it's breaking right, Indicators or inside at Steamer's Lane.
Southern California: Haggerty's in Palos Verdes.
Mexico: Santa Cruz in the state of Nayarit, Baja California, Grandfather's, in San Jose del Cabo. Puerto Rico: Tres Marias in Rincon.
Hawaii: Hanalai Bay on Kauai.
Shaper: Johnny Rice.
Shop: Freeline, Heat Wave.

---

for seven years. "I hold my ground a whole lot better than I used to . . . I'm not as compulsively nice."

Juanita Ortiz rides a mini-longboard and started surfing in 1983 because she was dating a surfer and knew that if she wanted to see him she'd have to get in the water. She got hooked and now makes a point of getting in the water every day, no matter what.

Besides surfing, Ortiz, who is a nurse practitioner at a clinic in Watsonville, belongs to an informal group of women who run three to four miles and swim a half-mile in the ocean 365 days a year, rain or shine. "We call ourselves the mermaids," she said.

"I really like the feel of the ocean. It's a good way of being one with the water, with the earth," Ortiz said. After a session in the water, she's calm, serene, confident, and ready for the rest of the day.

"I've learned a lot about balance and priorities," said longboarder Cynthia Landes, who's been surfing regularly for six months. "I know when enough's enough. . . . It's taught me a lot about my limits . . . There's something very magical about surfing, even just the sound of the water hitting the fiberglass. . . . No matter how shitty a day I've had, I have a completely different attitude when I get out."

When Nevius, who is now a student, first

started surfing, in Southern California, she didn't have a problem.

"A lot of people thought I was a boy," she said, "I used to surf in trunks and no shirt."

Once she started growing breasts, things changed. "[Guys] started taking off on waves in front of me and stuff."

Over the years, she's tried different things, from ignoring the remarks, to verbal confrontation, to being as obnoxious as they are.

"If they start snaking me, I'll start snaking them right back," she said.

"I sit there and think, I'm an Amazon. The ocean is my higher power. I deserve every wave out here!"

"You get the really rude guys," said Ortiz. "They want you out of the water, because they think it's their wave. I've said to them, 'If you're so good, go find a bigger wave.' . . . Well, they're shocked. They just get quiet and paddle away."

Forman has a variety of tricks, ranging from trying to befriend the dominating surfers to pushing guys and their boards off of waves when they drop in on her. The latter technique, which has a high shock value, since Forman is only about five-foot-two and 110 pounds, usually works rather well.

It only backfired once, when a guy went off, called her a "big bulldagger" and threatened to drown her. ("He's got to weigh 100 pounds more than I do and he's got to be at least ten inches taller," she said.) Forman talked to a friend who's a well-known surfer in Santa Cruz, the friend talked to the guy, and the guy has since apologized and befriended her. As for her sexual preference, "Now it's like he could care less about who I sleep with. [Men] seem

to think that that's the end-all of end-alls to call me that, but I just laugh. That's like going up to a piece of kelp and calling it a piece of kelp."

Dee Ann Cecil, who works as a firefighter in North Santa Cruz County when she's not surfing, said she just can't deal with male attitude sometimes.

"It depends a lot on my mood," she said, "a lot of days I'll get out of the water and just do something else." But, she said, she knows every time she holds her ground, "I push it that much further for women who want to get out in the water."

The sport relies heavily on upper-body strength and many women find they aren't strong enough at first. Weight training helps, but just keeping at it builds up strength, and using a longer board can make a big difference. Not knowing about equipment, not having money, and not getting proper instruction also keeps a lot of women out of the water or unnecessarily frustrated.

Landes, who works at a women's health clinic in Santa Cruz, had surfed a couple of times in her youth in Brazil and several years ago in Santa Cruz, and was afraid to get back in the water again earlier this year because "I knew I'd be hooked, I knew I'd want my own equipment, I didn't have the money." But a friend gave her a board on long-term loan, and she picked up a used wet-suit for fifty dollars at a local surf shop. Eventually she put together enough money for a nearly new board of her own.

Forman barely caught any waves and never stood up for the first six months she surfed.

She started out with this "old, crappy piece

of shit longboard" and kept trying to ride it until one day a fellow surfer took pity on her and let her borrow his board.

"I caught the next wave, stood up, turned and rode it to the beach," she said. Then she went out and bought a better board. She recommends that beginners "find someone who knows how to do it, who's a nice person you can trust. Someone who can explain things, take you out and show you how to keep from hurting yourself and other surfers. Don't go out in big waves until you feel safe."

"One of my dreams has been to compete," said Nevius. She did compete once, and came in second, but hasn't tried again.

"I knew I was good enough, but I was intimidated because of my weight. I was just so intimidated by all the bikini girls," said Nevius, who is chunky but most certainly not overweight.

All of the women interviewed love seeing other women out in the water and especially like to see young girls learning to surf. "That really makes me happy," said Ortiz.

"I check out all the women doing it," said Cecil, when asked if she has a mentor. "I'm totally impressed with every lady out there."

To the Beach and Back:
Adult Surfing-Convert Leslie Lacko Takes Roxxie to the Beach

by Roxxie

Leslie Lacko grew up in Orange County, California as an avowed punk rocker who hated surfers. Somewhere along the way there was a turning point, and now she owns her own surfboard and goes on surfing vacations. Sports sleuth that I am, I headed out to the beach to investigate. Although I had never surfed before (I am also a bad skateboarder—I don't have the right rhythm—and a bikini-losing water-skier), Leslie proved very tolerant and helpful. The result of the adventure? The following story, and sand in my ears for a week.

Photo © Richard Zoller

WE STRAP ON THE SURFBOARDS

We meet at her Oakland, California, home. Leslie takes me to the back of the house where the surfboards are kept. She shows me her surfboard, the top side is covered with sticky goo.

"Sex wax," she says, pointing to the goo, and smiles. We carry the surfboards outside her house and strap them on top of her red-and-white 1969 Toyota Land Cruiser. The Land Cruiser's gearshift growls like a hungry animal. We head off in the Land Cruiser.

14

Destination: the beach of Leslie Lacko's choice. The following interview was taped en route.

Roxxie: *Does anyone else in your family surf?*

Leslie Lacko: I'm the only surfer in my family, but I never surfed when I was a teenager living in Orange County, California, because of the "scene." It's a not-friendly kind of surfing "scene."

R: *What was the "scene" like?*

LL: Certain groups of kids from high school were the "surf rats," and they were terminally cool. It was a boy thing. I never knew a single girl who did it. Besides, when I grew up, I was a punk rocker, and we hated the surfers.

R: *Why was that?*

LL: It was the thing to do, I guess. They were a different clique.

R: *Where are the best places to surf in the Bay Area?*

LL: Probably the best place to surf here is Steamer Lane in Santa Cruz. It's a huge point break. You don't surf there unless you're good.

R: *What's a point break?*

LL: Point breaks are the best kinds of breaks! You ride the waves in and then paddle out around the waves. Paddling out is really difficult. It is the hardest part.

R: *Is paddling out the worst thing about surfing? Or is it what your sisters will think of you when they find out you've become a surfer now, or is it the cold water?*

LL: Definitely, for me, the worst thing about surfing is some of the guys that are out there. It is intimidating to be the only woman out there with a bunch of guys. Especially when I first began. It's like going out to play pick-up basketball with a bunch of guys—only as

a beginner! I only started surfing about five years ago.

R: *When you go surfing, do you forget about everything else?*

LL: It's a focused sport, but not as focused as soccer, basketball, or a constant action sport. It's important to keep your eyes on the horizon and see what kind of waves are coming at you, be aware if a big set of waves is coming. If there's a big set out there, you have to paddle further out there, because it breaks further out there. You don't want waves breaking on you.

WHEN WAVES BREAK ON YOU

R: *What happens when the waves break on you?*

LL: [laughs] You get washed ashore.

R: *With your board?*

LL: Yeah.

R: *Do you ever get thrown off your board?*

LL: All the time. That's why you wear a little leash to your board. Even though the old-time surfers didn't wear them, and might frown on them, it's better than having your board washed ashore every time.

R: *Are there any, um, great white sharks at the place we are going to?*

LL: No, it's fine. It's just a nice little cove.

R: *Phew!* [Big sigh.]

SHARK SAVVY

LL: But great whites are definitely a concern in this area, so I recently went to a shark behavior lecture. The biggest tip I found out was always surf with a partner.

R: *But would you know if a shark was coming?*

LL: No, they rely on a surprise attack. They come up from the bottom and they chomp.

R: *They just chomp?*

LL: They go for the midsection. They try to avoid arms and legs. They probably think they're avoiding fins and claws.

R: *Be fun to interview a shark.*

LL: Be kinda neat. See what they think of humans. Maybe they aren't mistaking us for seals after all.

R: *What else, besides sharks, is scary about the ocean?*

LL: If you grow up around the ocean, it isn't scary, because you know about waves. You know that waves come in sets and have patterns to them. But if you don't grow up around the ocean it can be scary. For example, Patrick Swayze didn't actually surf in the movie *Point Break*. He couldn't "get" surfing. The ocean scared him. Maybe it was too unpredictable, or overpowering.

R: [A moment of silence ensues: Uh-oh, I think to myself. I didn't grow up around the ocean. I grew up around cornfields, and they had very obvious patterns. I wonder what I'm in for.] *Oh.*

LL: [almost reading Roxxie's mind] Have you bodysurfed or anything like that before?

R: *No.*

LL: Uh . . . O.K. Well . . . it takes some getting used to.

ARE YOU ANY GOOD, AND OTHER SURFING COMMENTS

R: *What sorts of things do surfers say to each other when they are surfing?*

LL: Surfing is a pretty nonsocial sport. People don't talk to each other much. If men are going to give you a hard time about surfing, or being out at their local beaches, I've found out the men will not talk to you. Most of the comments I've heard that weren't flattering were from people trying to be nice, who stuck their feet in their mouth. Usually people come up and say things like, "How long have you been surfing?" or "Are you any good?" I get asked if I am good a lot.

R: *What do you say to them?*

LL: I say yes! But the truth is, I'm not that good, I haven't been doing it for that long. Surfing around lots of men is different than working on construction jobs with them. The company I work for is really cool, the guys have adjusted to me, but when subcontractors come to work on our job sites, the guys who don't want you there let you know it.

R: *What do they do?*

LL: They'll call you . . . Butch. Which, to them, is supposed to be an insult. Stuff like that.

R: *Why do straight men think that's such a big insult? To many gay men, that's a compliment.*

LL: I guess they think it means that you are a dyke. Now why they think that's such a big insult, I don't know.

WE ARRIVE AT THE BEACH

LL: The first thing you do when you get to the beach is you get out and check out the waves. What you look for is the shape and the size—you want them to curl over, but not closing out. Closing out means the wave breaks all at once. When it peels, it breaks at one point and you can ride it as it breaks along the wave's length. This surf today is called "mushy" surf. It doesn't have really great shape, the waves are rolling on in. Basically, you can apply any term to surfing you would apply to food.

R: *Like "over easy"?*

LL: Like mushy, or crunchy, or . . . over easy. [She laughs!]

We arrive at the beach—it's really crowded.

R: *This looks like fun.*

LL: This is fun. Soccer is still the most fun, but this is a lot of fun.

At this point we get out of the Land Cruiser and get ready to surf.

MY FIRST WET SUIT EXPERIENCE

Leslie has an extra wet suit for me, because Northern California coastal waters are so cold. It is easier to get into than panty hose, and much thicker.

"Getting out of it is more difficult," she tells me. The wet suit is dark colored and zips from shoulder to shoulder behind the neck. I slip into it, she zips it for me—I feel like a seal. I jump into the water, which is not cold now. The only places that can get cold are my hands and feet, and they're numb after a minute.

Leslie shows me basic bodysurfing. She shows me how to "catch" a wave, and how to dive and swim beneath an oncoming wave's crest. The waves are stronger than I would have guessed. After I get used to the motions, we head back for our boards. My board is light green, with lots of sex wax, and black detailing. It's such a nice board that a stranger came up and complimented it. It's a big longboard. I feel like a midget next to it. I try not to trip over my leash as I walk, board under arm, to the water. We paddle out a little ways. She ducks the surfboard head under the oncoming wave-crest and paddles under and through each wave. I try it too and it works. It feels like I'm faking out a wave. I'm enjoying working my new "moves" on the ocean. It works for four waves in a row.

"Good," she yells at me, "You're getting it. Let's head out there."

She paddles out ahead of me. I scramble to catch up.

Suddenly a large wave grabs me before I can blink, or inhale. I'm traveling backward quickly and feeling weightless. I realize that my friends weren't kidding when they said that the ocean plays with people. Salt spray covers my face and I suck foam. I hold my breath, some icky spray included. I'm still being dragged backward. The wave has me in its grip. I try to turn myself around or get out of it, with no luck. The wave suddenly slams me on the beach sand, and my board slaps into my knee. I'm no love-child-of-the-ocean, I quickly get out of the water in fear of the next wave. My arms are tired, I've got sand in my ears, salt water up my nose, and the ocean is big.

Ultimate Thrills

by Alison Gallant

It's a warm sunny day in Santa Cruz and the university fields look well trimmed and dry. There's a slight breeze coming in from the bay. The temperature must be around eighty and the afternoon sun is low in the late October sky.

There are three soccer-sized fields on this little plateau. About a hundred Ultimate Frisbee players, men and women, college age to their forties, are tossing discs (as Frisbee players prefer to call them) and waiting for the next round of games to begin. The Frisbees criss-cross the air lackadaisically.

This is Western Regionals for Ultimate Frisbee and the winners here will go to Nationals. Some of the best teams in the country are here: the San Francisco Maniacs, Women on the Verge from Seattle, Safari from Santa Barbara; and San Francisco's Double Happiness. Since this is an international sport—Ultimate is played in Venezuela, Sweden, Japan, Australia—I guess you could say that some of the best players in the world are here.

I grew up a tomboy and I've played every sport I could find—rough downhill skiing, rock climbing, skydiving, triathlons, mountain bike descents down Whistler—and nothing, absolutely nothing, is as gnarly and physically demanding as Ultimate. Nor is there a sport as beautiful, fluid, and graceful.

Ultimate is played on a field that is 125 yards by 40 yards. Each team plays seven players each on the field at a time. The object is to score a point by moving the disc down the field into your end zone, like in football. You cannot run with the disc. You must move the disc downfield by throwing it to an open teammate. And the only way to get open is to sprint, not run.

If you're fast enough to shake your "marker" (defender), get open and catch the disc, you have ten seconds to pass the disc off to another teammate, while somebody is in your face, marking you (covering you, trying to block your throw). If you're able to get the disc to a teammate in your end zone, you've scored a point.

If you were just scored against, you can at least console yourself with the thought that between points you can catch you breath, and if you're really winded, now's your chance to sub out (if you're lucky enough to have subs). You play two halves, and games are usually to fifteen. If there's a tie, there's a time cap that's put on the game at an hour and a half, and then it's the first team to win by two.

Now let's talk about grace. I always thought that part of what made Frisbee so beautiful was the Frisbee itself. When a well-thrown Frisbee rides the air, it really flies. Sometimes it floats. Sometimes it glides. But any way you slice it, it travels in style. Not like a ball that, let's face it, really just lobs around and comparatively seems so much clumsier and clunkier. And there are some people on the field who can really work it—backhands, forehands, "hammers" (overheads), hucks, inside outs. You never realized, until you've seen an Ultimate game, how many different ways there are to throw a Frisbee.

Sometimes the catch is even more incredible than the throwing. There's one expression that every Frisbee player knows and speaks with reverence—the "layout." Sometimes you need to make a diving catch because there is just no other way you're going to get there in time (a disc that is dropped or hits the ground first is a turnover). Now you've seen wide receivers do it in a football game. But in football they're wearing all that padding. But here you are on the Frisbee field, in shorts and T-shirt, running full-speed and about to stretch

completely horizontal. Now the body's natural instinct is to protect itself, but great athletes transcend their bodies. Your body says: Let it go, don't try to fly. But your mind, completely in the throes of passion, says: Get it! You're airborne, you grab the disc, and brace yourself 'cause you're going to hit the ground hard, chest first. This is one of the disadvantages of being a woman and playing the sport. As soon as the pain subsides you can hear everybody cheering you, your own team and the opposing team, and all you can think is, Gee, I hope somebody got that on film. But you got to get over yourself pretty quickly 'cause the person marking you has already counted up to four and you've got to get rid of the disc.

An average game lasts about an hour to an hour and a half unless there's a gross imbalance in talent.

Now that I've gotten my ya-yas off about the physical part of the sport, let me tell you

Photo © Phyllis Christopher

what makes Ultimate Frisbee the most incredible team sport experience you'll ever have. It's what Frisbee players call "spirit of the game." If ever there was a sport that was antipatriarchal, it's got to be Ultimate. And maybe that's why so many women play. Men and women are segregated into their own leagues during the season (there are exceptions—the men's team from Calgary has a woman who plays with them), but in the off-season play is coed. Because Ultimate relies so much on speed and finesse and stamina and less on brawn, women not only hang well with the boys, they sometimes outplay them. And women don't have to put up with patronizing handicaps, like four strikes instead of three. The sport is egalitarian and nongender favored, and queer-friendly.

I spoke to Annie Kreml of the San Francisco Maniacs about Ultimate and queers.

AG: *When did you start playing the sport?*
AK: In 1982. I was in college at UC San Diego. I thought now here was a totally cool, alternative sport.
AG: *Go on.*
AK: Well, the San Diego women's team, Safari, at the time I started hearing about the sport, was a bunch of crunchy, hairy-legged earth women who worked at the co-op. They were totally cool.
AG: *And accepting?*
AK: Oh yeah. But then things changed a little a few years later when all these young people joined up.
AG: *What do you mean?*
AK: Well, they were just a lot younger and I think I scared them.
AG: *Because you were queer?*

AK: No, because I was an intimidating presence on the field. And I used to play in my Jogbra. You know I was the one to start that? I was the one who was doing it way before it was fashionable.
AG: *And now every woman Frisbee player plays in her bra. Huh. You probably scared them with those rippling stomach muscles. So did the youngsters come around?*
AK: I deprogrammed them. Like there was this one player from La Jolla, a La Jolla brat, kind of like a Marin brat, who would show up at the field with her pastel-peach water bottle who I teased incessantly until she came around.
AG: *Well, that was college. What has it been like in the club circuit up here in the Bay Area?*
AK: Well, I thought I was breaking ground being out and playing Frisbee up here, but then I found all those women who were out up north [Seattle?] and there are plenty out on the East coast. There have been maybe five or six queers on my team at one time or another over the years I played.
AG: *And you and your girlfriend, who plays on the same team, have been totally open?*
AK: Absolutely.
AG: *And what about the guys?*
AK: Well, there's at least one guy that I know of in the Bay Area who is totally out and playing Ultimate with a men's team.
AG: *Just one guy? Those are not great numbers.*
AK: No, but then again, is it possible at all for a gay man to come out in any institutionalized sport in this country? Is there one out queer in the NBA, the NFL, in baseball? I mean, Frisbee is still such a new sport, forging new ground, and it's already come so much further. And it's so much less image-conscious. . . .

"Spirit of the game," says Rose Duhan from Spike in Ann Arbor, "is really why I love this sport. Excessive competitiveness and testosterone are what ruin other sports, that whole winning-at-any-cost attitude." Rose is twenty-five and has been playing Ultimate since it was introduced to her at Wesleyan. "You can't get away with being an asshole. It's more important to play with integrity, to play fairly. Unnecessary aggression doesn't fly. You'll get a lot of flack if you act macho."

"If you really think about it, having to be the best in a sport or in anything is such a stressful and absurd goal to maintain. I mean, you have no control over what your own natural limitations are. And you have no control over other people's gifts. But what does make sense, and what Ultimate sort of fosters, is pushing yourself to your own limits. Maybe that's where the name came from."

Ultimate is not played with referees. The sport is self-officiating; it counts on personal integrity. You make the call, and when it's not your call, respect what the other player has called. But what probably makes it truly subversive is the sports' stand against becoming commercialized. The UPA (Ultimate Players Association) has rejected many offers of corporate sponsorship to keep the sport pure, although recently the association has accepted José Cuervo's sponsorship of a major tournament. There are a lot of players worried about the sport becoming mainstream and losing its marginal status. "So many sports get corrupted by middle-American values which emphasize winning—you know, winning-is-not-everything, it's-the-only-thing mentality. I mean, it's great to be competitive, but you have

to keep everything in perspective. The whole point is to be out here and have fun and push your own limits," says Duhan.

Anybody who's ever been to a Frisbee tournament knows what a countercultural scene it is: guys playing in skirts, players on the sidelines getting stoned, an occasional self-mocking group of men and women holding hands in a circle singing "Kumbaya."

3:07 P.M.: Walking toward the fields that look over the bay, I run into Kelly Longren, the tournament massage therapist. I stop her and ask her if this is some California New Age thing to have massage therapists at tournaments.

KL: No, no, no. This is the kind of sport where you can easily rip up your muscles if you aren't prepared. I massage people pregame and postgame to keep people warmed up.

AG: *Well that's awfully nice of you.*

KL: No, it's not. The UPA pays me a flat fee to set up my table here and I charge five bucks for ten minutes.

AG: *Oh, I see. And what is it people need you to work on?*

KL: I deal mostly with hamstrings.

AG: *Huh. Why are they called the hamstrings, by the way?*

KL: Because it sounds better than porkrope?

AG: *Oh. All right, just one more question. What is it that you love about this sport?*

KL: You meet great people, it's competitive . . . it's not political like most games are, and you always have a good time.

As I walk around the fence into the fields, I notice that the wind has picked up a little. Wind sucks for Frisbee. You could throw a perfect pass and the wind can take the disc, flip it, toss it, and send it back in your face. It makes the points longer, and makes the game hellish. There's a strategy for playing with wind. The defense will often throw a zone defense, just like in basketball. Because it's windy you know that the offense, the team with the disc, won't be throwing long passes. By throwing zone defense, you make it more difficult for them to work it down the field in short, neat passes because you cut off all the openings.

I see down on the third field the San Francisco Maniacs playing some team that I don't recognize. I walk down there with my camera, hoping to catch the Maniacs doing their thing. These are the hottest women athletes you'll ever meet. One of the players gave up her soccer scholarship to Berkeley just so she could play Ultimate.

When I first moved to San Francisco I played a little with the Maniacs. I went to a tournament with them in Arizona and I felt like George Plimpton in *Paper Lion*. But when I actually started playing, it wasn't that bad. These chicks were so smooth, so tight, they brought up my level of play.

When I got to the field I threw off my lens cap and started taking pictures of some of the Maniacs who were just hanging out on the sidelines. They're photogenic on the field and off. One of the funniest women on the field, Martha of the Maniacs, walks up to me.

M: Hey, Buick, where the hell have you been? (*I got the nickname Buick for doing something unprintable at a tournament once with somebody I picked up. We did it in the back of a Buick and got caught by the Buick's owner.*)

AG: *Hey, big mouth, is that all you can remember about me? Who are you guys playing?*
M: Ketchum.
AG: *Where are they from? (I thought she meant Catch 'em, a nickname.)*
M: Ketchum. It's a town in Idaho.

Idaho. How the hell did they pull together a women's Ultimate team in Ketchum, Idaho? Huh, this sport is getting too popular. I watch the Maniacs trample this team and then leave to go catch some other games.

4:15 P.M.: I walk back to the first field and find a few guys hanging out who look eager to talk. They also look a little older than the rest of the crowd.

AG: *So what's your name?*
Anonymous: Barn Dog.
AG: *And your name?*
Anonymous : Johnny Mo.
AG: *Looks like you guys have been playing for a while.*
BD: Yeah, I've been playing since 1977.
AG: *You started in college?*
BD: Oh yeah, and here I am playing masters division.
BD: What age do you get thrown into Masters?
JM: Thirty, for the men, I'm not sure about the women . . .
AG: *Thirty? You're a master at thirty in this sport. In PGA golf I think the master division starts at 85 or something, right?*
BD: Yeah. In Ultimate, you're an old man at 30 . . .
JM: Yeah, the first sign is when you start taking Advil as a matter of course, before you start playing, in the middle of the game, at the end of the day . . .

AG: *You guys are really depressing. Thanks for the interview.*

BD: You just can't keep up with these young guys. They just run so hard . . .

I walk away because it is all too true and I can't bear to hear it. Ultimate forced me into a midlife crisis at age 28 because 23-year-olds were running me into the ground. Here I was thinking I was hot shit because I could do five miles in thirty-five minutes. So what? You're eating dust of the heel of a twenty-three-year-old punk. You have the urge to trip them. Anything to stop them, to stop the searing pain in your chest . . .

5:35 P.M.: I'm watching San Francisco's Double Happiness play another men's team from Portland, Oregon. I stand on the sidelines with Rose Duhan who's out here visiting. Ultimate is a great spectator sport because the pace is very MTV. It moves fast, it's colorful, and everyone looks kinda hip-grunge. Rose and I stand close to each other so we can hear over the people screaming on the sidelines, screaming "up" calls. (It's really helpful to have teammates, etc., scream "up" when the disc is airborne because when you're on defense and chasing your person you're too focused on them to know the disc is on its way somewhere. Maybe it's about to hit you on the back of your head.)

AG: *So why do you think this sport is so . . . alternative?*

BD: Because, I guess, a lot of people who play it started playing in college, usually kind of liberal artsy, hippyish colleges . . . so the players are typically more liberal, open-minded.

AG: *The sport definitely has a feminist sensibility, don't you think?*

RD: Well, ya, maybe because it's player-run. There's no authority to defer to . . . it's anti-authority, no referees, no coaches . . .

Sheila Ellis from Atlanta, Georgia, has been playing the sport for two years. She's an avid feminist and was drawn to the sport partly for its feminist sensibility.

SE: It's the first time I've ever competed where the women were encouraged by the men and helped by the men; men were helping to promote the female end of the sport. The men work to try to get more women to play and get the women to play more aggressively.

The UPA has divided Frisbee officially into three kinds of teams: open, women, and masters. So what that means is that if you want to play with a guys' team you can try out—they can't keep you off. But if you want to play with only women, you can.

AG: *Rose, what else made the sport attractive to you?*

RD: There are more opportunities to get in because it's so new . . . if you don't get into soccer at age nine, forget it, you'll probably never the play the sport . . . but Frisbee is easy to pick up, and the Ultimate community is very open to new players. . . .

A roar comes up from the crowd. Double Happiness has just beaten Portland and all the players are shaking the hands of the opposing team. It's nearly six o'clock, and the sun, fat like an overgrown orange, hangs over the horizon. It's magic hour and the colors on the field are even richer than they were in the afternoon sun. Cleats, sweatshirts, and bandannas that have been tossed off lie scattered on the grass. Even they look tired.

Double Happiness and Portland are about to engage in a very endearing Ultimate tradition: the postgame cheer. After every game, both teams have to sing a cheer to the opposing team. The cheers run from the clever to the absurd. The women's teams usually put more effort into coming up with something witty and more personalized. The men's teams, either too lazy or too self-conscious to be silly, tend to recycle generic cheers. The women's team I played with in Upstate New York was the Bad News Bears when it came to Frisbee, but, man, we had the cheers. Once, after we got crushed by a team from New York, we cheered them with a song from *West Side Story*. It went something like this:

a girl like that, she run too fast, and
when you're not looking,
she'll kick your ass. one of your own
kind, play with your own kind.

7:05 P.M.: The sun has just set and we are walking off the fields toward the parking lot. I'm going to catch a ride back to San Francisco with this guy named Taro. I jump in his Jeep and close the door and try to remember what I felt like at this time of day, after a tournament. Your skin is salty from sweat and darkened from the sun and every muscle is pleasantly sore. And you're on such an Ultimate high you wonder if your body could take this for another ten years, or maybe fifteen years, or maybe twenty. . . . 'Cause you never want to stop.

Taking My Girlfriend Rock Climbing

by Susan Fox Rogers

It was a late fall weekend. There was an early morning bite in the air, which I knew would give way to a dry, cool, blue day, maybe the last perfect day before winter cold set in. It was a must-climb day.

It was about four months into our relationship. We were still in that stage where we would do anything for each other; try anything at least once. If I waited until spring to ask her to go rock climbing with me it might be past that window of bliss. She would smile sardonically, shake her head, and say "guess again," then install herself with a big bowl of popcorn in front of some lesbian experimental video. I had to seize the day.

I live directly behind the Gunks, a seven-mile-long band of cliffs, about ninety miles north of New York City. Because of its location and because the rock offers such a wonderful variety of climbs at all levels of difficulty, it is one of the most popular climbing areas on the East Coast, if not in the country. Rather than climb at the main cliffs, which I knew would be laced with ropes, at the end of which would be dangling New Jerseyites and Manhattanites in Lycra, I decided a brisk five-mile hike to a more remote crag was in order.

It's not that I don't like the crowds at the cliffs, it's that I hate them. Back in the old days, climbing had something to do with being outdoors, and most of the time people acted like they were in nature. You could hear yourself climb. The few climbers who did exist were mostly a motley, marginal bunch of hedonistic rebels for whom climbing was not a sport, but a way of life. That's what I came into at age fifteen in 1976, and I thought it was a lot of fun: I hitchhiked to Yosemite for a summer, spent another sleeping in the parking lot of Eldorado Canyon in Colorado. I climbed all day, ate rice and soup mix at night, and woke to climb again. My parents didn't want to know what I was doing, and it was agreed that when I was home there wouldn't be too many stories of long falls or unprotected climbs. In other words, I was in silence training for when I came out several years later.

And then something happened to climbers and climbing: We became athletes, we trained and lived healthily, competitions appeared, then blossomed, climbing walls were built in every city, and as a population we expanded exponentially. But above all, we became popular, the perfect image of daring and strength to be used on everything from perfume to insurance ads. It was sort of like becoming chic as a lesbian: There was something not quite authentic about it. I couldn't help but wonder if all of these climbers were real climbers, and I couldn't help but feel that the press was making us into something we are not.

So anyway, there we were escaping the madding crowds in search of the authentic climbing experience. "Authentic" only meant that we would be able to hear ourselves think, could enjoy the pleasure of moving on rock without worrying that rocks, gear, or a person might fall on us.

Skytop was deserted, and the climb I had chosen, Grey Face, was free. It was, as the name hints, a sweet face climb on smooth gray quartz conglomerate. A face climb means the rock was vertical or less than vertical and climbing would involve looking for holds on the surface of the rock. It was rated 5.6 on a scale that runs from 5.0 to 5.14. The rock was clean, the holds neat and solid, the line direct. In every way, it was the perfect introduction to the rock.

Photo © Todd Swain

Everything had to be right because I wanted my girlfriend to understand my passion. It was like introducing her to my oldest and best friend, my first love and lover.

I was in luck in that the technical side of climbing, which usually overwhelms new climbers, didn't stump her. In fact, she came complete with her own harness, which she had used climbing steel when she worked rigging sets for rock-and-roll bands. So while she slipped into her harness, I uncoiled the rope, ensuring it would feed out easily. I showed her how to tie into the rope with a figure eight and introduced her to the basics of belaying. The belayer is the one who holds your rope, feeds it out or takes it in as needed, and, if you fall, it's your belayer who catches you. Your belayer literally holds your life in their hands.

Climbing is the perfect sport for gear freaks because you can shop and shop: for hexes, and stoppers, and steel nuts, and polig nuts, and friends, and quick draws, and runners, and locking 'biners, and oval 'biners, and sticht plates, and tricams, and . . . And none of it is cheap. So I climb with a minimum of gear, mostly simple nuts that I wedge into the rock and that are removed just as easily.

I stepped onto the rock and caressed the first holds, searching for the perfect purchase. I stopped for a moment to show my girlfriend how I moved with my weight on my feet, letting the sticky rubber of the climbing shoes adhere to the slimmest of holds. I explained that because I was balancing I didn't have any weight on my arms. Then, because I'm a teacher who believes everyone should find their own way, and that no two people climb in the same manner, I was gone, moving upward, doing my own dance with the rock.

It wasn't that I was being cruel in leaving her with so little instruction. Climbing is a sport with no rules, and no set movements to practice and learn. It asks only that you be flexible and strong, both physically and mentally. You need to be able to look at the various holds the rock offers and then imagine how your body might fit and work with those holds to move upward. I've spent hours, even days, playing a sort of physical chess with a piece of rock less than fifteen feet high. It may sound silly, but it makes me feel free and happy.

This lack of structure bothers some climbers, who want to be told; they want the full beta, which would run something like this: "Left foot on that crimp near your waist, now match with your hands and mantle, then reach for that pinch grip and lay back off it while smearing your left foot. You're going for a real tweaker so suck it in. Don't forget to breathe."

The rock was warm, the holds solid, and I swayed and stepped, stopping only to place a piece of gear to protect me should I fall, or to dry my hands off with gymnast's chalk.

I arrived at a small ledge, clipped myself into a runner that I draped around a young tree that had made its home in the middle of that cliff, waved and called down, "off belay." My girlfriend could see and hear me, and I watched her as she laced up the climbing shoes she had borrowed for the day, and prepared to climb.

"You're on belay," I called down. "Here I come," she said. ("Climbing" is the usual call, but I knew what she was up to.) I expected her to take a while to adjust to the rock, figure out the first slightly awkward moves, so I held the rope in my hands, looked down into the valley at the wild colors of the changing leaves, and thought what a lucky person I was to have my lover at the end of my rope. Then I saw her step onto a small crease about fifteen feet above the ground, a gentle loop of rope over her arm. I sucked in the rope as fast as I could, imagining what would have happened if she had slipped and fallen on those first moves. Needless to say, I belayed attentively, never letting my eyes stray from her movements.

It was wonderful watching her move: She monkeyed her way up the rock, using her strong arms and shoulders to pull her through the trickier spots. I reminded myself that even though she was now a film freak, she was once a butch jock, best third basewoman the local league had ever seen. She knew what to do with her body—hold on and move—in an instinctive, playful way, like a kid scrambling away from her parents. Only now she was climbing toward me.

When she arrived at the ledge she was wide-eyed and breathing heavily. I was ridicu-lously proud and excited for her, and I moved to make room for her on that small perch seventy feet off the ground. Our sweaty bodies touched. I took her in my arms, the rope wrapping around us both, and I could feel her heart racing, the heat of her breath, and the excitement and warmth of her body. It came from a delicious combination of fear, exertion, and anticipation. We kissed.

I have shared hundreds of tiny ledges with dozens of partners, and I have always wondered: Is it the altitude? Or adrenaline? or her? Now I know.

Hot Rock Babes Scale Largest Plastic Peak in North America!

by Sharon Urquhart

A Lycra-clad climber scaling a rock wall at Joshua Tree National Monument held my undivided attention. Skill, finesse, mental endurance, and strength—she was a tightly packed bundle of all these things, clinging calmly to the shear wall. The questions of what she would do next and how she would get down kept my eyes riveted on her every move.

Climbing is about solving the problem of physically getting up a wall or rock. Climbing on rock walls and on manufactured climbing surfaces such as those found at climbing gyms is an exciting and challenging route to fitness. Strength, finesse, flexibility, and commitment are necessary in both the body and the mind. For this reason, climbing is accessible to many different types of people—not just the extremely fit.

Further, climbing demands that you take responsibility not only for your self, but for your partner as well. Trust takes on new meaning when you allow your life to be held in the hands of your partner. Climbing will erode the bonds of some relationships while it builds those of others because it demands trust, responsibility, cooperation, and communication.

Like most activities, climbing is only as safe as people make it. Even in a rock gym, climbing can be a dangerous sport. Used properly, climbing ropes won't break, harnesses won't fail, nor will carabiners snap. Most of the accidents and death that are climbing-related occur because people have failed to use equipment properly. It is critical to learn the basic safety skills of climbing thoroughly, from responsible individuals or organizations.

Climbing gyms are a convenient place to take a basic safety course. It won't get dark, nor will lightning strike, and a double espresso is always available! A basic safety course at a climbing gym should cost between thirty to fifty dollars, depending on what is included in the lesson and where it is taught (lessons taught outdoors often are significantly more expensive).

In your first lesson, you should learn about your harness, how to tie your knots, and how to belay. Belaying is the process of taking up the rope as a climber ascends and stopping the rope should the climber take a fall. While tying knots and belaying are not complex skills, they are necessary as building blocks for more advanced skills.

The next step is to gather your wits and give it a go! We organized some gals who had little or no experience on the rocks and asked them to try it out. It wasn't difficult to lure them into Pacific Edge, the largest indoor climbing gym in the country (in Santa Cruz), with the promise of a free climbing lesson, all the coffee and goodies they could eat, and immortality between the pages of *Girljock* magazine! The day started something like this:

Laurel bounces through the door at 8:30 A.M., all cheeks and smiles, ready to try something somewhat crazy. The other women, Janet, Ilene, Drama, Shannon, and Anne Marie follow somewhat cautiously. The signing of liability waivers inspires nervous jokes about "death" and "dismemberment," almost sending little Anne Marie out the emergency exit!

Strong French roast coffee and gooey "Powerless Bars" ("help for the honeless") from the Gravity Cafe in the gym eased the tension. We chattered about why everyone was there: to try something new; because it seemed fun and challenging; because it seemed scary; because Laurel begged everyone to come with her (besides the fact that Laurel had promised the Herland Carrot Cake Queen she'd deliver some Hot Rock Babes). The coffee and goodies got the gals to stay long enough for the class.

Leading the crew of six was Gladys Love, a climber and Pacific Edge instructor. Her volunteer teaching assistants Jenny, Shannon, Mikayla, and Rachel are part of an alternative high school program that includes climbing in its curriculum. These assistants were five to ten years younger than their students, making for an interesting dynamic.

WHAT HAPPENED NEXT TO OUR ROCK BABES . . .

First: the obligatory caution that climbing is dangerous.

Second: the harness. Most groups struggle to get their harnesses on, but these women were up to task; it almost seemed like they had done it before! (Make sure it fits above your hip bones and that the buckle is double backed.)

Third: the knots. Gotta tie them right or you'll fall right out onto the pea gravel, we don't want that. The assistants help each woman with the figure of eight follow through knot and the fisherman's knot to be used as a back up. The assistants are confident and the students willingly accept their teaching as gospel.

Next: belay practice on the ground. Simple yet demanding, "pull-pinch-slide" is the rule of thumb. Hook your locking caribiner through your harness, slip the rope through the belay device, drop the rope into the carabiner, close and lock its gate. Pull up the slack, pinch the rope with your free hand and slide your break hand toward your belay device. Keep going: "pull-pinch-slide, pull-pinch-slide, pull-pinch-slide." Never take your break hand from the rope.

Now: Belay each other up the wall. Tie the knots, put the climber on belay, double check the system, and go!

On the surface it was all clear and simple: A group of women were climbing and working together. Not so apparent was how climbing affected each woman.

ROCK BABES SPEAK OUT

Girljock decided the best way to let readers know what the climbers experienced was to let their words be heard. Here's what they had to say:

Laurel Elizabeth: "One of the hardest things I did today was charging up the 5.7 wall and finding myself stuck halfway up. I couldn't figure out what my next move needed to be. Everything seemed physically impossible at that point and I was so frustrated! It took me fifteen minutes to get past that one rock. It was so friggin' hard, but I was so glad I didn't give up!

"I surprised myself by doing and having an amazing time climbing the walls. Climbing wasn't something I have ever really given thought to doing before. Maybe I thought that I couldn't pull it off—I was surprised at how much I enjoyed myself!

"The thing I loved about today was being with a group of Amazon women doing something new to all of us together. I loved climbing that wall all by myself yet not being alone at it because my friends were at the bottom, supporting me all the way. That point of utter frustration was almost too much. I was so angry and physically exhausted. My hand was all scraped up and bleeding, but I kept with it. I loved working past that frustration. I got a high from being with that power. I was working with my body in a way I never have . . . I feel like we developed a new relationship. I learned I need to trust my body more. I wasn't trusting it, nor did I realize my own strength before. I would climb again to try different walls because all the paths up are different. It felt like a puzzle to solve with your body.

"I have been telling my friends to try it for the sake of doing something different and because it was damn fun. I saw my friends and myself face our fear of heights, our fear of quitting and of failure. This experience has given me a sense of worth . . . in the physical sense of 'I can do things with my body,' and that I am a strong woman, regardless of the messages society give us. Climbing is such a metaphor for life . . . it showed me that with commitment and perseverance we can do anything!"

Drama Rose: "I climbed the 5.5 wall; getting up on it in the first place was really tough. I had to try about ten times to even make the second step. I almost gave up, but I stuck with it and made it to the top!

"I really liked being with my friends, encouraging each other, and making it to the top when I never thought I could. Learning something new—especially something athletic (since I am not what you would call an athlete!) was great. I would love to try climbing again because it was fun, challenging, and a great work out. You don't have to be a big sports person to enjoy climbing; it seems like anyone could climb. You can start out on an easier climb and work up to harder ones.

"I loved this experience, though it's something I never would have done if Laurel hadn't talked me into it. I worked hard at climbing, but it wasn't impossible, and succeeding at climbing, tying the knots, and belaying made it so much fun."

Anne Marie: "I totally dreaded going to Pacific Edge for the first time. I worried about it all night the night before and almost succeeded in talking myself out of going. I think if it hadn't been a group of my friends in an all-women environment, I probably wouldn't have gone. I was worried about lots of things: certainly the heights; also, I was worried about being able to use the equipment properly, tie the knots correctly, etc. I told Drama, 'Take all the things I am most afraid of, most insecure about, put them all together and make a sport out of it—that's climbing!'

"At the risk of sounding cliché, I must say that climbing is among the most empowering things I've ever done. It was such a rush to feel that I could overcome one of my biggest fears. I get nervous on a stepladder. I was high for the whole rest of the day. I'm not planning on trying Half Dome anytime soon, but now that I know I am able to do it, I'll push myself (slowly!) to try harder climbs. I'm hooked—I'll definitely climb again!"

Ilene Stern: "It was really hard for me to trust people I had no reason to trust in terms of their climbing skills. Since I managed to get out of bed to keep this commitment, I decided to go for it anyway. I felt like I wasn't ready to really challenge myself with the climbing—I stuck with climbs that I knew I could do. I feel like soon I'll be ready to push a little harder. We walked into Pacific Edge as six individuals and emerged as one cohesive unit—a truly valuable experience."

Janet Harvie: "The hardest thing I did was to touch the last rock; I was three moves away. Those three moves were the hardest. I felt like I was going to bust at the seams when I finally grabbed the last hold!

"I surprised myself the whole time I was there: putting on the equipment, by not giving up, at my strength and endurance. I loved when my friends and acquaintances supported me on my journey up that wall. The only time I was really afraid was when I was told it was okay if I wanted to get down when I was frustrated halfway through. I was afraid I might, but I didn't!

"In my life, I have been known to be many unendearing things, and a quitter is one of those things. This experience was a powerful tool to reinstate some of the faith I have in myself. I had lots of support from people who were telling me that any amount of effort, energy, and presence for this activity was going to be respected. This really helped me to not quit because I knew that anything I did would be an accomplishment."

E. Shannon Stavinoha: "I felt unsure that I could belay Anne Marie; belaying is a big responsibility! I kept climbing even though I was scared, I felt really proud of myself and glad that I pushed my limits. I was surprised at how easily I built trust in my belayers and how I could talk myself through panic moments. When I was stuck for so long, unable to find a path to get higher, I was thinking, 'This is impossible, I can't, I can't!' Then I heard what I was telling myself, and I said, 'Shan, you can.' In a minute you'll be above this place and you will be working on a new problem. And then I reached the rock I needed, found the strength to pull myself up, and was at a new place. My next move was to fall off from fatigue, but that was okay, because I loved the whole process. I love that I believed in my ability to persevere.

"Being with women and climbing was wonderful, and having the young women teach us was incredible. They were really great because they were patient and coached us at belaying and climbing. Climbing got me in touch with my brave self, and I felt like a kid playing.

"P.S. It was nice to get to wear a harness in public!"

Bodybuilding's Secret Workout:
The Kitchen

by Roxxie

"The biggest part of a bodybuilder's workout is in the kitchen—where you exercise the motivation to stick to your diet," explains bodybuilder Alex Alexander. "Working out is easy. You don't have to spend a million hours at the gym. The goal of a bodybuilder is not just more muscle, but less fat."

"Bodybuilders' diets are the hardest part. It's hard to be strict with yourself," she confides. "Thirty percent of bodybuilding for me is workout, and 30 percent is attitude/motivation. The other 40 percent is diet."

Alex is a bodybuilding success. She's also a devoted soccer goalie and volleyball player. She bodybuilds in the mornings, or on the evenings that she's not occupied blocking goal shots or spiking volleyballs. She loves team sports (soccer is her favorite), but bodybuilding forces her to be introspective and to feel good about herself. "It comes from within," she says. "You have to see what you can do to make yourself shine. No one else can do it for you, and it helps my self-esteem."

When training for competition, she'll lose up to ten pounds to thin out the outer layer of body fat that obscures women's muscles. Usually she plans four to six months to prepare for a show because "three months is really pushing it. With dieting, easier is better."

And just how does she lose the weight? "Not everybody's routine works for every-

Photo © Alex Alexander Archives

body else," she warns. While she's training she eats six little meals a day. Big meals are slow to digest, and draw a lot of blood into the digestive tract—away from the brain and other important body parts. "You know that light-headed feeling you get after a big meal? That sleepy feeling? That's from big meals," she explains.

She drinks a half gallon of water every day. "Alahambra water is okay, but I prefer Evian—and it's important to drink all the water before 7:00 in the evening, so you don't have to go to the bathroom too late."

Here is Alex's special training diet:

7 A.M. Alex's first meal of the day: oatmeal, two pieces of unbuttered toast (occasionally she'll eat no-fat no-calorie jam), and juice. Her favorite juices are orange juice, grapefruit juice, or "the Ocean Spray combination juices."

9 A.M. Meal #2: a protein shake and a banana, or, a muffin.

Noon Lunchtime features baked chicken with no skin, brown or white rice "with nothing on it," more fruit, and lots of water.

3 P.M. Time for another protein shake!

5 P.M. (ish) A PowerBar, and a big container of water. Then . . . work-out time.

Around 7 P.M. Dinner: fish, chicken, or turkey, with rice and vegetables. Possibly some juice or a nonfat dessert. (Alex doesn't eat much red meat when training.) She steams her vegetables—because she doesn't like them raw—and goes for those with high iron such as broccoli or spinach. She loves green beans, and often will enjoy a broccoli-carrot-rice mixture.

Late-night snacks? Popcorn cakes, maybe a glass of juice.

"Cutting out sweets is really hard," she admits. She substitutes fruit, unsweetened applesauce, or natural fruit-juice sweetened cookies for heavy doses of sugar. She drinks lots of diet Coke.

And, the minute the competition she's been training for is over, she craves pizza! "A basic cheese slice," she explains. Her nontraining diet allows her the pleasures of cheeseburgers and a switch from nonfat to two-percent low-fat milk.

Protein Shake Power

Alex loves protein shakes.
Here's her secret recipe.
Take a banana, or a bunch of strawberries blend with
8 oz. of nonfat milk (she uses 2% lowfat when she's not in training) and
2 tablespoons of protein powder
("Most protein powders are basically the same," says Alex, "but I like Hot Stuff. It's got a lot of vitamins and minerals in it. It helps muscle growth, and maintenance of muscle size.")

Advice for Would-be Bodybuilders

"It helps to train with a friend."
"You can't really drink on a training diet (but then I don't really drink anyway)."
"It's good to talk with people who've got the kind of body you want to have . . . see what they do, but not everybody's routine works for everybody."
"Steroids are a drug—*don't do it*. They accelerate muscle growth but there are a million negatives . . . your liver, kidneys, spleen, heart get overloaded with toxins. Do it the natural way, it just takes more time and patience. Steroids are cheating, it's just to look good . . . a short cut."
"It helps a lot if your girlfriend goes on your diet with you."
"It helps a lot if your girlfriend is into sports."

Putting on the Gloves

by Stephanie Rosenbaum

"Thank you for calling the Bay Area Boxing Club."

It was with some trepidation that I phoned the Bay Area Boxing Club, a gay and lesbian boxing group, for permission to watch a training session just a few days before their next tournament. After all, the only lesbian boxer I knew was Frameline director Jenni Olson, who regularly takes out film festival stress on her in-office punching bag. From capoiera to tae kwon do, most of my friends have taken some kind of martial arts training, but competitive boxing was a whole different ball game.

"The Bay Area Boxing Club . . . the boxing club that actually boxes . . ."

What else would a boxing club *do*, I wondered as I left my name and number. It's not like the Bohemian Club, which you can be pretty sure isn't full of guys in goatees smoking reefer and reading Gary Snyder. Boxing is boxing, right? You put on your gloves, shake out the creases in your Everlasts, the bell rings and Bam! Clean left hook to the jaw, TKO, screaming fans, "He's down!" three, two, one, BZZZZ! But I asked around until a New York source told me there are certain boxing clubs where boxing is a euphemism, a code word like Plato's Symposium, where the activities are more along the lines of the wrestling scene in D. H. Lawrence's *Women in Love* than a Tyson-Spinks bout.

But the Bay Area Boxing Club is serious about boxing. Tough, sweaty, rule-abiding, competitive boxing for men *and* women—an anomaly in a sport where a men-only rule still holds in most training gyms. In fact, the hour and a half that the BABC works out is the only time all week that women are allowed in the gym where practices are held.

Tonight there are five men and one woman warming up in the gym around the punching bags, shadow boxing in the wall of mirrors with the concentration of Russian ballerinas. Everywhere, there are posters, photographs, banners, hand-lettered good wishes to locals heading off to distant matches—all testaments to the glory of boxing.

"My lover and I started this particular boxing club in our attic in 1977," says club trainer Greg Varney, watching the group's warm-ups from a corner of the ring. "It stayed underground for about a good thirteen, fourteen years. People boxed each other in garages, set up matches, and everyone, including myself, was a little afraid because you know boxing's got its rough aspects."

A professional trainer for over twenty years, Varney had to come out to his colleagues in order to make the club public. His fellow coaches took his homosexuality in stride. "We've gotten all the support in the world," says Varney. "It's been a good community thing." However, the club still doesn't publicize the whereabouts of its training workouts and tournaments, since they use facilities in a local recreational center often low on general supervision.

The focus of tonight's training is the club's second tournament, the *Second All-Gay Boxing Rainbow Championships,* with boxers coming from as far away as Seattle and Washington, D.C. The exclusion of boxing as a *New York in '94* Gay Games sport rankles Varney. "Because we're not officially included in the Games, this is our trial event for what we like to call the Games in Exile—the sports that don't quite make it."

Unlike previous exhibition matches, the tournament's ten to fifteen matches will be competitive, with boxers scored on the number of clean blows hit as well as overall form. However, as Varney is quick to point out, there will be no Rocky-style fighting. This is a sport, not a brawl, and the sort of take-no-prisoners mauling so popular among the Stallone set has no place in this ring. "We stop where there's blood, we give standing A counts, and we stop when a good blow is thrown. Unless it's very even, we don't let it go. There's no reason for anyone to get the shit beat out of them."

As the boxers move around the gym, it takes me a minute to pick out Elia, the one woman in the group. Compact and muscular, her attention never wavers from the mirror as she works on her jabs. "We've had some trouble getting off the ground with women," Greg admits. "A lot of that had to do with the fact that a lot of women wanted to have a woman trainer. I can understand that." While the club has always been open to women, Greg kept his

recruiting style low-key at first. "But then I came back and I said, well, there's not a lot of women boxing, and I don't know a woman who can box as good as me, so why don't I teach you? By using that approach, I started getting women in here."

Varney takes obvious pride in Elia's form and concentration, already honed after only six weeks of training. His only worry now is finding someone to match her up with in the upcoming tournament. Her moves are good, but she's a lightweight—130 pounds and dropping, and he's heard the women coming in from Seattle are big. They could have fifty pounds on her, easy—not a handicap a new boxer wants for her first tournament. But Elia's used to competition: She's competed in the Gay Games as a cyclist with Team San Francisco. Already familiar with karate, she started boxing as a way to cross-train.

As we talk in a corner of the gym, the men pair up for three-minute rounds with the punching bags. This is tough, Elia tells me. "You go for three minutes, and I swear, you feel like you're made of noodles by the end, like you don't have anything left. Cycling is fun—this is work!" And she means it. Obviously in great shape, she still comes out of the ring running with sweat after only a few rounds. She'd like to see more women boxing. As it is, she can name only a few women in the whole country boxing on the tournament level. On why there aren't more, she points out the exclusionary policies of most gyms. "If you can't even walk into the gym, how are you ever going to put the gloves on or get good technique?"

The training pauses for a pretournament pep talk. The boxers are reminded to be at the gym before four o'clock, ". . . and if you don't think I'll scratch you [for being late], just try me," warns Varney, sounding like everyone's tough-love high school football coach.

Members are warned against eating bananas (they increase the pain of body blows), reminded to use the facilities *before* getting their hands wrapped, and above all, encouraged to stay focused and relaxed before their matches. That means no talking to the other clubs, no forgetting of mouth guards or last-minute fussing. Have a San Francisco attitude. Use your head. Psyche 'em out.

When the practice resumes, I sidestep the swinging bags to talk to a few of the guys.

"I love to fight," says Mike, wearing a tight red T-shirt with the phrase "Come Into My Office" emblazoned under an image of a boxing ring. "And I was looking for an outlet besides the streets. Here, it's safe, it's structured—it's fantastic."

Tommy, on the other hand, started boxing as a way to combat his fear of the ring. "I wanted to get into another sport besides weight lifting, and it always kind of frightened me, the confrontation aspects of being in the ring and not being able to run. So I wanted to teach myself the ability to face that."

An hour and a half after the six boxers entered the gym, it's time to pull off the sweaty gloves and go home. The fierce, controlled violence of the ring dissolves into good-bye hugs and loose camaraderie. On Halloween, as the Castro fills with good fairies and wicked witches, gawkers and queens, these men and women will be swigging water, adjusting their Everlasts, and getting ready for some serious work.

The Joy of In-line Skating

by Cherie Turner

IN THE BEGINNING

"In-line skating is not cool, and besides, it hurts my feet and it is scary. I'll just stick with my roller skates."

That's what I used to think of this sport that is sweeping the urban streets of our world. Overtaking the roller-skate market of my youth, in-line skating is not only a lot of fun, it's practical. These skates, as opposed to those of yesteryear, allow you to go so much faster that they make for a great way to get around town or just get out, exercise, and have fun. I'm getting ahead of myself. Let me explain how I got from the beginning of this story to where I am today, a mere nine months later, having competed in an in-line race and made skating a part of my everyday existence.

It took a friend and a little frustration to persuade me to put back on the Rollerblades I had bought six years before and had since given to my brothers. They had been uncomfortable and difficult to use without falling. They just weren't fun. But now, after befriending a skater and trying to keep up with him on my quads (conventional roller skates), I decided I'd give in-lines one last shot. He just

Photo © Cherie Turner

seemed enthusiastic about them.

First I learned that my skates did not have to squeeze all the blood out of my feet in order to fit correctly. They became comfortable. Then I learned what you can do on a pair of skates. Admittedly, the first few times I went out in unknown territory I was leery, and when I saw what other skaters could do, I figured they were either very experienced or very crazy. Certainly I'd never feel so able on a pair of skates that those moves would not be frightening. I simply did not realize that with practice and some basic skills you can go anywhere and do anything on a pair of in-lines.

As I became more interested and practiced, and more able on my four wheels, I began to meet the skater crowd. The one thing that struck me as really intriguing was the diversity of the people interested in the sport. There are tall ones, heavy ones, smokers, elite athletes, children, mothers, grandfathers, and professionals. The list is endless but the interest is the same; we all enjoy gathering together and zooming, dancing, or jumping around on our skates. A whole new subculture, and what a joy. Unlike any other sport I'd ever been involved with, skaters seem to offer the most unique blend. There is no stereotype.

So love for skating developed like any love does. At first it was just the joy of something new to explore. Then, after the initial bases had been covered, there was the chance to settle in and explore a wider range of possibilities. I learned that skating gives you freedom. In-line skating is flying on the ground. In a natural human stance, fueled by your own energy, you are able to glide over the otherwise motionless surface of the ground. Unlike any other sport, skating gives you the liberation of wheels without the need for motors or extravagant equipment. The small amount of equipment needed makes locomotion convenient and easy, whether you are sight-seeing or commuting. You need little more than you would regularly drag around if you were just walking, and you can go so far so fast. They are easy to stow away when you want to enter work, a store, or a restaurant. Just a pair of light shoes in a pack and you're in there!

As you can imagine, it wasn't long before the enjoyment of in-lining permeated my life to the point that skating has become a part of my existence. I have begun to explore the speed skating side of things because I truly enjoy just going *fast*! This has brought a whole new dimension to my interest, a whole new realm to explore.

What follows are some of my thoughts on how to get involved in this sport. As you might guess, I am not a lifelong expert on the in-line industry. Rather, I hope that my recent entrance into the sport, along with a lengthy athletic history and the advice of some of the most experienced, impressive skaters I've ever met (I have come to learn that San Francisco has a very large number of awesome skaters in many disciplines), have given me enough knowledge, mixed with a fresh outlook, to speak to the novice as well as those who have gotten past the basics.

THE FIRST ATTEMPTS
You'll Need

1. An adventurous spirit. The first couple of times that you skate can be scary, frustrating, clumsy, and out of control. More than most sports, in-line skating makes you feel helpless because your feet never touch the ground. This can be somewhat disconcerting (especially for those of us who are control freaks). You must therefore approach this event as an adventure and go with the flow; it won't always be this difficult.

2. Willingness to look like an idiot. I have yet to see one novice skater who doesn't look like a complete dork (me included). You wobble, your body jerks around trying to establish balance with your arms flailing. You resemble someone walking across ice with slippers on their feet. Go with it. Trying to look cool and in control only makes you look like a self-conscious dork. I found learning to skate a wonderful time to laugh at myself.

3. To take a deep breath in the face of fear. The first couple of times you skate you're likely to slip, slide, and fall. This can be scary. But instead of freaking out

and tensing up (which can be the deciding factor in making you fall), take a deep breath and relax as much as possible. Your body really does know how to stay upright. Let it do its thing.

4. Equipment. Skates, pads, and a helmet. Make sure that the skates are very comfortable. Ask around for the shop with the best, most knowledgeable staff. Believe me, it's worth spending the time to find skates you like: Uncomfortable skates can be the difference between fun and misery.

Purchase a skate made by a major skate manufacturer—these companies know how to make skates and you will be able to find replacement parts. You are also less likely to have structural problems. The price of a particular skate is often determined by the features that come with the skate and the quality of the wheels and bearings. Therefore, the boots and frames are not necessarily better on the more expensive skates. Make sure that any features you pay for are important to you, and remember, you can easily change the wheels and bearings.

Wheels differ in size (measured in millimeters) and hardness. Basically, the bigger the wheel, the faster you can go. If speed is an interest, you may want to consider buying skates with a frame to fit large wheels. The hardness of a wheel determines how well it will grip the surface and how fast it will wear. Hard wheels—indicated by a higher hardness rating, which is found on the wheel next to the millimeter size—last longer but they don't grip the surface on which you are skating as

well. Bearings are rated by Abec numbers that range from 1 to 5. The higher the number, the more precise the bearing balls and, thus, the faster the bearings should spin. Most moderately priced skates come with Abec 3, which is fine for general use. Pads and helmet are a must!

THE FIRST STEPS (UH, I MEAN ROLLS)

When you put on that first pair of skates, it's important to learn how to balance, break, and avoid obstacles. To begin, find a flat, smooth surface, preferably with grass on at least one side so that if all else fails you can head for the grass and bail out. Many big cites have areas that are closed to cars on certain days. These tend to make great spots to learn. Also, many skate stores will offer a free lesson with the purchase of skates. Ask around to find out if this is available in your area.

Start by balancing on your skates. Hold on to something stable and shift your weight to find out how the skates react.

Photo © Cherie Turner

41

You will find that keeping your weight forward will give the most stability. Again, wear all the protective gear so that you don't sustain any real injuries. (You look more silly flailing around without pads than you do with them.) Start rolling with your knees bent and arms forward. Once you get going, learn how to use the break. The best way to do this is by "sitting" with the leg on the break side while holding the other leg slightly forward. Best advice: Watch someone who knows what they're doing and imitate them. This holds true with all lessons of skating. Watching someone gives you a visual of what your body should be doing.

Other things to work on once you get rolling and stopping are avoiding obstacles, changing surfaces (going up and down curbs), and skating over different surfaces.

Proper form can dramatically affect your ability to skate. The problem that most skaters exhibit is allowing their ankles to roll inward. Focus on keeping your wheels perpendicular or, preferably, slightly rolled out when you're rolling. This aids in stability, builds the correct muscles to hold your feet in the correct position, helps you have a more efficient stroke, and gives you style points.

On the note of stroke. Ideally, you want to start with your legs together ankles rolled slightly out; push your leg outward and at the end of the stroke flick your skate outward. You'll notice that by starting with your wheels slightly edged in (ankles outward) you can get a more full stroke than with the wheels angled out (ankles in). This should help you keep away from the one posture to watch out for, the A-frame skater. This is someone who has

their legs spread wide and shifts back and forth from one leg to the other without ever stroking and gliding on their wheels. This position gets you nowhere. If you find yourself here, don't despair. Bring your feet together, slightly bend your knees, and stride.

The most crucial step to take when you become proficient is to remove that pesky brake. Horror!! Terror!! How will I ever stop? Well, let me tell you from a 'fraidy-cat's point of view, taking the brake off is the most liberating day of skating ever. The brake elongates the skate and makes it harder to maneuver. In order to stop without a brake you need to learn the T-stop. The T-stop requires that you drag one skate behind you at a right angle to the skate you are rolling on. Certainly, practice this a lot to build up confidence before you actually take off the brake. Or, do as some of my anxious friends did and just crash a lot. Either way, you'll find yourself more mobile and more confident in your abilities. As you advance, you can also learn other ways to brake, such as slaloming (turning quickly back and forth), "street plowing" (skates angled slightly in like a snow plow), power slide (turn, extend one skate behind you, and slide to a stop), or the hockey stop (jumping sideways with both skates to stop abruptly).

Once you are able to get around comfortably, you can branch out and work on new skills. Some of the more popular practices are speed skating, jumping, slalom, dancing, grinding, hockey, and ramp skating. All types of skating are done on four-wheel skates except for speed skating, which is most efficient on five wheels (although you can learn to go very fast with whatever you own). For all of the other disciplines, there are generally specific places that you can practice these skills. Just look or ask around to find a place near you.

As you can see, there is room for everyone in this sport. If you tire of one realm, you always have the freedom to learn something new. Since you don't need a whole new set of equipment, you won't be limited by your bank account.

On a final note, you will quickly learn that skating equipment can get very pricey. There are wonderful $800.00 speed skates, lovely leather hockey skates, wheels for every occasion, and frames that are made for your every whim. . . . The possibilities are endless.

SKATE MAINTENANCE

It's very important to keep your skates in good working order, which is very easy. Even those of us who are not particularly fond of equipment fiddling, skates require so little care that the attention you do pay to them is painless. The reason for this is that skates have just a few parts: the boot, frame, wheels, bearing, and wheel bolts. Care of the boot is as follows: This is a major part of your skate's identity. Keep it clean and decorate it with cool stickers and paint.

Keep the frames clean too.

Wheel bolts should be cleaned. Apply a little grease when they become dry.

Bearings are a matter of preference. Some will tell you that bearings should be cleaned with soap and water, or some other degreaser, and then lightly oiled. This is the safest advice. But to keep you informed, some say to do the above but leave out the oil because they claim it slows the bearings. And then there are those who have told me not to touch them at all but instead "skitch" (grab onto a car and let it pull you) at about forty miles per hour. Anything that should not be in the bearings will be forced to leave. This is illegal and I do not recommend it to anyone, but, quite honestly, I've never seen wheels spin so well as with this method.

Wheels need to be rotated which means that they need to play musical chairs with each position in the frame. One side of the wheel wears faster than the other and the pattern in each position is different. It's the same concept as rotating your car's wheels. The general rule of thumb is to rotate the front and rear wheels to the center and the center wheels to the front and rear, and switch the wheels from the left to the right and the right to the left. The goal is to wear the wheels evenly so that they don't get lopsided. That's the end of skate maintenance. If you use these techniques, you won't have to replace parts very often and your skates will be *bitchen*!

FINALE

That's it. I hope that this encourages you to search out the joy of skating, to recognize the versatility of this sport. Realize the freedom and experience the fun!

Bees on Ice

by Roxxie

They love big hair, women, cool jerseys, and skates. They make things travel at speeds of eighty miles per hour and they wear tons of padding. They believe big hair and big muscles should go together. Their worst fear is a groin pull, so they're always stretching "down there." They define themselves as, "BEE•Hive (be'hiv'), n. lesbian on skates with *Big Hair* and a penchant for black rubber."

With female hockey players making national news by breaking into the men's pro leagues, a new national trend of female interest and participation in ice hockey has taken off. Even women who love big hair are drawn to this helmet-mandatory sport. The Boston Beehives, a lesbian ice hockey team, even sport T-shirts with an ultrafemme icon—a big-haired woman powdering herself in the mirror. Why are so many women of all hair types drawn to this fast-moving well-padded sport?

This pressing question drove *Girljock* to find the behind-the-scenes story about Boston's Beehives, big hair, pads, and lesbian skating action.

Girljock **Reporter Roxxie:** *What stylistically separates you from other hockey teams?*
Beehive Maria Vetrano, Queen Bee: And we're not talking ice dancing, here. We are babes on blades who fire a puck eighty miles an hour. We are women of the blue line. We love ice rinks, hockey sticks, cool jerseys, women, and big hair. I suppose you could say we have a sense of camp, because, unlike your typical team, with names like "Sharks" or "Chargers" or "Barbarians" or whatever, we are the "Beehives," and we want to play hockey and exploit humor at the same time. Why should gay men have the corner on camp?

R: *Good question. What does it take to become a Beehive? Do you have special initiation rituals?*

M: Well, if a new player were six feet tall with nineteen-inch hair, we'd roll out the red carpet for her. We'd probably be so distracted we couldn't even practice. She wouldn't need an initiation ritual; some of us might even kowtow to her. Now, if a more typical sized player wanted to join the Beehives, we would ask her about her political affiliations and make sure she wasn't a vegetarian. Not really, we'd ask how long she'd played hockey, what her favorite colors are, has she ever wounded anyone with a slapshot . . .

R: *Do you recruit musical players as well?*

M: YES! Beehives love to sing and otherwise carry on. We could always use more Divas. When we were in Montreal last April for the first Gay & Lesbian North American Hockey Challenge, we won the Talent Competition.

R: *What did you perform?*

M: An original spin-off of "Mr. Sandman" and customized version of "It Had to Be You," which we sang to my friend, Al, who was wearing a wig, heels, and one of my mother's dresses. He looked like a very butch Patsy Cline with facial hair.

We sang before and after practices, we sang walking down the street, we sang at the Montreal talent competition—that was actually pretty competitive, what with a men's team from LA being there and all. We even sang at Boston's Gay & Lesbian Pride Parade in June.

R: *So what's the hockey like on your team? How competitive are you?*

M: We have a mixed level team. Some players will go on to the U.S. Nationals this year, some are moderately competitive and experienced. Almost all of us play every week in one of the Boston women's leagues and one coaches girls' prep ice hockey.

R: *What are the main hockey injuries and how do you avoid them?*

M: Well, the one which I detest the absolute most and can be very limiting, shall we say, is the groin pull. If you're skating a lot, it's important to stretch the groin—or say goodbye to your love life during hockey season. Knee injuries, like ligament strains and pulls, are also fairly common. I've seen some nasty things over the years—broken collarbones and one broken pelvis—but those are few and far between.

R: *Can you cruise the other teams during games or is the play too fast?*

M: It's very hard to cruise someone who's wearing a helmet. It's not like the old NHL days when players skated around *sans* head protection. So, you really can't see anyone's face in great detail. Maybe her skating style and puck handling will drive you crazy, who knows? Cruising is usually reserved for pregame and postgame celebrations. At the postgame party in Montreal, some of our players engaged in mega-adult "Truth or Dare"; more than one of us walked up to the opposition, delivering kisses on mouths and navels.

R: *Did drag queens influence the evolution of your "big hair" style, or was it a leftover from childhood?*

M: Drag queens, no. Doris Day, yes. The big hair thing flies in the face of how hockey players usually define themselves—macho, virile, all of that. Beehives are a contradiction in terms: We are silly women with a femmy icon who can *really* play hockey.

R: *Of all hair options, why big hair?*

M: Because we get sick of cruising cute blond boys on the street, having mistaken them for women. We think big hair *and* big muscles go together.

R: *Do you keep "big hair" when you play?*

M: No, it wouldn't fit under our helmets—and it would look really terrible after a game of hockey. "Big hair" is a way of life—a Beehive mentality. We are "big hair," so we don't always have to wear it. We do have some official wigs, though, and one of our be-

wigged players once metamorphosed into a suburban housewife while we weren't looking. It's a sad story. We now call her Louise. Last I know, she was buying a Volvo. Tragic.

R: *Do fans wear wigs?*

M: Only our male ones, for some reason. I guess our female ones are too concerned with catching our attention. Unlike the other team, they're not wearing helmets. So we can see them quite well. Our fans also perform a Beehive cheer of sorts—it's called the "Beehive Buzz." When a Beehive scores a goal

or a Beehive goalie makes a great save, they do this buzzing thing. This happened in Montreal. Unfortunately, some of the Montreal fans caught on and they started spraying our fans with imaginary Raid. It wasn't pretty.

R: *Do drag queens get jealous of your wigs or hockey drag?*

M: The drag queens again! Are your best friends drag queens? We've never had any protests by drag queens or anything—and I think they have fancier wigs. As for our hockey drag—it's not the most attractive garb in the world, although some women do seem to look hot in it. I don't think a drag queen would be caught dead in a hockey uniform. It doesn't have any sequins.

R: *So, what does your uniform look like?*

M: We aim for classic line and color—we have white jerseys with black line art. The art is of a Beehive woman in uniform on skates. We also have matching socks and some of us wear lipstick under our helmets.

R: *How do you Bees get ready for games?*

M: We usually sing in the locker room in a little pregame psyche-up ritual. Sometimes we also hum the theme from "Mission Impossible." We've only sang on the ice once, but look forward to more opportunities in the future.

R: *Are bigger hockey sticks more macho, or are hockey sticks all the same size?*

M: Some sticks are more macho than oth-

ROXXIE REPORTS ON THE FEMALE SIDE OF PROTECTORS

Not everyone calls them jills. Cooper, the company that makes them, says they are "Women's Protective Pads." Bay Area Valkyries winger Angie Dennis says, "I grew up on the East Coast calling them jill straps. People call them 'women's protectors,' or 'jill straps,' or you can call them your cup, too."

The jill strap is made of hard plastic and foam padding. The plastic is on the outside, and the foam padding underneath, protecting the groin area from trauma. Jill straps are mandatory equipment for collegiate hockeywomen, but not everyone playing recreational hockey wears them.

"Some people won't wear it cause they say it feels like a sanitary napkin, but it doesn't even go down past your clit," Valkyrie Dennis explains. "All defenders wear them, 'cause, when an eighty or ninety miles per hour slap shot hits you in the crotch, you're going to be sorry. Offensive players don't always wear them but they should wear them too, 'cause many times they have to play defense too, or offensive players can get a stick in the crotch, too. I've seen women crawl to the bench after a hard crotch hit, and lay there moaning for the rest of the period."

Body temperature plays another factor in the jill strap issue. Hockey, although requiring cold ice, is a sweaty sport. The big padded shorts hockey players wear, called "breezers," have a guesseted crotch made of mesh or sheer material. The wind blows through the crotch area, severely cooling the crotches of non-jill-strapped women. "You get really cold," says Dennis, who sounds as if she's skipped wearing hers at least once, "I feel naked without one. Jill straps are like a tiny little clit cup."

Jill straps give Dennis and many other female players a new feeling of equality with men. Dennis explains, "In hockey, locker rooms are given out per team. If you play coed hockey, you share locker rooms with men sometimes. Hockey isn't modest, at all. People will even change in the hallway. When I'm getting dressed in a locker room with men, and they put on and adjust their jock straps, I get to adjust my jill strap, and it feels good."

---

ers—they're called goalie sticks. I'm one of the Beehives' goalies, but I'm not feeling that macho right now, so I'm learning defense.

Goalie sticks are much larger. They're designed for deflecting shots; forward sticks (used by defense, wings, and centers) are designed for shooting and controlling the puck. Some players are more "macha" than others, but that's got nothing to do with the sticks.

R: *What kind of padding do hockey players wear and where does it go?*

M: Well, I think I'll start with forward equipment; it's easier to explain. Forwards wear pants, knee/shin guards, shoulder/breast pads, pelvic protectors (more important than you know!), elbow pads, gloves, helmets, and skates. Goalies wear all the padding they can get their hands on. Sometimes they look like Michelin Tire Women on skates. Goalies wear special pants, big leg pads that extend from their lower thighs to their skates, pelvic protectors, goalie skates, arm and chest pads, spe-

47

cial gloves—a blocker and a catcher, and a helmet with a throat protector. Goalies don't travel as fast as forwards.

R: *While wearing full hockey uniforms, can you tell the difference between a man and a woman? A butch and femme?*

M: You can't always tell the difference between men and women. It's those helmets again. If Mary Stuart Masterson wore one, I wouldn't even recognize her—and that would be terrible. So, you can't always tell gays and lesbians apart, either. There are some excellent lesbian and gay male (not drag queens) ice hockey players. One of the guys on the Montreal team used to play in the NHL, and he didn't wear a helmet. He also had a mustache. I knew *he* wasn't a woman! As for butches and femmes, it's like I said before. We're all butch and we're all femme. Almost all. One of our players, Donna, is really pretty femme. If she lost her Lancôme, all hell would break loose.

R: *What are good ways to stay in shape for hockey?*

M: Biking, StairMaster, racquetball, weight training, jogging (if your knees are okay) are all good. Hockey requires both strength and speed, sprints and endurance. It's flavorful, yet piquant—know what I mean?

R: *Will there ever be women's professional ice hockey?*

M: I don't know. Will there ever be women's professional basketball or softball? Both of those games have more participants nationwide. Even men's hockey isn't as big a sport as baseball or basketball, so I don't think that women's hockey will be one of the first (other than golf, tennis, or beach volleyball) to go professional. Also, one of the sick things about men's professional hockey is the contact—

checking and fighting. These things are not (generally) part of the women's game. I think that women will have professional hockey when all the homophobes and most of the men are sent to Idaho to live. When our neo-Amazonian society is in place, then women will have professional hockey. I'm hoping that will be soon.

There's a woman goalie who's playing professionally now, and I think she's the first woman to ever get a real contract with a pro team. Her name is Manon Rheaume, she's only twenty years old, and she's a native of Quebec. On September 23rd of this year, she was the first woman ever to play in a major league men's professional game. She played one period (that's twenty minutes, not five days) for the Tampa Bay Lightning, an NHL expansion team run by Phil Esposito. After the game, she signed a three-year contract with the Atlanta Knights, the Lightning's International Hockey League affiliate (minor league team).

R: *Do you think she'd like to be a Beehive?*

M: I think she's straight, and a lesbian team wouldn't be the place for her. Besides, she's much more serious than we are. I would love to see her play. Any Beehive in her right mind would. One of our coaches, S. T., who's an excellent goalie in her own right, ran out and bought Manon Rheaume's rookie card. She was psyched. We all were.

R: *What would you say to Manon Rheaume, if you could?*

M: I'd say (in perfect Canadian French), "It's an honor to meet you. Your accomplishments and your courageousness are awesome. . . . Hey, you're cute. Have you met my friend, Louise?"

Gay Gaming:
Gay Games IV, New York City

by Nancy Boutilier

FRIDAY: THE DEPARTURE

The terminal is overflowing with queers and their sports gear. My departure for New York reminds me of the airports during the March on Washington, but this time nobody calls me "sir." Instead, a student sees me and comes over to say hi. Her parents follow. I introduce them all to my partner. The father asks about the tennis rackets I'm carrying, and I tell him we're on our way to the Gay Games. "Cool!" says my student, and she means it.

"Oh, that's great," says the father as their flight is called. "Good luck," the mother calls back over her shoulder, waving. And I think about how lucky I am that the people of California defeated the Briggs Initiative that would have banned lesbians and gay men from being high school teachers.

Still, it's unusual to be out as a teacher, even more unusual to be out as a high school coach. In part, that's why I'm going to the Gay Games. That's why the work of those who fought back at the Stonewall Inn twenty-five years ago was only the beginning.

SATURDAY: DAY OPENING CEREMONIES

After a long wait lining up, milling about, finding a few friends from lives I lived before moving to San Francisco, we finally head for the stadium. Opening Ceremonies catch me off guard. I choke up as I march in with Team San Francisco. Where did all these people come from to fill the stadium? The procession of athletes goes on and on. So many flags. So much cheering. Sure, this might be about showing the world the narrowness of stereotypes, these images might reshape someone's view, but for now it's us, the queers in the stadium, celebrating ourselves and each other. How wonderful it is to see the new South African flag flying over the dozen competitors from that country. I cheer the courage of the two participants from Alabama. I wonder what it's like to be a lesbian in Cuba? A bisexual in Cyprus? A gay man in Venezuela? a transsexual in New Zealand?

There's camp, celebration, and fun. Some political welcomes, including the noticeable rumble within San Francisco's sizable contingent when Mayor Frank Jordan offers greetings. A short film pays tribute to Tom Waddell and his vision of the Games as an event fostering inclusion and the quest for one's personal best. Video greetings from Greg Louganis and Billie Jean King. Athletes' and officials' oaths taken symbolically by Dave Kopay and Dave Pallone. We all fall silent to remember those who have lost the biggest match of all, their lives. I feel tremors, and when the dance production that culminates in the lighting of the flame, I know only what it's like to be me.

SUNDAY: SUBWAYS

Getting to and from events is always a mass transit adventure. The Gay Games badges around our necks make for a week-long visibility fiesta. Gays and lesbians are visible in all five boroughs heading for more than thirty sports venues. We often travel in teams, in groups big enough to make up the majority of a subway car. We hold hands, make jokes, talk about our events. Everyone on the train knows we're queer.

With the celebration of the New York Rangers' Stanley Cup victory, the World Cup soccer matches, the Knicks losing the NBA title, O. J. Simpson's fall from grace, and Barbra Streisand's Madison Square Garden appearances, there are plenty of reasons for New Yorkers and the media to be distracted. But here we were in the thousands with proud T-shirts, pins, and badges, in every subway car. Even in New York, we cannot be ignored!

Gay and lesbian New Yorkers commuting to and from work, not involved in the Games, eagerly approach to engage in conversation: Where are you from? Have you seen the Stonewall exhibit at the public library yet? The news reported that some world records have been set. . . .

One young social worker told me how the visibility of others had allowed her to come out to some of her coworkers.

Again and again, they talk of the wonderful way their city has been invaded—11,000 athletes, hundreds of cultural events, 20 different languages, everywhere queer!

It's too much to say New York will never be the same, but I do believe our presence put a dent in the consciousness of all.

TUESDAY: TENNIS

My main event. A fulfillment of a childhood dream to play at the site of the U.S. Open. My parents come to watch. I play well enough to secure a bronze medal for myself, but, in the end, it is hardly the point of my being here.

WEDNESDAY: POLITICS ABROAD

One small but active presence is that of Gays and Lesbians in Zimbabwe (GALZ). Beverly Clark of GALZ is eager to raise awareness of the growing gay and lesbian movement in Zimbabwe. "We're trying to build a community that gives social support. A lot of gays and lesbians in Zimbabwe are scared of being too political," said Clark.

Three years of Gay Pride Weeks have helped GALZ create a multiracial organization of 150 members. In addition to the four athletes who participated in the Games, two representatives of GALZ had been sponsored to attend the ILGA conference held concurrent with the Games.

Clark understands why South African politics have been in the American media's spotlight, yet she also knows that each country struggles in its own way. While she called South Africa "a small, cosmopolitan country," Clark sees Zimbabwe as "a small, backwater area" where the treatment of gays and lesbians is, in some ways, "harsher" than in South Africa.

Censorship is tighter in Zimbabwe, where her organization cannot even get newspapers to run classified ads offering counseling services to gays and lesbians.

GALZ does publish a quarterly magazine,

which Clark edits, but both Clark and her partner have had their offices raided by police.

"We're hoping that Mandela will influence Mugabe's attitudes" about gay rights, she says.

THURSDAY: POLITICS AT HOME

At Ellis Island I look for my grandmother's name on the wall of immigrants. What I find in the museum is a crude button hook used to inspect the eyes of potential immigrants for trachoma, a contagious eye disease. The museum displays explaining the quarantine and medical exams conducted to prevent foreigners with contagious diseases from entering the country. While the exhibit reports the procedures as if such demeaning inspections are only past history, the strings that Gay Games organizers pulled to allow for HIV-positive participants to gain entry into the U.S. with an exemption from the ban on their entry reminds me that today's immigration policies remain as crude as those button hooks.

It seems as much a step back as step forward when I hear praise for the exemption. Better the ban be lifted altogether than our country's current welcome: "Give me you tired, your weary, your HIV-negative . . ."

FRIDAY: MEDALLING AROUND

What fun to stroll through Greenwich Village with my medal on. When else will I ever get to wear it? Where else will it ever be so appreciated? Gays and lesbians nod, smile, and offer congratulations. Others in medals of their own ask "what sport?" and I return the favor so they can tell of their own victories.

The straight couples are filled with questions. They have seen something in the news—coverage is pretty good—and want to know more about these Gay Games: How good is the competition? Had I seen pairs figure skating? Is Mario Cuomo really playing basketball?

A grandmotherly woman—strong, short, Italian American—high-fives me for my victory.

SATURDAY: CLOSING CEREMONIES

The metaphor is right that we march into Closing Ceremonies not in geographically defined contingents as we did at the Opening Ceremonies, but as one enormous tribe. I am reunited with an old friend swimming for Denmark. I meet Lisbon's only participant, silver medalist Lita Gale, who had no Portuguese teammates for the opening march and now has 11,000: *Unity '94*.

The walk into Yankee Stadium, yes, a filled Yankee Stadium, is amazing. To see Marga Gomez, Roberta Achtenberg, Rikki Streicher on stage before the thousands is a San Franciscan dyke's dream come true.

Rumors have been flying about possible performers—Elton John, Melissa Etheridge, Aretha Franklin, Madonna, Queen Latifa, maybe even Barbra herself.

None of the above show, but nobody notices because there's a host of drag queens strutting on stage as Cindi Lauper bounces around singing "Girls Just Wanna Have Fun."

Then, when Patti LaBelle wants a mike stand and gives a warm and wonderful hug to the techy dyke who brings one, we're all melting—and not from New York's heat. LaBelle calls the dyke "Sugar" and then belts out something even sweeter, the most memorable and loving rendition of "Somewhere Over the Rainbow" I ever hope to hear.

If Opening Ceremonies celebrated our gathering, Closing Ceremonies is sending a message for us to carry back home: Come out, come out, come out, keep visibility on the rise.

Along with an inspiring account of the cheers that welcomed her wheeling to the finish of the 10K race, Janet Weinberg, Disabilities Services Committee Chair, urges participants to retain the lessons of the Games. Just as we've learned to cheer our diverse community in athletic endeavor, she said, "let us not forget to do the same when the Games are over."

I want to give Tai Babilonia and Randy Gardner gold medals for public acknowledgement that figure skating has been hit hard by AIDS. How bold it is for them to step forward to say, "We feel, as figure skaters, that our sport is not doing enough."

When Armistead Maupin speaks, I am too focused on fighting the lump in my throat to write down his words, but his tribute to the courage and creativity of those people living with AIDS has my body chilled with a combination of pride, admiration, gratitude, and rage. By pointing to those people we've all seen or known to have been diagnosed and then written their best work, directed the most important of films, scored operas and symphonies with genius, Maupin destroyed the myth that a person get AIDS and dies. His assertion that one-third of the athletes here are HIV-positive strings me with disbelief—I do not want to believe it—and then seals my resolve to march, not in the official parade on Sunday, but up Fifth Avenue with ACT UP.

SUNDAY: STONEWALL 25

Gathering outside that small pub with the neon sign: Stonewall. Police everywhere, but it doesn't look like confrontation. ACT UP monitors take charge and we leave Greenwich Village behind.

Two hours into our trek toward Central Park—somewhere between the Empire State Building and St. Patrick's Cathedral, a guy marching beside me says, "Hey, you were in the Games, weren't you. I saw you on the news last night." Sure enough he had remembered what I had said to the reporter from Channel One, but unfortunately, they had edited out the most political part of my comments. No surprise there.

Anyway, he admits he isn't a sports fan, and he's disappointed to see us focus seven days on sports and only one on activism. Then he points to a sign that reads: STONEWALL 1969 REBELLION. 1994 RECREATION.

I know that, for some, the Gay Games are the most political act they will partake in all year. Many who played yesterday are not marching today. But, others are. The Games are a way to take activism to new fields, new courts, and new rinks.

The way I see it, the Gay Games offers seven days of sports every four years, including leap year. That leaves another 1,454 days for activism.

The chant is a familiar one. We must repeat it and others, and find ways to make our voices heard. ACT UP. Fight Back. Fight AIDS. Even if we have to shout all the way to Amsterdam in 1998 for Gay Games V.

Wrestling New York:
Amsterdamer Marianne Ijnsen's Adventures in the Big Apple

by Marianne Ijnsen and Dafna Van Delft

Photo © Rachel Corner

FRIDAY, JUNE 17, 1994

Our flight to New York is due to leave at 3:40 P.M. At 10:00 A.M. the phone wakes me: Sonja, a fellow Tigerlet who will be competing in martial arts, wants to know how and when to get to the airport. We agree to meet at the train. After breakfast and a last phone chat with Mum, my backpack and I hop on the back of Lieke's (my girlfriend) bicycle and she pedals us to the station. While waiting for Sonja we run into Margon who managed to scrape together a basketball team. At the airport we start getting slightly nervous. Lieke begins to realize it's a pity she's decided not to come. I agree wholeheartedly. After our goodbye at customs I really am on my way.

The plane only makes a quick transfer stop in Amsterdam; it is en route from Karachi. To the Pakistani passengers are added Dutch Gay Games participants and Dutch football fans on their way to the World Cup—this makes for an interesting mix.

In New York we pile into two taxis which take us to Juanita's house in Brooklyn. Juanita and Laurie are our hosts; both are New York wrestlers and both live in Brooklyn. Their reception of us is absolutely fabulous. Juanita lives in a terraced house with a small garden and little stone steps in front.

Later that night we find out the boys' hosts have let them down and left them without a place to stay. Juanita bails them out and lets them stay at her house while she moves in with her girlfriend in Manhattan.

My teammates Cinta, Mieke, Liesbet and I move on to another wonderful welcome at Laurie's house. We sing her "Tulips from Amsterdam" in Dutch.

SATURDAY, JUNE 18

After breakfast we go to the Pennsylvania Hotel to meet up with our teammates and get accredited. We meet some women wrestlers from San Francisco. The first thing they ask is our weights: They are in the same categories as Liesbet, Mieke, and me. I trade the Gay Games pin Laurie gave me for a purple "volunteer" one.

Once inside, registration goes smoothly and

I am very satisfied with the photo on my athlete's ID-card. Rachel, our photographer, runs into some difficulties even though she has sorted her press-card credentials and everything before we left Holland. A lottery decides what press are allowed where and she loses out on everything including the wrestling. This, we are told, means she will not be allowed into the venue despite the fact she is part of our team (the only foreign team in the entire sport), traveled halfway across the world with us and this is the only event she absolutely wants to photograph. All this seems rather strange, especially since some press-folk seem to luck out in every lottery and can attend all events. . . . Is this what happens if you are foreign and have no connections?

On the eighteenth floor I find the k. d. lang stand and succumb to a T-shirt.

At night we take the subway to the opening ceremonies. Oops, the train zips past our intended station and we find ourselves in the middle of the Bronx. It takes us an hour to get back to 96th Street and change trains. This then seems to be the right one, it is jam-packed with Gay Gamers. After a two-hour wait we can finally enter the stadium, to be among 12,000 fellow gay athletes is very impressive.

SUNDAY, JUNE 19

It's wonderfully warm again. Laurie's living room, now our bedroom, does have windows but you have to look up at a slant to see a piece of the sky.

This afternoon we weigh in, then it's decided what weight class we wrestle. Dafna (our trainer) phones to say she has found practice space at the Y across from where she is staying.

At the Y they don't want to let us use the accommodation; a while ago someone popped it (died) due to playing indoor sports in hot weather, so now above 90 degrees Fahrenheit only swimming is allowed. Eventually we do manage to get permission.

At first all goes well, but then it happens: Somehow my right elbow tries to also bend the other way. It hurts incredibly and I scream down the entire building. Luckily everything can still move, and provided with a sling and an ice pack I proceed to the weigh-in wondering if I will be able to wrestle at all tomorrow. I am extremely upset.

We find you can check your weight before the official weigh-in. Both Liesbet and I weigh more than we thought. The top limit for the class below ours is 136.5 pounds, about 62 kilograms, and we weigh 138! We have until 6.30 P.M. Liesbet decides to run around the block to lose the one and a half pounds, she even removes her tampon. I can't be bothered, not even knowing if I will be able to wrestle tomorrow. After a visit to the toilet I decide to try the scales again and the impossible seems to be true: in my birthday suit I make 136.5! Now if only my injury doesn't get too troublesome . . .

We end up in a pizzeria in a subway station, with a view of passing trains. We stuff our faces since weight is no longer an issue, if we put on some all the better.

MONDAY JUNE 20

Today is the big day. Laurie has made us pancakes for breakfast. My elbow didn't bother me at all during the night, perhaps because

I popped an aspirin in advance? I do intend to try at least one match, we'll see how it goes.

The tournament kicks off. At first we reasonably manage to coach each other (which we have practiced), but as the day progresses it gets harder and harder because everyone seems to be wrestling all at once. Considering the injury to my elbow we have made the following deal: If things don't work out, I either roll over on my back or step off the mat, thus giving up. If, however, I get stuck so badly I can do neither, I will start screaming and the coach will throw in the towel.

Dafna tapes my elbow so at least I can't overextend it again. The elbow-pad seems to function as some sort of pressure pad although apparently putting pressure on an elbow is dead dodgy due to some nerve there. During the rest of the day I continuously keep checking the sensation in my arm and fingers.

My first bout is against Barbara from San Francisco. Without too many difficulties I pin her, although I do find it annoying to wrestle someone who's wearing headgear.

Meanwhile, many other Tigerlets have shown up to cheer, Sonja and Elske keeping their end up. Also, my coworker Rick and his brother Rosseel who are on holiday in the U.S. come to watch.

A TV-team from a national network is filming our performances and interviewing us. We will be on the nationwide news in Holland. Hello Mum!

My second opponent is Cathy from Chicago. Mieke drew her in the first round and managed to last 16 seconds before getting pinned. I take Mieke's advice to heart and last 42 seconds. The prelims are now over and due to my results I have made it to the next round.

Rosseel leaves to find a legal parking spot and Rick buys a ten-dollar ticket for the semifinals.

Unfortunately I lose. My opponent holds me in a stranglehold and I yell at the referee that this is not allowed (which it isn't). Then he says the match is over and I have lost. Still groggy from the strangling I don't understand. What happened was Dafna, who couldn't quite see what was happening, heard me scream and according to the deal (I would scream if things went wrong with my elbow) she threw in the towel. We then find out there was only one second left to the match and I was ahead on points. But, alas, peanut butter (traditional Dutch saying similar to the Americanism, "that's the way the cookie crumbles"), it had been impressed on us by our coach we shouldn't interfere with the refereeing. Being self-opinionated didn't serve me this time.

Liesbet does move on to the next round: She will wrestle Cathy in the finals. Liesbet wins the gold and we are all very happy with such a wonderful result. Our coach (the only female one in the tournament) is in tears.

At the first aid stand the medics remove my tape. I explain what happened and ask for their advice. They tell me chill, move a little, don't exert. I recognize this from an earlier similar experience with the other elbow.

Back in Brooklyn we go for ice cream, three scoops please. These turn out to be gigantic. American scoops are about three times as big as ours. The ice cream is delicious. We do not know what is in it, but no dram or spliff can beat this. It makes us very giggly.

A good ending to a beautiful day with splendid results.

Welcome to the Arena—

Going 24/7 in
Women's Sports

PART TWO

2

All Dinah Shore Golf Action

by Roxxie

When I found out that I, a non-golf fan, was going to the Dinah Shore Golf Tournament in Rancho Mirage, Palm Springs' neighbor, California, I called my friend Norma, a southern California golfing expatriate, and asked what people wore to such occasions. The Nabisco Dinah Shore Golf Tournament is reputed to attract the largest lesbian gathering in the known universe. Southern California lesbians, who are among the most likely to attend this event, are rumored to have more glamorous dress codes than the rest of the country. Is it caused by the Hollywood effect? People even say straight men wear makeup in Los Angeles. I didn't want to be inappropriately dressed at the ultimate lesbian cruise-a-thon and golf watcher's delight. Norma told me, "You've got to wear Izod Lacoste polo shirts."

I was mortified. I shrieked.

She counteroffered, "Okay, you can wear a button-down short sleeve plaid."

I said, "I'm not wearing plaid! I wore too much in the seventies."

"But plaid is the meat and potatoes of golf! Well, I guess a solid shirt will do. But, be sure and wear white tennis shoes, and no cut-off jean shorts."

She was right about the white tennis shoes, but I still couldn't bring myself to do it. I wore black soccer flats, designed for Astro Turf, with mismatched shoelaces—one black and one white. I stood out. The only other pair of black tennies I even saw was on a journalist wearing an Izod Lacoste polo. Hairspray was everywhere, fancy clothes, expensive sunglasses, visors with golf equipment names on them. People wore saddle shoes and gold watches. Most of the golf fans were white. Although some people of color watched the tournament, most of the professional golfers were white, too.

Golf fans are no different than other fans, they dress like their pro-golf idols. Baseball fans wear baseball caps, and carry their gloves in hope to catch a fly ball. Rock-and-roll fans dress like their favorite musicians. k. d. lang fans have been kidding about being Lawrence Welk fans since k.d.'s tour last summer when she publicly announced, "I have something important to tell you. I'm a [what followed was the longest running letter *l* sound musically possible in the history of the American musical stage, just long enough to think she's about to say *lesbian*, when she finally says . . .] Lawrence Welk Fan."

Lawrence Welk isn't cool, and never was. Is k. d. lang cool? She lost me eternally with that embarrassing confession.

Is the sport of golf cool? I've never been drawn to it; however, the National Golf Foundation says that 11.2 percent of all U.S.

residents play golf. Some of them must be pretty hip.

Yet there is some discouraging news: On the back of the Nabisco Dinah Shore tickets are coupons for a play one round, second round free, at Lawrence Welk's Desert Oasis Club. Was this some pre-arranged deal between k. d. and the Welkies? Scary.

Is there some master plan out there to schmaltz-ize modern lesbians?

Like any other reporter going to a major athletic tournament, I applied for a press pass. But Donna Hahn of Hahn Communications, the public relations office handling press passes to this event, turned down my application. Donna Hahn told my editor that the thought of a lifestyle piece on the Dinah Shore Tournament made her feel uncomfortable.

I called the Nabisco Public Relations office in New Jersey. Had my reputation as an irreverently queer sporting journalist preceded me? Why wouldn't they want *Girljock* at a Golf Tournament? P.R. man Mike Falcowitz suggested, "You aren't exactly popular with big corporations because sometimes you're cynical about corporations, and besides, you haven't given me a free subscription yet." He sent me a tournament directory, saying it was almost as good as a press pass. "It's got all the right phone numbers in it," he consoled.

With no press pass in sight, I decided to attend the weekend undercover as a golf fan. That way, I figured, more people would feel comfortable speaking with me. I knew it meant making fashion compromises. I'd forgo SILENCE = DEATH T-shirts, Doc Marten boots, and my black leather motorcycle jacket. I left the welder/skier form follows function thick

sunglasses at home. I bought cheapo designer shorts and short-sleeve blouses at a discount store. For more visual normalcy, I lathered my jet-black extra-curly leg hair with women's shaving cream and mowed it down. I wanted to fit in.

Friday morning I flew into Southern California with a friend. We picked up a rental car to drive to Palm Springs and the long-haired pretty rental car lady offered us a special rate. She'd spotted us as other "women in the know," and without saying the word lesbian, queer, or homosexual, she told us she was going to Palm Springs, too. She gave us a red T-Bird, and told us which bar she'd be at for drinks at 5:00 P.M.

She said, "I'm off work in a few minutes."

I offered her a ride with us.

"I wouldn't ride in that piece of shit," she said, "I've got a brand new BMW waiting for me."

When we drove into the mythic city for fleeing movie stars, wealthy retirees, and golf addicts, my friend and I counted eighteen lesbians on the streets. They wore athletic outfits with white tennis shoes. My friend commented, "The lesbians all look like they are out of the movie *Personal Best*." The downtown Palm Springs area looked like a city from the fifties. Golf and tennis stores were as common as casinos in Vegas. I stopped for gas and directions to the golf tournament. The gas station attendant was an avid golfer himself (there are twenty-five public golf courses in the Palm Springs area). As he explained, "If you live here either you play golf or you don't do nothin'."

We headed for the Riviera Hotel, the legendary heart and soul of the Dinah Shore lesbian party scene. A special table at the front offered free copies of *OUT* Magazine, and the *Lesbian News*, which had the scoop on all the lesbian parties during Dinah Shore Weekend.

The lounge area was crawling with lesbians. There were 32 parties for women, some naughtier than others, like the Whipped Cream Wrestling Contest at Daddy Warbucks, a local gay bar; a Bra Contest at the Desert Pals Inn; and the Jaegermeister poster models autographing their posters at the Riviera's poolside.

The Riviera lesbian cruising was so intense I wondered how the women could walk through the hotel without tripping over furniture.

In the hotel lounge, I asked some Los Angeles women about the scene. "People come here," said one, "to socialize and make a show of their unity. Look, this hotel lounge is like a women's bar, I mean, there's diversity here."

"Diversity?" I said.

"You know, economic diversity, and multicultural."

After a quick glance around I saw one black couple out of about a hundred women.

The Hotel bell captain told me the lesbians were good tippers.

Dinnertime. We headed for Sizzler, which was filled to the brim with locals, tourists, and lesbians. Cute lesbian after cute lesbian. Bodies to die for. The salad bar looked OK.

As we left, a man sitting at a table asked his wife, "Did you hear what the table next door to us was talking about?" His wife answered in a loud tone, "Yes I did, strap-ons." The word strap-on echoed throughout the restaurant.

My traveling friend and I ran outside and burst into laughter.

Big names get booked for Dinah Shore Weekend lesbian parties. Two years ago, Grace Jones performed; this year, Deborah Cooper of C&C Music Factory, Sabrina Johnston, and Kim Syms performed. The lesbian event promoters promised huge crowds. Posters advertised romps like the "Night of 3,000 Women." I was dubious about those figures until I walked into the sea of women at the Palm Springs Convention Center comedy program called "Funny Girlz," starring Ellen DeGeneres, Kate Clinton, and Lynda Montgomery. I'd never seen Ellen DeGeneres before, so I went up closer for a look. She's hilarious, adorable, and from New Orleans.

I asked her if she liked golf.

"My mother wanted me to be a pro golfer," said DeGeneres. "In high school I played golf out of desperation because you can do it by yourself. After I had friends, I didn't need to do it. I used to imagine walking on the golf course and waving to all the people. Little did I know that I would end up with a career in comedy, waving to all the people."

The next morning I drove to Mission Hills Country Club for the tournament. I'd dressed in my golf fan outfit to check out the action. Walking into the Country Club grounds, I asked a group of Southern California lesbians, "Do many women actually came to watch the golf?"

Their estimation—"Half the women never even go to the golf. They are too hung over. When we get back to the hotel, our friends will ask, 'Who won the tournament?' so they can go home and make it sound like they were there."

"We just came to look at the women," said Susan, an engineer from San Diego attending the golf tournament, who declined to give her last name.

When I reached the Old Course, a tough course, the crowds were full of golf fans, senior citizens, Mission Hills Country Club members who looked down their noses at people who weren't wearing a member badge, and lesbians. Lots of lesbians. The sun was hot and I was drenched in sunscreen and sweat, wishing for an espresso, admiring the accuracy of the pros and the politeness of the crowd.

Golf spectating is for people who follow rules. Tournament officials hold up their hands while players hit the ball as a sign to be quiet. The silence when a player hits is almost eerie. The port-a-potties even have signs saying DO NOT SLAM THE DOOR. After the shot is made, the officials' hands fall, the crowd reacts as a group with a sigh or with applause, depending where the ball goes.

There's no catcalling in golf. The only fan/player weirdness occurred after a player stormed off in a huff, after finishing her eighteen holes. Her caddie warned off a fan who wanted to speak with her. "I wouldn't try and speak with her if I were you. She's had a really bad day, and she can get very mean sometimes." The caddies' outfits made them look like they were on the road crews at the Indianapolis 500.

An older male spectator, a Canadian tourist, took a minute to tell me why he thought women's golf was so popular. He said, "Aside from being a sexist thing, you don't want to see your daughter or girlfriend battered across a hockey rink or a basketball court."

I like watching women's basketball. I love women's hockey. I grew up watching Roller Derby. Big women wearing fancy clothes, hitting little balls around a beautiful course, flanked by picturesque mountains is another matter.

Though I golfed in high school gym class, it always seemed so sedate, a sport where everyone had to behave. I liked sports where you run a lot and get really winded and sweaty, like soccer. I've always believed that sports gave people a chance to work out their violent frustrations, providing a regular calmative for one's animalistic inner self. Yet my soccer buddies all know that when we are senior citizens, we'll either be playing golf, or the world's slowest game of soccer. Several of us made a pact to learn golf now so we're ready for our later years, sort of a sporting pension plan.

That evening I went back to the Riviera for Monte Carlo Madness. Three lesbian party producers, Mariah Hanson from San Francisco's Girl Spot, Robin Gans and Sandy Sachs from Los Angeles' Girl Bar teamed up to produce a weekend-long series of events, and Monte Carlo Madness was the second. I took Ted Soqui, a photographer. Hiram Walker employees greeted us on the way in. Hiram Walker and Jaegermeister had both sponsored the Hanson/Gans/Sachs events. This year was the first time two major corporations displayed an interest in the lesbian events.

Monte Carlo Madness was full of thousands of women looking like they just stepped out of *Glamour* or *Elle* magazine. A sea of beauties, a laser light show, and go-go dancers.

There were so many other parties we

couldn't even get to. We dropped in at a Bra Contest minutes after it ended, missed the Boot-skootin' Boogie Time, and didn't have time to go to the Outrageous Women in Uniform Party. Thirty-two parties is a lot.

Some lesbian party producers told me the tournament producers wouldn't connect themselves with any lesbian events, so I called the Nabisco Dinah Shore Tournament office to see what they thought of the lesbian party scene. Director Mike Galeski insisted, "Whatever else is going on in town is in no way connected to the golf tournament."

He followed with a lesbian anecdote. "One time a man at a Palm Springs service club asked me 'What are you going to do with all the lesbians that attend your tournament?'"

Galeski responded, "I don't know how many lesbians attend, I also don't know how many Republicans attend. We don't check sexual preference at the door. We just show-case the best women's golf in the world."

As I pondered that response, I thought back to something Kate Clinton had said to me the night before. I'd asked her, "Do you think any professional women golfers will ever come out?"

Clinton responded by asking me, "Do we really want queers in golf?"

Golf is a stronghold of mainstream-to-Ivy League America, the sport of those with lots of free time, the fifties suburban American dream sport. Why are so many lesbians today drawn to it? Ten years ago the biggest lesbian event in the world was the Michigan Women's Music Festival, a lesbian separatist, camping, nudity-positive, queer Woodstock, an attempt to create new lesbian realities. If you shaved your

legs to go to Michigan, you'd be harassed. Today, if you go to the Dinah Shore with extremely hairy legs, people either think you are European, cross-dressing as a man, or a feminist extremist.

This new hotel-and-affluence culture is a retro opposite of the hirsute, vegetarian, camping lesbian music festival. Separatists, dull dykes, lesbian activists, and extremists have widened the ranges and possibilities of lesbian culture enough to allow for this flood of lesbians into the mainstream. Does the new mainstream American lesbian culture still welcome the freaks, the mannish, the political lesbians, the bull dykes? I kept looking for lesbo-identification marks at the Dinah Shore—out of thousands, I saw only two politely disguised gay T-shirts; everyone else wore nice clothes. Today's Dinah Shore lesbians are going after the American dream: vacations, beauty, alcohol, nice hotels, hot dogs, golf, money, Hollywood entertainers, party-party.

The Dinah Shore is such the American thing, that even Marines are in on it.

As I walked into the last day of the tournament, I met Rob Maruschak, a volunteer scorekeeper and a Marine from Twenty Nine Palms, a local military base. I asked him what he thought about working at a Tournament with so many lesbians, or, had he noticed the lesbians?

His answer, "No Comment. We go with whatever our Commander-in-Chief says."

During the closing rounds of the final day, thousands upon thousands followed leaders Helen Alfredsson, Betsy King, and Dawn Coe-Jones, from hole to hole. I immediately liked Alfredsson because she was big and strong, she could really move the ball around the picturesque course, she had the most uncannily accurate long shots, and the coolest shorts of anyone at the tournament, including the fans. Her shorts had a goofy looking flower pattern on them.

King and Coe-Jones were both great players, but Alfredsson dominated the last nine holes. The others couldn't catch her, they'd get close, then mess up. Alfredsson stayed ahead. She had the edge.

Alfredsson showed more emotion towards the ball when she was playing than the other players did. "Dang," she'd yell at the ball, "What are you doing?" Once she even kicked the ground. I loved it. She'd even jump for joy when she made a great putt. She was an exciting athlete to watch. She'd make the little ball fly around the trees. She'd land the ball on the greens with amazing backspin. The crowd oohed and aahed for her. When she won, she hugged her caddie. I clapped as hard as I could, and everyone else did too.

After she received her trophy from the legendary women's golf backer Dinah Shore, she was escorted to the Press Tent, but ran off to hug Amy Alcott, last year's winner, on the way. Since I couldn't go to the press conference, I decided to approach Alcott. It was easy because I looked like a golf fan. After she found out I was a reporter, she was happy to speak with me. Alcott was very happy for Alfredsson. She said, "She's my best friend on the tour!"

When Amy Alcott won in 1992, she jumped into the lake around the eighteenth hole. I asked Amy, "If you would have won again, would you have jumped in the lake again?"

"Yes," she answered, "I thought Helen might do it after she won."

It was more exciting to watch the women golfers than I had expected. After the tournament, I put a soccer sweatshirt over my flowered short-sleeve golf-fan blouse and headed back to the Riviera Lounge, hoping to catch a little more of the Lesbian Dinah Shore action. I saw a woman in an LPGA emblem jersey who was suntanned and bronzed and dressed like a golfer. I offered to trade her my ultimately cool soccer jersey for her LPGA emblem jersey. Somehow I felt I had been won over to the excitement of women's golf.

She said she couldn't part with her jersey, she was an LPGA professional golfer, and her jersey represented too much to her. She then gave me a brief interview on the dilemmas of the women's pro golf scene, sexism in golf, how hard it was to be a lesbian on the tour, and how hard it was to be a woman. By then I realized that she was drunk. After she started to repeat herself, I, like a good reporter, knew it was time to wrap it up.

Later that night her friends told me she wasn't a real professional golfer. I called the LPGA to verify this the next day.

After I got over the embarrassment of being taken for a sociopathic ride, I realized that it was only fair, right? I'd tried to pass as a golf fan.

Search and Destroy

by Dafna Van Delft

Photo © Monique Vanhyfte

AN INTERVIEW WITH MICHELLE A'BORO

DVD: *Where, when, and how did you get started?*

MA: I started kickboxing when I was nineteen, it must have been '88 in Brixton. I lived in Peckham south London, which is about two districts away (in south London). I grew up there. A friend of mine was kickboxing, he lived in Brixton and he thought everything that boys could do good, I'd be able to do. Everything, like BMX-riding, he would always drag me along 'cause then he'd say: "Yeah, you could beat all the girls." So I went and started training.

DVD: *What is it you like about the game? What gripped you?*

MA: It was because they allowed women to do this sport. Because, before, I'd done a little bit of karate, kyokushinkai, but it wasn't enough, it was restricted. And then I wanted to box but they never allowed you to box. Especially in England with the ABA, the boxing board, it's all old men that still have old ideas. But now it gets a little bit better 'cause they allow you to box in clubs, but not a lot of clubs will allow you to spar with men. But I was lucky because I knew a guy who had a boxing school so he'd allow me to go there and box too. After that I started kickboxing and then you could box and you could kick and you could do it full-contact and you could get into the ring and fight too. This is what I like because in boxing, I could train there but I couldn't fight competitions so you couldn't see if what you were learning really worked in a situation that's not made up for you. So that's why I got hooked onto the kickboxing. Because I thought, Yeah, I can compete, and if I train hard I'll get better, and it gave me a goal to strive for.

DVD: *And then there's the adrenaline of competition.*

MA: [Laughs.] Yeah! Exactly. The hook that

gets you. You have your first fight and then it's over, forget about anything else. I just carried on competing all the time. In the ring it's left to you to be able to see situations and to be able to get out of things, to be able to think fast enough not to be hit, or to counter, or whatever. This is what I like too because then you don't only physically beat somebody, you mentally beat them. This person is as willing as you are to win but just by what you're given, nothing else, you are able to overcome their will to win. You have to analyse her strong points and work out: How can I make sure she isn't able to use this strong point by the techniques I will use? To try and take away anything she is capable of doing that's good.

DVD: *You fight like a chess player, very cool, but then I've also seen you lose control and kick a girl when she was down . . .*

MA: [Laughs.] Yeah, when I was younger I had a very bad temper. I would go "click," and then I would see nothing. But the kickboxing helped me to channel it. But sometimes, you know, with the pressure of competition. . . . A basic one was the September fight. Everybody really expected me to win this competition so I had very much pressure on me. And I knew from the beginning of the year that this competition was going to happen, so all the time through the whole year all my fights were building up to this one fight in September. So by the time I got there I was like this volcano, ready to erupt, and then I just totally clicked at the last minute. I really believed the girl wasn't on the floor. I thought I pushed her in a clinch and I believed that her bum hadn't hit the floor yet. But it had and it all happened so quickly, maybe ten minutes after the fight I

realized what I really had done. Out of all the fights I've had, even fighting Lucia, this was the biggest one for pressure. And I've fought tournaments, it wasn't the fact that it was three fights in one night. It was just coming in as the favorite. I take Amsterdam as my hometown now and when so many people come and see you fight there's even more pressure on you.

DVD: *What's a nice English girl doing in a place like this?*

MA: If I was a nice girl I wouldn't be in this sport, ha ha! It's not for the timid or shy, that's for sure. If you don't fight as hard as them, the guys are going to whoop your arse. After my debut in Amsterdam this Dutch woman fighter came up to my trainer and said, "She's good but she looks too much like a boy, don't you think you want to get her to change the way she looks?" I'm not going to put on my lipstick and eyeliner before I jump in the ring. As long as what I do in the ring is good, I don't care what I look like, I'd rather look like a serious fighter then like somebody that's there for a fashion show!

I came here through fighting Lucia. After I fought her, Johan and Lucia invited me over. So I came about two months after I fought her.

DVD: *They respected you because you put up a good fight.*

MA: Yeah, and the same when I fought her in Frankfurt, they didn't believe the fight should have been stopped so soon because they said I wasn't hurt. And the first fight we had, both of them really respected me because no matter what she done I wouldn't go down. It was just that from the second round my ligament had ripped in my leg, and I knew if I wasn't capable of moving from her I would have slowly but surely been took apart. Because she is very systematic in the way she fights you. After this fight she said, Yeah, come over, and I stayed with her and she trained me. And then Johan trained me.

DVD: *You emigrated for your sport.*

MA: Yeah, but from when I first started I never looked to no English fighter or other fighters, I only looked to Holland. Any video I would have would be of Dutch fighters. The only woman I ever watched fight was Lucia. The rest of them, I would watch men fight because of the way they fight. I don't know what it is that makes women and men fight differently, but some women are able to lift theirselves into the same realm, where others, they just don't have this explosion and power. But Lucia had this and so I really enjoyed watching her fight, and other Dutch fighters. Because of their technical ability, too. I always wanted to come to Holland.

DVD: *You managed to get into Vos, one of the top Dutch gyms. What's it like there?*

MA: At the Vos gym I am treated the same as everybody else, I'm given a lot of respect, as everybody else is given there—I'm really looked after.

DVD: *Are there other women at the gym?*

MA: There's one girl now, she's only had two fights, one loss and one win. I train with her sometimes but she's still a novice. Apart from that, there's women that train, but mainly recreational. They have a group of their own which used to be taught by Lucia. I'm in touch with the other women because they come and ask me some things or certain techniques, and sometimes I will train in the class

with them. Because I think it's good for them to have somebody they can kind of look up to, it gives them more inspiration to train harder.

DVD: *Do you have any fans (apart from me)?*

MA: Not that I know of, ha ha. In England when I told people what I done they looked at me freakyish. Like: You must be not all the ticket, (i.e., a couple of sandwiches short of a picnic—not playing with a full deck) did they drop you on the floor when you was born or something? But here in Holland I find people respect you because you're doing what you want to do. Whereas in England, I don't know what it is with their mentality, it feels like everybody is doing what they really don't want to do. They're just doing it because society believes they should be doing this.

DVD: *But do the people who say it's really cool that you're a fighter actually come to your fights?*

MA: This is a problem 'cause most of the time the support you have is very minimal from the group that you're in. Most of the people that come and see you fight, they're either from the gym or your family or so on. A few very close friends but that's about it. What you're doing is literally pushing yourself into a man's world, and then without the support it makes it even harder.

DVD: *You get better fights if you're a crowd-puller.*

MA: Yeah, exactly. That's the truth. You get put on bigger shows, you know, because they know they're going to make their money from you.

DVD: *Where's all the right-on women that say it's so cool what you're doing?*

MA: They don't want to come 'cause it's too expensive or something. Most of the time you hear "Yeah, I wanted to come but it's too expensive." They think it's a great idea what you do and that it's positive for women and it gives younger girls growing up a positive role-model and whatnot but ehh . . . no. There's nobody there to see it.

DVD: *How often do you train and what do you do?*

MA: If I have a competition then I'll train twice a day, six days a week, and run every other day in the morning. And weight training, too. The training consists of pad-training, bag training, sparring, weight training, running, and cardiovascular training like the step-machine, climbing machine, things like that. Maybe in a day I train between four and five hours. That's for competition, but if I don't have a competition then I train maybe four times a week, I'll run maybe twice a week, just to keep my condition at a level so that I can pick it up at any time. But most of the time, yeah, I take it very easy when I don't have a fight.

DVD: *So you can recuperate.*

MA: Yeah. Before the next competition. Because last year I had maybe nine months of total training, I had a one-week break in these nine months. So it was a heavy year last year. Now this year hasn't been so brilliant, no fights. That's why I started fighting at sixty kilos, which isn't my weight, to get fights. Instead of just fighting between fifty-four and fifty-seven, I thought, Well, I'll go to sixty and then I can fight the women at that level. I found I could handle the weight even though I gave away sometimes four or five kilo's, it wasn't so much of a problem. And then I got more fights. But now it seems again, I fought all last year at sixty kilos and this year it is very difficult to get a fight at sixty or under. Here

in my weight in Holland there's only one woman, the next one on the list, but I've fought her already two times and I've beaten her two times, so really it's not worth, for me, at this moment in time, to fight her. Because when I fought her and beat her I was just climbing, getting better. I'd really like to fight Corinne. She's a lot bigger but I would fight her at her weight category and any rules. Still, it's been very difficult to get a fight with her, I don't know why.

DVD: *Federation politics?*

MA: Probably. There's all this bullshit going on, instead of just saying "this is a good fighter, that's a good fighter, let's fight." For you to be put onto a big bill, you're very lucky sometimes. Last year there was the K-tournament they had here in September, they had one in Moscow in June: an all-women show too with only two men fights, which was great. And then they had another one in Japan which was a cage-fight, a whole women's event. And then they had the one in Amsterdam in September so I fought these three tournaments back to back. I lost the one in Japan 'cause my first opponent was a hundred and twenty kilos. But it was a good fight, I whacked her and I kicked her. She was a judo world-champion so when she grabbed me she laid on top of me, shoved her tit in my face, and nearly suffocated me [laughs]. That was it.

DVD: *So you fight different styles.*

MA: Yeah. I won last year, ISKA, a tournament title. ISKA means kicks above the waist, you must kick at least eight times per round, no low-kicks, no knees, no elbows. It was the second time I ever fought it, 'cause I usually fight Thai Boxing or WKA all the time. I really enjoyed this competition because it's some–thing I don't think I'm good at, and for the first time I fought out of my weight at sixty kilos. I fought three fights in one day and I managed to win the tournament. Which was miraculous in a way, really.

DVD: *What makes a good fighter?*

MA: A good attitude, I think, determination, discipline, and a flexible mind. To be able to take things in very easily: a situation, how to control it, how to learn things quite easily. A good brain, somebody that's able to ascertain,

For those of you not yet familiar with the (less than?) noble art of kickboxing, here's a quick introduction.

The Game

Two opponents step into the ring. The only protection they wear are boxing gloves. For several (anywhere between two to twelve) three-minute rounds they proceed to try and either knock each other out (literally) or win on points. Points are scored by punching (hooks, jabs, uppercuts) to the head and body, kicking (using either feet or shins) to the head, body or legs, kneeing to the body and legs (sometimes by mutual agree-ment also to the head) and, depending on the rules, elbowing. Kicks to the legs are called low-kicks. The game is full-contact, which means hit and kick as hard as you can.

WKA

World Karate Association. No knee-strikes.

ISKA

International Sport Karate Association. No knee-strikes, no low-kicks. Minimum of eight kicks per round.

Thai Boxing (A.K.A. Muay Thai)

Includes low-kicks, knee-strikes, and elbow-strikes to the legs and body. In Thailand and sometimes elsewhere also to the head.

K-tournament

Eight fighters of roughly the same weight get paired off. The winners of the first fights con-tinue into the second round, the winners of these fights meet for the final bout. This means for them it's their third fight in one evening. Only the winner gets a prize (between $10,000 and $100,000 dollars).

Cage fight

Same tournament system. The opponents meet in an octagonal cage, there are no rounds. The fight continues until one of the competitors is unable to go on. Fighters wear no protection and all techniques (including grappling) are allowed, except for eye-gouging and biting. Outlawed in several states and countries.

Some people mentioned in this story are:

Lucia Rijker

All-time great undefeated champion. She ruled for more than a decade and beat all other women no matter what the rules. Rumor has it she is now living in Los Angeles and moving into boxing, in search of new challenges.

Johan Vos

Owner of Vos gym in Amsterdam, previously Lucia's trainer and now Michelle's. (Also, Vos in English means Fox. Their symbol is a fox in boxing gloves.)

Corinne Geeris

High-ranking Dutch fighter. Michelle wants to fight her, even though Corinne is bigger and heavier.

take a person apart systematically. I like fighters like that, systematic fighters. Search and destroy, that's my motto. Maybe because where I train, at the Vos gym, most of them are very systematic. They slowly but surely break a person down. With Lucia the emphasis was on the surely! Left punch, right hook, the girl goes down, and on the way down a kick to the head. This is one of Vos's techniques that he teaches everybody. And I think that was the problem in September, it was the same thing. Because when you're trained by Johan you drum in the combination. What happened was a combination, the one-two grab, push down, knee. And I totally ran through with it instead of thinking, Oh, the girl's arse is on the floor. Once it's in motion there's no stopping. And that's what kind of fighters I like.

DVD: *Were you also upset because you got paired off with this girl who was so obviously out of your league?*

MA: Yeah, I think I tried to get rid of her too quickly. I just wanted to steam-roller her, get her out of there as quickly as possible. Which was the wrong way of thinking. Because there's so few good ones, you have to fight the bad ones too.

DVD: *And then it looks bad and it makes the audience say women's fights are crap when it's beginner fights that are crap, and women move up through the ranks much quicker 'cause the ranks are so small. So a woman B-level fighter is not necessarily as good as a man B-level fighter, not because she's a woman.*

MA: But because of the amount of fights she has had. I can remember I fought Lucia after just three years of training and that's ludicrous! No guy if he had a brain in his head would be

doing this, but there was no other way for me to go. Because everybody I had fought I had beaten, I hadn't lost a fight yet. She was the only one I fought that had a fair chance of beating me. Somebody that could test me to my fullest. This is what I wanted, somebody to push me. That's what I thought when I first fought Lucia: There's no way I'm going to lay on my back. You have to really literally kill me if you want to win from me. I would like to have more fights, of course, everybody wants more fights, but I like the way Johan is building me up. When I came here he said: "We take this from the beginning." To him I am like a new fighter, even though I'd won a world title already. He brought me back straight to the beginning, learning how to punch again and kick correctly. Really, to me this is my career started again. In England in my second fight I fought for a British title. That was six months after I'd begun fighting. And I won these things because of my will to win, because technically I shouldn't have beat these people. And it was my determination, I just stayed there and totally exhausted them. 'Cause my conditioning was always good and I would just pressure them totally 'til they either gave up or I knocked them down. And it's sad because you know it rubs off and if you go to your first show and you see a women's fight like that then it stays in your mind. Lucky there was somebody like Lucia to be an ambassador for the sport: Then you strive to be at that level. If there wasn't a Lucia then I wouldn't strive to even train harder now. It helps tremendously because then people give you more of a chance. The only good thing about my trainer in England was he didn't see no gender. So if you couldn't put up with it, see ya. This is how hard you must train and that's the bottom line, you know, male or female. I don't like people that always think you're not capable of this because you're a woman. They break you down, put a barrier in front of you for you to break down again and again and again, instead of saying you're capable of doing this, you know. And this is what I like at my gym because I train with some of the best guys there. So then you know when you get in the ring there's no woman going to hit that hard or be that technically good. Already you're at an advantage and I think that's what Lucia had. Because she always trained with guys and her look on fighting is like a man. I believe you should always strive for the best to get the most out of somebody. Like the women's class Lucia taught, fair enough, to some women who maybe had something wrong with them she will give them a break. If say they had to do frog-hops and they had a bad knee she'll say, Okay, but it doesn't matter if it's a woman or a man. When she used to train with me for fights she said, Yeah, because you're a woman you have to train harder. That's the way you'll win and you'll become good. So I would train twice as hard as the guys that would be fighting maybe on the same bill as me, who were fighting maybe the same rounds as me. To make sure when I fight it's at a good level.

DVD: *Is it your experience also that some feminists say they like strong women but when they actually see them, sympathize with the underdog?*

MA: I believe you should be who you are and just live your life as you feel you should live it. Not because it's right because you're a woman

or a lesbian or whatever, you should just be yourself. Not because you have to be that way for any little group, because then you are just making yourself smaller by putting yourself into an even smaller group. With these literary feministic women, they're all good to point the finger: "You should do more for women." I just say to them, basically, When it comes down to it, when are you there for me?

DVD: *What do they expect you to do?*

MA: To speak up more. I do an interview for myself, for sport, it's not about my sexuality or anything to do with it. Some of them say: "You're in a place in your life where you can do something for gay women." I say, Yeah, but at the end of the day what do gay women do for me? Come on, it's as clear as the sky is blue that I'm a dyke, you can see it from a million miles away. So I think that's enough, I show it in myself, I don't have to scream it out. That's the way I think it should be, doing, not talking. Most of the people that support me are my straight friends or family or people from the gym, guys from the gym. And they know what you're going through, how you're feeling and everything else, whereas these women, they would never be able to comprehend in the slightest what happens.

DVD: *Do you have any advice for women wanting to get into the sport?*

MA: Just be dedicated and believe you can do it. Because we're born with everybody telling us we're women, we cannot, we're incapable of, we're not strong enough. And then you have limitations. So just believe in yourself, that you are capable of anything, and don't just look at average women in the sport, look at the top men or the top women. But not just top women who are okay, but top women like Lucia Rijker, don't settle for second best and always look to make yourself as good as that person. Then you'll grow. Because that's how I thought about it, I said, Yeah, I want to be the best fifty-five kilo fighter in the world on all bodies, WKA, ISKA, Muay Thai. So then you can say that you really are a world champion: You got to unite the titles to make it real, to make yourself of any worth. Like Lucia did.

No other woman has done that—hold all of the titles in one weight category. There are just a handful of people that excel, untouchables. These very special people that are born to do this. You can see it in them, they're made, really it's weird, especially just for this thing. And it's good to see because they're the people you should look up to and want to be the same as. Not just look up to them admiring them, but say, "I want to be just like that!"

The Queens of the Court

by Maria Vetrano

After the '92 summer Olympics had ended and I'd gone into a small tailspin from women's sports spectatorship deprivation, I found the Tao of women's professional beach volleyball. On the beaches of West Dennis on Cape Cod, I saw world-class women athletes serving, smashing, digging, and gutting it out in one of the toughest two-person sports I've ever seen.

Though it's often marketed as a "babes on the beach" sport (with Coors as a sponsor, one can only wonder why), beach volleyball is nothing of the sort. The women who play it have generally emerged from stellar four-year performances at the elite college level, where they played the traditional six-woman indoor game. WPVA stars, such as Karolyn Kirby, Liz Masakayan, Lori Kotas, and Barbra Fontana, all had excelled in college level games.

When I heard that the WPVA was coming to Boston on July 4th weekend of this year, I scratched all other plans and resolved to get myself some interviews with these neo-Amazonian athletes of the beach-clad variety. I gathered my raincoat, my *Girljock* hat, and my six-foot-two girlfriend (a middle hitter herself and a great WPVA fan), and slogged down to the Tent in Quincy, Massachusetts, where the two-day Coors Light Boston Shootout was about to begin. After a morning of evil rain delays and half-played muddy matches, I found myself face-to-face with the number two team on the tour, Lori Kotas and Barbra Fontana.

My heroes have never been cowboys, but always earnest and powerful women striving to make a difference. Lori Kotas is one of these—with all the qualities that little Girljocks should emulate. At thirty-four, the six-foot-one Kotas is a seven-year tour veteran. She's competed in over ninety events with five different partners, including sixty-nine events with one-time partner Gail Castro. This year, the big-hitter Kotas teamed up with one of the best all-around tour players, twenty-seven-year-old Barbra Fontana. Kotas's experience blocking and hitting, and Fontana's incredible athleticism and fitness brought them the number two and number three positions all season long. Notably, Kotas and Fontana were the only team other than Karolyn Kirby and Liz Masakayan to win a WPVA final this year, when they triumphed at the Coors Light Austin Open on May 15 and 16. Kotas deserves extra recognition for toughing out the season with a chronic knee injury. By the end of the Coors Light Shootout, it was obvious that her bad knee was giving her trouble—I knew making those vertical jumps and big hits had become a superhuman feat.

I caught Lori Kotas in the tournament director's tent during an afternoon rain delay. She graciously offered an interview. How could I refuse?

GJ: *You've been on the WPVA tour since its inception. What was it like in the early days of the tour?*

LK: When we first started the tour, we were playing for really minimal money. I traveled around with money out of my own pocket. Now it's pretty much evolved into what you see now. The last couple years it had gotten a lot bigger, but this year we've scaled down and we're running in the black. Most of the top players have been able to make a really good living off it now.

GJ: *And your partner is Barbra Fontana.*

LK: Right—she's one of the rookies on the tour. This is her third-year playing. She's a young player—runs around like crazy. And we've done real well.

GJ: *Tell me about life on the road.*

LK: This stop, they're paying for my hotel. My sponsors cover my flights. I'm sponsored by Arena Sportswear and Killer Loop and they take care of almost all my expenses. When I'm

on television, I get incentives. TV is where you get a lot of the good money from your sponsors. I like to travel. Some of the players have families, like Barbra, who's got a boyfriend, but I'm single—so I really don't mind it.

Photo © Helen Privett

GJ: *What's your schedule like?*

LK: I fly on Thursday afternoon or Friday morning, so that's a day off for me. And then I play Saturday and Sunday and fly back home [Oceanside, CA] on Sunday afternoon. On Monday, I don't do anything. Tuesday, Wednesday, Thursday, I travel to LA to train with Barbra.

GJ: *Do you have any favorite tournaments?*

LK: The ones we win!!! This year, Austin was my favorite tournament! New Orleans was another favorite tournament because the nightlife on Sunday night was just unbelievable! But I have to say that at some of the California tournaments, Hermosa and Manhattan [Beach], we get eight to ten thousand fans.

GJ: *Do you have a least favorite tournament?*

LK: Las Vegas. It's about 104 degrees and they're manmade courts—sand on cement. People gamble on the games.

GJ: *Do you have any rituals/superstitions and what do you do to get psyched?*

LK: I get away from all the other players before the games, so I can strategize. And I won't wear a new swimsuit.

It used to be bad luck if you skunked a team 15–0, so we used to give them a point. But nobody believes that one anymore. Actually, Barbra and I get together and strategize and talk about the teams that we're going to play.

GJ: *Is there a special physical warm-up that you do?*

LK: We have fifteen minutes to warm up. We start by peppering the ball. After a couple of minutes, we start hitting. When we've got four minutes left, we do serve and return.

GJ: *Okay. So what do you eat for breakfast?*

LK: Bagels or oatmeal—carbohydrates.

GJ: *Is there a volleyball goddess or anything to whom you pray?*

LK: No, I don't have one of those.

GJ: *Did you have any sports idols when you were growing up?*

LK: Yes. Kathy Gregory. She's one of the players who retired from the tour. I looked up to her when I first started playing; I wanted to be like her. And Martina Navratilova, I really appreciated her, her style of play and her longevity in the sport—and her quotes. I cut out one of her quotes and carried it with me. It was something like, "commitment to the game is like bacon and eggs. The eggs are playing the game and the bacon is committed."

GJ: *Would you like to be a sports idol for girls growing up today?*

LK: Not so much an idol, but a role model. I practice some of that off court by going to high schools and lecturing kids about why they should stay in school. After I dropped out of school in eleventh grade, I started school again at a different school and met a coach who asked me if I wanted to play sports. I said, "Hey, no, I'm just thinking of a way to get out of this class." This coach kept me after school and on the team. She gave me a coach's trophy and I stayed playing volleyball. So, I'd like to think that I could be a role model for somebody, maybe make a difference for one person.

GJ: *What's it like being a team of two?*

LK: It's intense. Gail Castro and I played together for five years. We're the team who stayed together the longest and it felt like it was a team. Now I play my game individually, but before I was always so in tune with Gail that it affected my game. Now, as I've gotten older, I realize that all I can do is take care of my game. Individually, you have to make sure that your game is solid and good.

GJ: *Billie Jean King was a player who always used to "beat herself" up when she was having a bad game. How do you handle having a bad game?*

LK: I notice that when I'm not playing well I shake my head—and now I've stopped doing that. I'm able to put the bad things away and play in the moment. It's something that I think takes time to acquire. It's too bad that you acquire this mental attitude at a later age, when the physical is older too.

GJ: *But don't most women peak in their early thirties?*

LK: I think most women peak between 27 or 28 and 32 or 33. And then you win games mentally. We played a rookie team a couple weeks ago in Santa Cruz and they were ahead of us the whole game. In fact, we beat them 15–11. Physically, they were playing so much better. They were young; they had it all. But at the end of game, they just crashed.

GJ: *Would you say that there's an up-and-coming team on whom we should keep our eyes?*

LK: One team who's up and coming is Kengelin Gardiner and Christine Schaefer. They're both six foot and very athletic with all the good shots—and in their early twenties. They're one of the teams of the future.

GJ: *Did you know that you wanted to be a professional athlete?*

LK: Not when I was growing up, but when I was in college. Sports came easily to me, so I knew that I could be a good athlete. I was invited to try out for the Olympics, but didn't have the money to fly back East—so I didn't get to do that. Then I started playing on the beach in amateur tournaments. When I won a couple of the amateurs, I knew that I could do it.

GJ: *Do you ever get sick of the sun?*

LK: People say, "You have such a beautiful tan," and I say, "You have no idea!"

I use a lot of sunscreen, I get checked by my dermatologist yearly to make sure everything is okay. Some of the girls have skin cancer. But I'm not going to quit playing because of this. This is my window of opportunity.

GJ: *What kind of progress do you think women are making in professional sports?*

LK: I think women are doing very well in tennis and golf, but I think they're outpricing themselves. I think that more sponsors are going to be looking at smaller sports like women's volleyball, which is good for us.

We're way behind when it comes to men. I try to justify it by saying that this is their thirteenth year and our seventh year. It's not enough that the men are making more money. They sold all their banner space [advertisers' names surrounding the court for which sponsors pay dearly] and had no more room. They had another company come in with lots of money and they thought they could sell more banner space through the women. . . . These men are making three or four hundred thousand dollars a year and they're handing these [women] players twenty thousand dollars. It's a joke. They could have done it differently, but this was a hostile takeover. Although the prize money is lower and some of the players have left, I think that this year the women have banded tighter together than they have in the past. It's actually made this year more pleasurable than all of the years that I've played. And this has been one of my better years on the tour."

Just as things were wrapping up with Lori Kotas, Barbra Fontana, the newly crowned divinity for the ripped and the agile, walked into the players' tent, ever eager to be interviewed by your world-famous *Girljock* staff. At twenty-seven, Fontana's a trifle young for a Renaissance woman, but she qualifies for the title by being: (1) an aweinspiring volleyball player; (2) a practicing attorney; (3) president of the WPVA; (4) Italian. With over forty-five aces in the first eight tournaments of this year alone, she possesses one of the toughest serves on the beach. And at a mere five feet six inches, which is petite by pro beach volleyball standards, Barbra's made up in endurance, speed, and athletic ability what she lacks in height.

Girljock's Spectator's Guide to Pro Beach Volleyball Talk

By Helen Privett and Maria Vetrano

So you've whiled your life away watching tennis and basketball. You've known the difference between a cross-court smash and a jump shot since birth, but have no clue about the dialect of this hot women's professional sport. Here's a Berlitz-like guide to the very special language of beach volleyball.

ACE: Food for those statisticians, it's also adored by the crowd at large: an in-bounds serve with no return. At mid-season, Barbra Fontana held the record for the highest number of aces on the WPVA.

You'll often hear a player shout one of these terms to her partner:

ANGLE: This is a power shot. The player goes up and blasts the ball across her opponent's court at a sharp angle.

CUT SHOT: A terribly clever shot to use when the defense has set up a block. The hitter looks like she's going for a deep kill, but at the last minute, turns her elbow in or out, and hits the ball down at a sharp downward angle. Similar to the angle shot, the cut shot requires more deception and less power.

FLOAT SERVE: Staying on the ground for a change, the player makes a short, crisp contact with the ball. Because the ball has no spin, it will waver with the flow of the wind. It is difficult to know where a float serve is going; even genius-type physicists are often left stumped.

Serving to the **HUSBAND AND WIFE** position is good strategy. Aiming for the area between her two opponents, the server hopes that they will lose the ball between them. Usually causes quarreling and frustration on the receiving side.

HIGH LINE: This shot is aimed down the line and deep. Hopefully, it's placed where the opponents are not.

JOUSTING: Not the medieval variation. A Joust occurs when the ball is set directly on the net and both the hitter and the blocker go up for the ball. Each player tries to out muscle the other while in mid-leap. It's very Mary Martin.

There are also a plethora of serves. The most common serve for the professional is the **JUMP SERVE.** The server throws the ball high into the air. She then steps and launches herself into the air (quite spectacular looking) and hits the ball down into her opponent's court. These serves are powerful and difficult to return. One WPVA player increases the effect of her awe-inspiring serve through high decibel yells—she's Marla O'Hara, a.k.a "Cave Woman."

KILLS: Not to worry—it's a term, not a Schwarzenegger-thing. Statistics are often kept on the number of kills a player makes (giving those accountant-types something to do). When a player hits a hard-driven ball into the sand or her opponent's 'face' and the ball is not playable, it's a kill.

POKEY: The pokey is a kind of a knuckle ball. Rather than hitting the ball with her whole hand, the player uses her knuckles to punch the ball over the block.

More from the Shot Repertoire

RAINBOW SHOT: It's kind of like a deep lob in tennis. This ball curves gently over the opposing blocker's head and lands in the back of the court.

BEACH BLEMISHES: A common error in beach volleyball is the **SHANKED PASS.** A player receiving the serve flubs it, and makes a dig that is unretrievable by her partner. When a player overpasses the ball, she actually sets it for her opponent, not her partner. A real birthday present, this usually sets the stage for a terrific kill by the opposition.

SKYBALLS are the most unusual serves and often get the crowd psyched. With an underhand punch, the server launches the ball as high as she can while trying to retain some modicum of control. Not a great idea on a blustery day.

TOOL THE BLOCK: A great way to use the opponent's block to one's advantage. The player hits the ball directly into her opponent's block so that the ball sails out-of-bounds—off of the opponent's hands. Since the ball was last touched by her opponent, the point or sideout goes to the hitter.

Thus concludes the *Girljock* guide to the beach volleyball lingo. Now you will be able to spectate, not only as a happy enthusiast, but as an educated one, as well.

GJ: *Barbra, reveal for me, if you will, the untold story of your partner history on the tour?*

BF: My first year, I played with a gal named Holly McPeak. We were both rookies, and ended up being ranked sixth. So we did real well our first year out. My second year, I played with Deb Richardson. And this year I'm with Lori.

GJ: *What's it like playing with just one other person compared to playing the six-person game?*

BF: I really prefer the doubles game. I like working with someone closely, almost in a relationship-type way. I find it easier to work with just one person. You can develop a tighter, more cohesive team.

GJ: *How do you cope with being on the road?*

BF: We pay for everything—the tour just puts up the purse. I don't mind life on the road. I like to travel, and I don't have a problem with flights.

GJ: *Are you signed with any sponsors so far?*

BJ: This year I'm only signed with Killer Loop. I'm waiting for that big hit.

GJ: *And you're also a practicing attorney?*

BF: I graduated from law school in 1991 and then passed the bar. I practiced part-time in a firm last fall and now I do freelance legal work in the off-season.

GJ: *You're Amazonian by modern standards. What's your workout like?*

BF: I take Monday off during the season to rest my body. Tuesday, Wednesday, and Thursday, I lift and do cardiovascular running, and then I do a two to four hour beach workout. I take Friday off and play Saturday and Sunday.

GJ: *Do you have a big tournament bathing suit?*

BF: I did have a favorite suit—it's this green

lace one. We didn't win that [big] game in it—so it's not my favorite suit anymore.

GJ: *What sports did you play growing up?*

BF: I played beach volleyball, growing up in Manhattan Beach.

GJ: *What made you go back to beach volleyball from law school?*

BF: A friend of mine handed me a package from the WPVA, which included a tournament schedule, the prize money, and a list of people who'd won money the previous year. Because I grew up on the beach, I had played a lot of the players for years. I looked at these people, whom I knew and I'd beaten, and I shot down to the money, column and said, "I think I can do this." I always liked beach volleyball. I think it's my best game by far and I want to play while I'm young. I also saw a lot of potential in the playing and legal aspects of volleyball.

GJ: *What's the connection between volleyball and law?*

BF: I like to negotiate and I'd like to help athletes be represented so they're not being taken advantage of.

GJ: *Did you have any sense that you would be a professional athlete when you were growing up?*

BF: Absolutely not. When I was growing up, I wanted to do a variety of things. Originally, I was going to be a doctor, but I decided I didn't want to see injured people all the time. And I really struggled with it when I graduated from law school. I kind of thought that being an athlete was selling yourself short because if you have intellectual capability, you should use that to improve yourself and help people. That's why I still keep it [law] in, because I like to do things on the intellectual and the athletic side. Although I must say, since

I've attained the level I've attained, there's a lot to it. Sports also involve intellectual challenge.

GJ: *How are women's professional sports doing in the nineties?*

BF: I think that volleyball is going to grow tremendously. I think that tennis, golf, and volleyball are going to be big for women. I think that there are particular sports in which women are more likely to succeed. It [success] depends on the nuances of the game and how you can televise it; it depends on how you can sell it. It's not until you master the ability of how to capture a sport on film, that you can really sell it.

Tara Vanderveers's All-Female Basketball Fantasy Camp

by Roxxie

College women's basketball has grown in popularity to a point where some women's teams, like Stanford's, outdraw the men's. The initial successes of the ABL (American Basketball League) and the NBA's creation of a women's NBA or WNBA demonstrate exactly that. Jane Schroeder, former University of Illinois women's basketball coach, thinks the men's game of basketball may not even be the best. Although men have the height and strength advantage over women, women play with more finesse. Schroeder says, "It's like comparing the flyweights with the heavy-weights, and they are very different."

Now image this: some of the finest women's basketball coaches in the country, and you get to train with them for the weekend. It's star Stanford women's basketball and U.S. olympic team coach Tara Vanderveer's "Wanna Be" Camp, for adult women basketball-o-philes of all skill levels. All that's required are socks, a note from your doctor, and gym shoes. "No experience necessary! Get a great Workout!" the camp flyer promises. "We suggest you wear two pairs of socks at all times to prevent blisters." What adventurous athletic woman could turn down a chance like this?

FRIDAY, APRIL 30, 6:45

Maples Pavilion, Stanford University: I walk into a stadium filled with T-shirted women shooting baskets. I get my own ball, and a Stanford "Wanna Be" camper T-shirt. The ball is glorious, new, and it bounces really high. It says, TARA VANDERVEER'S BASKETBALL CAMP in large letters under the Rawlings brand name. The assistant coach writes my name in big letters on my ball. My first ever personalized basketball, it has the 1992 NCAA winning coach's name on it, and she's a she. This is really fine.

I put on my all-leather Nike high-tops, hoping that this time they won't stink too noticeably at the end of the day. I change clothes and dribble onto the court, toting my little reporter notebook, hoping I don't look like too much of a nerd. After a while Coach Vanderveer gathers us into the center of the stadium for a welcome.

"The biggest two problems with our summertime girl campers," Vanderveer warns, "is keeping them under the curfew, and the boy football campers. I can see that won't be the problem here. Our biggest problem here will be not wearing any jewelry."

We "wanna be" campers laugh. Coach continues, "The purpose of our camp here is to help you to develop an inside appreciation for the sport when you're watching basketball—and of course you all watch Stanford, right?"

I've always watched Cal (Univ. of CA/Berkeley) but I've got an open mind.

"We have a great trainer, and I hope you don't need her. Remember, this camp is about a three letter word called *fun*. Be sure and start out slow, we want you to make it through the three days. You may be sore after this weekend."

A friendly-looking camper on the other side of the room is wearing a PLEASE DON'T HURT ME T-shirt. I realize I'm smaller than most women here. I wish I was wearing that shirt too.

Coach Vanderveer and her staff take us through a basketball crash course. We attend lectures on basic offense, basic defense, and watch b-ball movies. Different coaches work with us each session. The all-star coaching line-up includes former Cal star Carolyn Jenkins, former Ohio State University stars Amy Tucker and Julie Plank, and former University of Illinois/Champaign women's basketball coach Jane Schroeder.

We learn the friendly way to describe basketball's full body blocks, used to block a teammate's defender momentarily so your teammate can shoot, is called "setting a screen." Setting a screen is physically demanding—you cover your breasts with your arms crossed, while the opposing screened player literally bounces off you.

We also learned the essential concept of the "Triple Threat"—your options each time you get the ball. When the ball is passed to you, square yourself towards the hoop as if you could float the pretty ball right in, and then you have the following three choices: shoot, drive (another term for dribble), or pass.

LATER FRIDAY NIGHT

Basic shooting drills lead to a game. Stanford assistant coach Carolyn Jenkins, known as CJ, formerly an awesome University of California/Berkeley player, instructs us. When CJ graduated from Berkeley with four years of college b-ball and an economics degree under her belt, she spent a year working as a financial analyst. "But I missed the sport," she explains. CJ's been coaching at Stanford for two years now, and says, "I'll probably stay with the game the rest of my life."

I ask CJ how her Cal friends reacted to her Stanford job. She answers, "I got teased when I went to work at Stanford, but it was all very friendly."

Is "friendly" the word to describe a sports department whose 800 line ticket number is 1-800-BEATCAL? At least it's memorable.

CJ talks strategy in our pregame huddle. She tells us to pass to the wing, and screen. "OK," CJ says, "This is my team, the Cal team." Everybody laughs.

"Is this a lifetime assignment?" asks a die-hard Stanford fan. Another pleads, "I want to transfer to Kansas."

The fantasy camp was only advertised to Stanford Women's Basketball game-goers. My friend Norma, who told me about the camp, attends Stanford women's games with a fervor. There aren't other adult female fantasy basketball camps in the Bay Area, but some highly successful women's college programs in the country have offered them for their fans. Coach Vanderveer explained earlier, "Really, this camp is for the over-thirty crowd who never got to go to sports camps. This is to help them develop an appreciation for the game by learning about it from the inside."

Yet a zealous camper explained, "The fans were begging for this."

There is some wild fan/sport chemistry going on at Stanford. The women's basketball program has grown from Vanderveer's early days at Stanford, where only thirty people would attend the games, to today's sell-out games—complete with a set of women fans of all ages and skill levels begging for a chance to play themselves.

Norma's a camper, too—she played college basketball at Loyola Marymount University in the late seventies. Norma and I laugh at how we miss-run the screen plays, and she says, "I still can't get all this screen stuff down. In the old days they just taught us the fundamentals of basketball, not all this screen stuff."

I ask, "The fundamentals?"

She replies with a serious look on her face, "Our team fundamentals in the late seventies—Where can we find a woman coach, and how can we get uniforms and shoes."

Norma and I both spent our childhoods playing neighborhood sports alongside boys. We both remember the painful age of heartbreak that athletic girls reach, perhaps nine, or ten, or eleven, when you realize that, although you play sports with boys, you are not a boy, and boys have more athletic opportunities available. We'd always get the leftover weird times to practice in the gyms, baseball diamonds, swimming pools, because boys' teams always had priority. My high school hired girls' swimming coaches who knew nothing about swimming—after a while I fled to practice with boys' teams. Norma and I both remember being sporting second-class citizens in high school and in college.

SATURDAY MORNING: BEFORE MUSCLE SORENESS CREEPS IN

Late in the season, the varnish starts to wear off the shiny wood floors. Varnish or no, I am slipping all over the floor in my thrashed Nikes, hoping that my double pair of socks will absorb the foot odor all leather high tops create. The leather holds so much moisture in, it doesn't let your feet breathe. I decide not to take my shoes off around other people.

The forty or so "Wanna Be" campers are a wide range of ages, but all over nineteen. One woman on my camp team played college basketball in 1967. "I'm reliving my college years," she tells me. She's got a knack for shooting the ball in the hoop. She's a Fast Break Club member, the Stanford Booster Club.

The coaches call out instructions to us, and after a while they sound like a mantra, "Pass to the wing, screen away. Pass to the wing, screen away."

Campers watch Coach Vanderveer with reverence. They wait in turn to go up and talk to her. She pops onto the floor to play in a game against my team, the Cal team. She's still wearing her watch. It's okay, watches aren't jewelry anyway and she's Tara Vanderveer, and she's brought women's basketball at Stanford out of the dark ages.

She believed that women's basketball could be something someday and so she's created the what would have been unbelievable ten years ago—a women's game so exciting they get more fans than the men's team does. She's very supportive and nice when she plays.

When we play offense, and the other team screens us, I notice painfully how small I have become. The last organized basketball I played was high school intramural, when other arms didn't reach as high, the weight of a body crashing into mine didn't hurt as much. Back then I had a knack for getting the ball to the rim of the basket, where it would do a little circular dance, and spill out, not in. I missed most of my shots.

My brother's best friend in high school, an amiable but wild fellow named John, loved basketball, and would spend hours as the shot-doctor, trying to fix my funky shots.

"Not the right arc on the shot," he'd tell me, "you've got too much spin on that ball." Eventually, I learned John's best two fakes, a reverse spinning turnaround jump shot and a jump backwards and shoot in the air shot. These shots improved my game, but we didn't get a girl's basketball team at my high school until my junior year. By then I was short, and a confirmed swimmer. I left the sport of basketball with memories of pimples, and missing shots under pressure.

It didn't surprise me that I still missed shots, and my rusty, sixteen-years-out-of-practice fakes had become comical. But when my thirty-two-year-old, sweaty basketball camper face started to break out again, I had to wonder what basketball did to me.

SUNDAY A.M. THE MUSCLE SORENESS ARRIVES

I'd asked coach CJ if this weekend intensive could prepare me to go out and join a men's basketball pickup game on any playground. Before she could answer me, a wanna-be camper pipes in, "Who would want to join into a men's pickup game?"

Who has the time to arrange segregated sports pickup games? If I really want to play, I take what is available. I just hope my body's not too old for the sport. Muscles I didn't remember having are complaining to me. My hands are covered with weekend warrior basketball calluses. My neck hurts.

I'm privileged to have played alongside Tara Vanderveer, Amy Tucker, Julie Plank, Jane Schroeder, and all the rest. In another day it will be worth all the stiff muscles. Now I know about screens. I wish I could go back to my childhood playground where I played alongside the boys, and out-play them with my newfound, all-female basketball camp knowledge. Can we have more fantasy camps for women in other sports too, please?

Sunde White, Skateboarder

by Pollyanna Whittier

Photo © Pollyanna Whittier

"This will be a little fakey kick flip," she announces. The ledge really isn't that tall, impressive, or even remarkable. Most passersby hardly notice the flaked paint, chipped concrete, or colorful enamel streaks from the bottoms of innumerable skateboards. If you don't skate you probably walk by it every day, never realizing that people come a long ways just to grind along its edge.

It's places like this that draw people from around the world to nondescript yet legendary skate spots in San Francisco. There are legions of skaters that know the city like the back of their hand based solely on skateboard video spots. "I know where that is, it's right by Wallenberg. That's the Presidio right by that hand rail, or Pier Seven, or Embarcadero, or whatever," Sunde parodies. Most of these places are just a ground down cement ledge on a really busy street, but they are manna nonetheless.

"Here comes some attitude," she says with a knowing and slightly weary look. I squinted down the street and through the heat haze could just make out a dark figure waddling briskly toward us. I wouldn't have noticed him if she hadn't said anything. Sunde White lines her skateboard up for another crack at the ledge she's been grinding for last ten minutes.

I'm in the Mission District shooting pictures of Sunde White, a local skater of considerable ability. She's young and brash, with an unnerving amount of self-confidence and subtle wit. Sporting the regulation baggy pants and Airwalks, she looks like any urban hip-hop knock-off. But wannabes are a pale imitation of the real thing, without the tell-tale holes worn through the instep of their shoes or the bathtub caulking filler roughly patched on to make them last a little longer.

A middle-aged man carrying two bags of groceries walks by on the sidewalk in the opposite direction. He takes no notice of her until Sunde's board crashes against the concrete step five feet behind him. He whirls and starts, eyes glaring as if she'd thrown a rock at him. Sunde ignores him. He doesn't get it and she's not about to be the good-will ambassador today. He snarls at her back in English and Spanish as she rumbles up the street out of range.

Another skater glides over like his board is on rails. He rides with a grace and ease that makes you think he was born on the board. The soft clack of his wheels on the pavement is in sharp contrast to the *whap, kick, flip,* and *crash* that Sunde is making. *"¿Que Pasó?"* he inquires politely. There is a lengthy tirade from the man, including what I judge to be some pretty colorful metaphors. Sunde seems to be taking it all in, at least her jaw's tensing up at all the right spots in the conversation. For a blond, blue-eyed Anglo, her Spanish is better than she lets on.

Sunde loosely hangs out with a local group known as LOS, Latinos On Skateboards. A couple of them are around today watching and skating—good looking, relaxed young men in baseball caps and untucked flannel shirts. It's an incongruous mix of youthful Latinos and one very white female. Her flashing, slash-and-burn skating style seems to have earned her respect, or at least acceptance from this group.

They are cool and reassuring. No pointing out that our fiery-eyed antagonist wasn't in any danger of being struck, no business about sharing the sidewalk, no overt militancy. The man walks off in disgust with some pointed threats about the police, and the attitude arrives in the form of a rent-a-cop in an ill-fitting blue uniform. He's surprisingly polite but firm. We don't even wait to hear what he has to say, it's always the same.

This spring I got the crazy idea to photograph female skateboarders. I'd been perusing the newsstand skateboard magazines, *Thrasher, SLAP, Big Brother, Daily Bread,* etc. Some had done girl-skater stories in the past, others featured a few sponsored pros, but women were mostly segregated to the clothing advertisements. I figured it had great visual appeal and might be a novel tap into the great well of urban youth culture angst.

In Berkeley I stopped a woman on the street and gave her my card. She was visually perfect for a photo op. Young and androgynous looking, baggily dressed with great natty dreadlocks and a skateboard that looked like it had taken a few knocks. The little pink triangle earrings didn't hurt the story either. She was direct and up-front, polite but wary. We talked and she sized me up. I asked her if she'd seen any articles on women skateboarders in magazines before. She skated away and didn't look back.

That was two months ago. Since then I've hit the skateparks, plazas, and obvious hangouts, but as I found out the hard way, serious female skateboarders are hard to find. I'm told they come in two categories. First are those that barely rate poser status. It hardly matters that they can't do technical tricks or Ollie or even stay on the board for more than a few seconds. They skate because it attracts novelty attention or because their boyfriend does. The second are serious skaters or wishful serious skaters who face an uphill battle of exceedingly low expectations from other skateboarders. The good ones, especially street skaters, are rare. As Sunde told me later, "You can't just put up an ad and expect the rad skate girls to show up, there aren't that many of them."

Skateboarding is dominated by men, young men. They are mostly young white urban boys living out a fantasy lifestyle as long as possible. Some parlay skateboarding into specialty small businesses or independent publishing ventures, depending on their native intellect and business savvy. A degree of isolation and even social retardation regularly permeates their closed world. Most of the women skateboarders I talked to had some choice words about male skaters, some of the most generous being, "They're not all dick heads." Sunde is more philosophical: "If you weren't independently minded you wouldn't go through the shit you have to go through to be a serious female skateboarder." I ask her why she skates if it's such a hassle. "I love it, fuck, like crazy," she tells me.

Photo © Pollyanna Whittier

The big break in skateboarding, as often as not, is to get sponsored. Equipment manufacturers, promoters, and even local outfits carry a small number of men and fewer women on their rosters. They do it mostly for their own self-promotion, but nobody's complaining. They put them on "teams" and set them up with exhibitions, but mostly they give them stuff. Urban skateboarders are almost universally poor and marginalized by society, so a couple of new boards and some shoes are a nice dividend. Pro sponsorship, or even the notoriety of skate video appearances, however, has the same two-edged quality of a great ledge next to a two-story drop. Everybody wants the free stuff, if only to give away to their friends, but with it comes the pressure to perform. The fun goes out of it, and it surely becomes a job, when there's a video production crew waiting impatiently for you to land that 360-degree kick flip over the four-foot bench.

It's late afternoon and Sunde is working nose slides on a long handrail. She kicks the board up so that the rail rides between the nose and the front wheel truck. Once up, you go downhill at an alarming rate of speed. It looks frighteningly great through the camera viewfinder. With calculated understatement, she points out that "they're really slick, no need for wax on those babies." After several elbow scraping, board dinging, ankle rolling efforts she announces, "I am totally not insane." I have no idea what that means.

I'm searching for a locale that says San Francisco Mission District, something that colorfully defines urban youth culture, but everything is dark pavement and gray concrete. The sun is low and I need some splash of color to break up the monotony and uniformity. No editor is going to want to see frame after frame of hot, dry streets, telephone poles, and little shops that advertise food for a dollar. I settle for a hackneyed cliché, photographing her in front of a large mural on the side of a warehouse. The faded stars, flowers, and rainbows that dominate these outdated murals reflect nothing of the street life and the thrasher mentality of skateboarding.

When she eats, Sunde is a burrito fiend, "Like crazy totally man extra, extra carne in my burrito with plenty-o queso." She rambles like this continuously about skating and life. I can hardly get it all down. "San Francisco is a total youth city, they come here and get as tattooed and pierced as possible, as young and crazy and homeless and heroin addicted as possible, as hip and hip and hip as possible. If I wanted that, I'd be on Haight right now spare changing."

But she's not. Sunde lives in the Mission because that's where her friends are. She takes sucky jobs that leave her time to skate everyday. Mostly, she is focused on technical tricks, kick flips, jumps, etc. More accurately, she is obsessed with her ability to do technical tricks. When we are out taking pictures she is highly critical of her performance. She explains it this way: "If you can only get a trick once every fifty tries or you can't land it all the way, you can't really do it." She has a surprisingly clear understanding of the physics behind board movement and that, no doubt, makes for better tricks. Sunde boils it down to a unifying principle. "All you have to do is kick at the right time and put your foot down in the right place." She makes it sound easy.

The next week we go out again, traveling to different skate spots in the city. Sunde fills the day with bizarre anecdotes from her life. Most days she suffers the usual hostility society directs at young women. Other days she is a crazy-person magnet. She relates a story that seems to be repeated about once a week. She's working a low ledge in the evening south of Market. A guy walks by and she fails to give him the little courtesy smile women know so well. *Hey, I'm busy. I'm working here.* He calls her a bitch and a whore under his breath, and walks on. She chases after him down the street, dogging him for a block. He's stunned by the anger of this seemingly insignificant target of his unfocused hostility. "What does me being on a skateboard have to do with selling my body on the street for extra money or not?" Now he's like a stone and won't look at her, but she's crossing Market and Third screaming at him, "*What the fuck, what the fuck?*" That's pretty much how the day goes unless the police show up.

"100A . . . 100A," I hear in a low voice. Everyone rolls away when the police come by. "Why do we get ticketed?" she complains to

85

no one in particular. 100A is the local ordinance covering skateboarding on a public sidewalk and carries a fifty-nine-dollar citation. "We're exercising, we're not selling drugs, we're being happy and healthy, well-adjusted citizens," she says with a slight touch of self-conscious sarcasm. "There are guys sniffing paint in the square where we skate, passed out and totally fucked up so they can't even move, and why am I getting arrested? For totally destroying property? If they don't want me to skate there, don't design a building (like the new library or the Embarcadero ribbon walk) like a skate park."

But it's bigger than that. In nature, erosion and weathering are the forces that inevitably wear down great mountain ranges and carve deep canyons. No rock stands forever against the irresistible forces of nature. On the urban landscape it is people that become the natural forces of erosion. Street skaters are more than urban vermin. They are the clear physical manifestation of modern youth culture, with all its ugly, antisocial, ledge-and bench-destroying consequences. Skaters tear at social conformity like they tear at the concrete around them. Their activities *are* the nature of things.

As I look through the last batch of three hundred slides the lupe tells no lies. Sharp focus, good balance to the fill flash, just a little bit of movement at the hands and feet, perfect. But everywhere Sunde said she was off on the jumps, she was. A misplaced foot here, not enough height on the board there, she was right pretty much every time. The pictures in front of the murals look especially dull and lifeless. Most of the slides go right through the shredder. The jumps, kick flips, and grinds that remain are still, pretty much, a gray blur of concrete, glass, and macadam. Only at the very end do I see what I'd been searching for but lacked the correct vantage point to see. In the last few frames Sunde is riding away from me on her board. Her dog tugs at the leash, pulling her down the rutted sidewalk like an off-center sled dog. The long telephoto compresses the perspective into a diffuse kaleidoscope of light and shadow. She stands out sharply against the background and, like those once bright murals, the colors all around pop out from the distance.

Mimi Meets Martina

by Mimi-Freed

By now you've heard there were a handful of hard-core queers protesting something at the nation's capitol.

At least that's what you heard if your only access to the March on Washington was the measly coverage provided by every major media outlet in this country.

Yeah, I guess the network players were too busy watching their asses to get any real count of how many people were there. But leave it to the qweirdo I am to have gotten some inside scoops to share with *Girljock*.

Photo © Mimi-Freed Archives

SUNDAY, APRIL 25, 1993
THE MARCH ON WASHINGTON
FOR GAY, LESBIAN AND
BISEXUAL RIGHTS

I performed on the Kick-Off Stage as a co-emcee with Nalty, C.W.A. (Comic with AIDS) for an hour. Silly me, I thought nobody would really be up that early (10:00 A.M.). There were over 20,000 on the grass in front of me. I was so happy they could all make it! I did my best to give them pro-bisexual humor and antireligious intolerance humor (i.e., I'm willing to bet that when we're not watching, most of the Fundamentalists are really singing, "And they'll know we are Christians by our guns, by our guns!").

Instead of doing any actual marching—it took all of seven hours for all the contingents to finish!—I decided to make the best use of my press pass. I left my New York sister and her gal-pals on the lawn close to the stage and easily found myself backstage at the Main Stage. Not that there weren't a bunch of surly, undersexed (?), and downright rude security types trying to stop me.

I just waved my performer pass around and flashed my brashest "I-belong-here" attitude and vaulted over them. My outfit helped. In true San Francisco sex-positive style, I wore bright red jeans, a red lace bra and an open black vest with necklaces and passes hanging down my cleavage.

I ran around and tried to talk to as many people as I could that wouldn't run from my chest. Cybill Shepherd was surrounded by too many handlers who insisted I keep my distance. As if I wanted to hide from the sun with her prissiness under her parasol. Get a tan!

It was easy to find the bull-dyke of comedy herself: Lea Delaria, the dyke to watch out for. You know she's broken the dyke barrier on Arsenio, don't you? Twice now! I asked her what the march felt like and she responded: "This march to me feels like: If I were locked in a pastry store in Paris overnight and I couldn't get out and I was then told that I could eat anything I wanted and not gain an ounce, *that* is what this march feels like to me."

And Scout, one of the four National co-chairs could only respond: "I'm having a twelve-hour orgasm. I'll probably have to sleep for two weeks to recover, so sorry to all my girlfriends. You know, the thousands out there. But please, catch me later in the month."

But the epitome of the March came for me when I thought the mighty woman of sports herself was cruising me. I'd stopped to reload my camera and caught her peering out from the camper door I was standing outside of.

No time to think—Act!

Here is the entire interaction I was graced with between myself and the Amazon herself:

"Can I just come in and interview you?"

"Is that all you want to do?"

"Yeah. Well, I could do plenty more. I'm dressed for it, okay? Hi, Martina, Mimi Freed. Nice to meet you. I'm freelance reporting for anybody who'll buy this story and . . ."

Navratilova laughs. "You have too much hair."

"I just got a haircut."

"Ha, ha, ha," Navratilova laughs again. "What a shame."

"I did the best I could do. Were you at the '87 March?"

"No, I didn't know it was even happening. In fact, the first I read about it was when I read that *Time* and *Newsweek* didn't report on it," she answers. "That's the first I even heard about it. I didn't know it existed. I would have gone then, I'm sure."

"I won't ask you the difference between the two marches then. [Brilliant observation, Freed, good journalistic instinct.] How do feel about this march? I've seen you at the Honoring Our Allies event and you were at the Gala last night. How does it feel to be at this one?"

"Overpowering. To see all the people out, it's fantastic. It feels like a positive experience. It's one of those days obviously that none of us will ever forget.

"But for me, because I've been the underdog so much as far as public adulation or acceptance even, and I've always been in the minority. It's nice to be in the majority here. I mean, I've had the crowd really come on to my side in the last couple of years, but to get this kind of rapport and respect and love, it's overwhelming."

"This may not matter journalistically," Freed confesses, "but I appreciate what you said about Magic Johnson. I'm sure you took a lot of shit or flack for that."

"What is funny is that everybody asked me, 'Have you gotten any negative response?' But I really didn't, it was only in the questions they were asking me. 'Did you get any bad mail?' And I didn't. Everything has been positive, except for maybe the questions, people thinking that I would get negative feedback from it and I really didn't."

"Great."

"So there was like one bad letter out of thousands," Navratilova admits.

"That was not the assumption at all. Everybody thought you were going to get hit for speaking out . . ."

"And I didn't. Everybody said, 'I'm glad you said something. We all thought it but you said it.' And they all said, 'Did you get any negative feedback?' And I'm like . . . 'Why should I?'"

"Because you said the truth. You shouldn't."

"I said the truth. I cannot get bad feedback."

"Can I ask a favor?"

"Maybe," Navratilova responds coyly.

"Picture please?"

"Sure."

"Okay, you want to have brown hair?" [I put my hair on top of her head.]

"Yes!" [Her friends laugh. We take it off.]

Just then, Michelle Crone, the woman I've been searching for during the entire march, comes into Martina's trailer.

"Is that Mimi Freed?"

"Crone-y!"

I rudely ignore Martina in favor of adoring the woman that got me a space on the kickoff stage. I hear Martina say on the tape, "She's unbelievable. I mean, look at that hair!"

"I'll have some to spare the next time I get it cut," I hear myself reply.

"Send me some," the *Girljock* goddess demands.

"I will."

Right. Does anybody have her address?

[ZLATA HOLČIČKA -- GOLDEN LITTLE GIRL]

Love, Ace, Match:

Interview with Martina Navratilova

by Heather Findlay, from *Girlfriends* Magazine

"It's great to have all my gay fans here." You could have heard a pin drop in the press tent. The greatest tennis player in history, holder of more titles than any other tennis champ, male or female (167 to be exact), winner of over $20 million in official prize money, imperial playtomboy of the tennis world, *had just acknowledged her gay fans.*

Then again, the speaker was Martina Navratilova, the former Czechoslovakian who, in the late 1970s, risked her career and personal happiness by telling immigration officials that she was bisexual. Only ten years after Stonewall, she spoke openly to a sports editor about her affair with out lesbian novelist Rita Mae Brown. During 1993's March on Washington for Lesbian and Gay Rights, she delivered an unforgettable speech from the podium. She campaigned publicly against Colorado's Amendment Two and, in the wake of Magic Johnson's revelation of his HIV status, criticized the double sexual standard prevailing in the sports establishment. Now, by talking to *Girlfriends* on the eve of her retirement, Navratilova becomes the first international superstar to grant an interview to a lesbian publication.

On that November afternoon in Oakland, in a coliseum stocked with debonair, Adidas-clad dykes—some carrying banners with pink triangles reading WE LOVE YOU MARTINA, WE'LL MISS YOU—it would have been hard *not* to acknowledge us. The Bank of the West Tournament has always been one of Navratilova's favorites, in good part because of the rowdy gal crowd and their characteristic foot-stomping.

After nudging past the likes of Amy Frazier and Debbie Graham, Navratilova fell prey in the finals to the relentless passing shots of Spanish powerhouse Arantxa Sanchez Vicario. The loss did not, however, deter her Bay Area fans. Foregoing the traditional tennis obsession with underdogs and girlie-girl youthfulness— a topic Martina touches on in this interview— they remained loyal to the war-horse of women's tennis.

Navratilova has a staying power with her lesbian fans that will persist well into her retirement. Beyond her unforgettable game, Navratilova's direct and unaffected clarity about her love for women has changed forever the way the public thinks of lesbians. And not without cost. Citing her revolutionary serve-and-volley game—an aggressive net strategy so *unladylike* in a field dominated by Chris Evert's baseline tenacity or Tracy Austin's sky high lobs—Navratilova insists that sponsors avoid her for reasons other than simple homophobia. But lesbian-baiting seems always to lurk in the margins of Navratilova's mainstream sports coverage. Whether it's grumbling about how she's "too good for the women's tour," or *Sports Illustrated*'s snide remarks about her former coaches Renee Richards and Nancy Lieberman (a.k.a "Team Navratilova"), the implication is that the suped-up immigrant plays like a man and hails from some queer, inhuman family. When the sports pages cover gay *male* athletes, explains Navratilova in the interview below, it's a different ball game altogether.

Navratilova's staying power also stems from her status as a lesbian heartthrob. Bawdy dyke comics *love* Martina material: Suzanne Westenhoeffer claims that Navratilova's erotic aura sent her swooning when they first met, and after feeling the Navratilova thigh at the March on Washington, Lea DeLaria jokes that she'd be afraid to go down on her "cause my head might get crushed." Among young gay women—some of whom claim they came out because of her singular influence—Navratilova boasts a Midas touch. When Rita Mae shacked up with Judy Nelson, lesbians everywhere drew the conclusion, however imaginary, that the only replacement for Martina is a Martina ex.

These days, Navratilova's Czech reserve and her experience with vicious tabloids causes her to be reticent about her retirement and her latest love. *Girlfriends* did, however, spot the lucky woman in the stands, and suffice it to say, she's a graceful, curly-headed femme and a dedicated dogsitter to Killer Dog, the miniature fox terrier that keeps company with Navratilova's entourage. She's smart, too: Claiming that flash photography might trigger a seizure in the aging K.D., the European-looking beauty kept all paparazzi at bay.

Some lesbian journalists have recently blasted Navratilova for not granting interviews with lesbian media. Yet Navratilova is not a professional lesbian. She's a professional tennis player who "happens" to be gay, and considering her political track record in Washington, D.C., and Colorado, we can't fault her for extracurricular laziness. Cynics may raise an eyebrow at her occasional jingoism, her new novel *The Total Zone*'s rambling plot and disappointingly straight heroine, or her head-in-the-sand defense against Nelson's palimony claims (which the former Maid of Cotton recorded, after all, on videotape). Nevertheless—unless you're Nelson—it's hard to complain.

In this exclusive interview, Navratilova talks about her activism inside and outside of the tennis world, her new relationship, "the game that eats its young," and more.

HF: *My idol has always been, well, before you, Billie Jean.*
NAVRATILOVA: Oh, Billie Jean!
HF: *Oh yes. Not Chris Evert. And I feel that both of you were really important not only in tennis but also in directing a women's movement.*
NAVRATILOVA: Well, Billie Jean, especially.
HF: *Who do you foresee doing that after you retire?*
NAVRATILOVA: I can still do it. I don't have to be playing to do that, but I'm sure that there will be some people who will step up to do it.
HF: *Now that you're retiring, are you really going to have a baby?*
NAVRATILOVA: I don't know. I never said I would. I only said I don't know.
HF: *There's a lot of talk in your autobiography about how, someday, you would like to settle down and—*

NAVRATILOVA: No, I never said I would like to, I just said that if I did, I would like Wayne Gretzky to be the father [laughs].

HF: *If you did have a baby, would you carry it, or would you supervise?*

NAVRATILOVA: One thing at a time! First I have to decide if I want one, then I'll worry about how to go about it.

HF: *To me and to so many other lesbians, you are the most desirable, eligible bachelor in the world.*

NAVRATILOVA: I'm *not* a bachelor!

HF: *I'm thinking about how Suzanne Westenhoeffer said that when she first met you she fainted.*

NAVRATILOVA: She lied!

HF: *Really? Do you have a significant other, then?*

NAVRATILOVA: Yes. I've been in a relationship for a year now. But, you know, she's a private person, so . . .

HF: *What about your book? Why a mystery? Why not a tennis instructional?*

NAVRATILOVA: I've done that already, a

THE MARTINA FACTOR

Forget the world-class drop shots. What is it that makes Martina Navratilova so, um, sexy? In search of answers, *Girlfriends* called JoAnne Loulan, author of *Lesbian Passion,* and friend of the great heartthrob herself.

"I think it's the vein," says Loulan. You mean blood vein? "Yeah, I think Suzanne Westenhoeffer has something about it in her gig, but I hear talk about it on the sidelines, too. She's got this vein up her left arm, her playing arm . . . and you know how those girls love those muscles."

Loulan also attributes Navratilova's sex appeal to her attitude (indeed, Martina is cool as a cucumber off court) and "her physical stance," the mere thought of which renders Loulan at a loss for words. "In real life she's very sweet, very dear, extremely genuine, given the kind of life she's had. That's a turn-on for me."

Is power a factor? "I'm not so completely turned on by the fact that she's the greatest tennis player in the history of the world, but I know some people are. To me, it's so amazing to watch a woman who is great at what she does, whether it's singing, teach-ing in a classroom, or playing tennis, whatever."

On a scale from one to ten, serious butch at one, high femme at ten, where would Loulan put Navratilova? "Oh, one!" says Loulan, not missing a beat. For one thing, Navratilova has, in recent years, ditched those cutesy tennis skirts for shorts. "She wore shorts years ago, and then she went to the skirts, and now she's back. I do love that. That's fabulous."

She seems, moreover, to go for femmes. "Although you know that Cindy Nelson wasn't much of a femme," says Loulan mischievously. "that's probably why it didn't last long.

"When we had dinner last week, I told her I'd just started exercising that day. I spent a total of two minutes on the treadmill. Instead of being horrified or putting me down, she was totally gracious about it, like any good butch would be.

"And, of course, I love her accent. That just sends me right around the bend. I know they're not from the same part of the world, but it reminds me of Garbo."

while back. It's fun to write fiction because you don't have to tell the truth [laughs]. You can make it up as you go along.

HF: *The book talks about the problems of young people growing up in professional tennis.*

NAVRATILOVA: Yes, absolutely. [Those problems] are very real. But what's funny is that we came up with the plot before this whole thing blew up with Jim Pierce [father of tennis youth star Mary Pierce, recently accused of child abuse]. The media criticized me, saying I'm just writing about what happened. Well, we made it up before it happened. It takes a year before the book can come into print. It was life imitating art imitating life.

HF: *It's really a novel about women who have lost their childhoods to tennis.*

NAVRATILOVA: Mmmm. There are a lot of them.

HF: *Look at what's going on with Jennifer Capriati, and now—maybe—with Venus Williams. the* San Francisco Chronicle *today said tennis is a game that eats its young. In that sense, your book is really timely.*

NAVRATILOVA: Still, it's the parent's problem, and we can't control the parents. You can blame the WTA, or the press, but it's the parents who ultimately make the decision. They have to see the future. And yes, these kids don't have a childhood. But I had a great childhood. Yeah, I played tennis a lot. I may have been on the court for three hours playing doubles, because it was fun. But I never practiced for more than an hour until I was 13 or 14 years old. And then we hit for two hours, and that was huge. But these kids are on the court four or five hours a day practicing, hitting balls,

working out. They're fourteen years old, and they don't even have time for school. Some of them do that at twelve faxing their homework.

HF: *So you're not a bachelor. I'm crushed.*

NAVRATILOVA: Don't you read the tabloids?

HF: *From what I could tell, they were making you out to be something of a Don Juan. One girl one week, another girl the next.*

NAVRATILOVA: Well, there you go. That's what you read. If I had the life people say I had, I wouldn't have time for tennis. God, I wouldn't have time to do all that anyway. The latest is [a British tabloid reported that], I had been driving around London in a red Porsche, I had rented a house with my girlfriend, I had been there since July, and I had been seen all over town. My friends were calling me, mad that I didn't tell them I was in town! It's not that there was some untruth to it; it's that the whole thing was made up. I've been linked with Melissa Etheridge and k. d. lang, both of whom are very dear friends, but neither one I've had an affair with. Two famous lesbians are in the same room, and everyone assumes they're together.

HF: *Exactly!*

NAVRATILOVA: "Oh, my god, they found each other! Isn't that great!"

HF: *There's also the idea that there are only two lesbians in the world, and therefore, they must be girlfriends.*

NAVRATILOVA: Right. I had a single life for a year, and I played around for a couple of months and it got really old really fast. It's the first time I've ever done that. Nobody knew about those women. But I got tired of that really quickly, and so I decided to look for a relationship. I took my time, and it sort of happened when I wasn't [looking].

HF: *What about the future of lesbians in tennis? After you, will it be safer for them to come out?*

NAVRATILOVA: It's still hard for everybody to come out because the endorsements are not there. Once the first company comes forth and endorses a gay athlete, more of them will be wanting to come out. Especially professional athletes like tennis players and golfers who can always play. It's much more difficult for a team sport player because they get blackballed out of the league.

HF: *Who will be the first sponsor to back us?*

NAVRATILOVA: Well, you might be surprised. I can't tell you yet. I'm trying to get a rainbow card going, a credit card for gays. I have some friends, and one's a banker. You'll read about it, hopefully.

HF: *You don't have any specific plans with the WTA to make tennis a safer place for lesbians?*

NAVRATILOVA: Oh, I think it is [already]! There are some gays on the tour who are very comfortable about it, but they're not talking about it. There really is no point in talking about it. The heterosexuals aren't proclaiming their heterosexuality. It would be a whole lot easier for all gays if there were more gays that were willing to come out. But there are a lot more gays in the entertainment business, whereas on the women's tour there are maybe four or five in the top hundred. The numbers are very, very low. So their coming out isn't going to change society anyway. I think it's time for male athletes to come out.

HF: *I liked that about your book, actually. It touched on that problem by having a gay male tennis player who is deeply closeted.*

NAVRATILOVA: The media are protecting the men. The media know the gay male football players, and basketball players, and they wouldn't dare ask them the question, let alone intimate it, or say in the press that they may be gay. But the women—they ask them the question all the time, whether it's personal, or "What about the lesbians on the tour?" They wouldn't ask male athletes, "What about the gay guys in the locker room?" They won't even broach the subject.

HF: *That's the general problem that faces women in sports.*

NAVRATILOVA: Right!

HF: *You're good at sports so you must be a dyke.*

NAVRATILOVA: Exactly. You have to prove that you're straight. Gay guys don't have to prove that. They play football, and therefore they must be straight. Not queer.

HF: *Or, if you're a woman, and you serve and volley, you must be a dyke.*

NAVRATILOVA: No, there are a few of them who are straight and who are serve-and-volley.

HF: *Actually, I can't think of any who are serve-and-volleyers any more, period.*

NAVRATILOVA: Yeah, really. That's true.

—with assistance from Diane Anderson and Erin Findlay.

Nike's "W" Soccer League

by Roxxie

"When people ask me to do something after work, its like: 'Oh, you have soccer *again*,' and it seems that all we do is work, sleep, eat, and practice, but we love it," Lady Roughrider Kim Conway, a former University of Virginia (Charlottesville) player, told me. The Long Island Lady Roughriders train three to four nights weekly from 7:30 to 10:00, and there are at least twenty other teams all over the country in the new women's National Soccer League training comparably as many hours. The new National League is designed to enhance women's competition by creating super-teams from different regions that travel and play each other. It's a two-month long summer league set up so college players can participate in it as well. Nike is a partial League sponsor, hence the name: the Nike "W" League.

The organization behind it is the USWISL, the United States Women's Inter-regional Soccer League, also known as the *Swizzle*. Upper level U.S. players have come out for this league, including some current and former U.S. Women's National team members, and Canadian national team players.

Each team provides travel arrangements, uniforms, and equipment for the players. Teresa Abrahamsohn, who plays on the San Francisco Vikings USWISL team, is a defender with an outstanding resume of soccer achieve-ments—Brown University/All American 1984, U.S. National Team 1987, Northern California State-Select since 1986, Amateur National Team since 1991. She told me, "For me this is the closest I'll ever see to a pro league. I've never been on a team since college where they pay for everything."

"The NCAA was concerned our teams were pro, but the teams are sending letters to the NCAA saying they are amateur," said Ron Griffith, USWISL Development Director. "People use the word semipro, but what does that mean, free shoes? College teams provide more than that. An athletic scholarship is worth up to $20,000 a year. College scholarships may be semipro. Out in the real world, leagues such as ours run from the heart."

So if you were a woman soccer player still reaching for your *personal best* in soccer, wouldn't curiosity be eating a hole in the bottom of your cleats? Wouldn't you head out to watch the league games? Or would you go out to a Nike "W" League team's practice?

Hey, I did.

I had to find out what the next level of U.S. women's soccer was like. It was a new mountain to climb. Besides, my women's over-30 soccer team, another San Francisco Vikings team, was training for the Amateur National Cup Finals, and I was already in pretty good shape. We'd been invited to come practice with the mostly younger squad of the USWISL Vikings. We'd played the USWISL Vikings team in a practice game and had a tied score: 0–0.

So was I scared to go work out with the USWISL Vikings? Just because they'd had tryouts and their uniforms, equipment, and travel were all paid for, and just because their roster sheets listed players with "All-American" after their names, or "All-this conference," or "Such-and-such player of the year," didn't mean the practice itself would be scary. It couldn't be that awful. This is amateur sports, after all, not a perfect world. Some signs of amateur-sports-wear-and-tear showed during the first mini-USWISL season in 1994. As the mini-season ended, there was an invitational tournament for their National finals.

"Last year when we were preparing to go to the Nationals," Kim Conway told me, she had to become a fundraiser. She said, "We were not being financed for the trip through the Roughrider organization. They did not even realize that we had a National tournament last summer. In about three to four weeks we raised three to four thousand dollars.

"We read in the paper a while ago that Tampax was asking the Tennis Association if they could be the sponsor and give them ten million dollars, but they turned them down because of the negative connotations associated with menstruating. When we heard about *that* we were like—we'd do anything, we'd wear tampons with earrings if someone would give us just a tenth of that."

So was I scared to go to the practice, okay, maybe I felt a twinge or two of fear, but

knowing there were USWISL players out there imagining tampon earrings helped. Besides, even if a USWISL league practice was going to be that awful, for me it had been a sports year of what-doesn't-kill-you makes you stronger. I was ready.

I was so ready, I went running that day at lunch. Just two miles in a lot of heat. It seemed like good training. An easy two, a soccer practice at night. No problem at all, right?

I even showed up a little early for practice, held at a local high school field. The grass was a little wet and the ground soft. The grass was that pregnant color green, where the grass blades are still lining up according to their own sense of order, not yet trampled upon by the cleats of twenty-odd women. The women arrived in summer workout gear, and their different colored soccer bags, and we all put on our shoes and got ready.

Here goes: We ran. We had timed intervals dribbling. We jumped over our teammates backs for minutes at a time. We did high jumps from standing where you raise your knees up high into your chest. We did awful stomach crunchy leg tosses with a partner where you, on your back, must not let your legs—tossed by the partner—touch the ground. For the first fifteen seconds or so, they don't actually hurt. But when they start to hurt it is an evil burn that goes way deep into the very belly of the muscles. It becomes the type of pain that makes you forget how to laugh. For the next three days, those crunches and jumps and compressions of the abdominal region leave their calling cards on your stomach. I was marked and I knew it.

We juggled balls with feet, with thighs, we

head-juggled, we juggled with a mixture; then, what killed me: We juggled with the left or nondominant foot only. I *accidentally* kicked my ball into a corner of the field during this drill, trying to hide far away from the coaches. It was pathetic: I could only do a couple in a row on my nondominant side (I knew what I would be practicing alone later in the week). I pretended to stretch my aching leg muscles, and put a pained look on my face. I sweated in nervous agony. Finally, the next drill.

We practiced two shots on two port-a-goals. The first shot was a normal shot, the other shot was turn and an outside-of-the-foot weird swipe shot resembling a tennis slice. My right knee was still recovering from a slight ligament strain a month ago so I was doomed to use only my left side. My shots were not even as good as a seven-year-old's.

It was time to start cracking jokes with the teammates. At least my sense of humor was still working. I got a couple of them to laugh.

Later, the coach, Danny Link, divided us into four teams, with different color vests on. Red, yellow, green, and my team: the blues. We were going to play a small game, only it had so many rules I couldn't remember them all. San Francisco lost the ball to lightning-quick young players who understood the rules. After fifteen minutes I started to understand. When your team took the field, you played against another color, staying on as long as no one scored a goal against your team. When you left, you took a position on the sidelines, and the players in the game could use you as a wall player for a stationary pass.   .

After twenty minutes my team realized we had one less player than the other teams. When we told the coach, he gave us another player.

Then we started to play better. My teammates, formerly a quiet bunch, started talking a little, only I distinctly heard people yelling at me, things like: Go! Get that ball! Step into your tackle!

Commands. I was being told what to do by players I could have baby-sat as children. However, that's the increasing reality of women's soccer. The women's soccer demographics look something like this: In 1979, there were only seventeen women's collegiate programs, but by 1994 there were 720, including the NCAA, NAIA, and junior college teams.

But prior to this league, outside of players involved in the National-team level, the only other hopes for postcollege players were to find club teams which play in competitive tournaments, or to head off to play professionally in another country. There's been the documented exodus of players to Europe, or the Japanese "L" league.

Finally I got a shot on goal—the kind of ball that sprays out from a miskicked defensive attempt to clear the ball away from the goal mouth. Like the hungry goal-seeking vulture all we soccer players are, I found a little extra speed in my legs and swooped in and got the ball. I owned it right then, and I was ready to crack that ball into the back of the net. I aimed, I did, but somehow I misswiped it. I cranked out a soft fluff shot that the goalie easily swooped up into her arms. Ouch.

The rest of the night my legs felt somewhere beyond tired, they felt like lead. I wanted to feel the next level of women's soccer and I'd found it. It was a truly physical, physical thing.

Sports change as you age. Strength and

speed decline as you age, so you have to fight your own battles to keep them at the right level that you need them to be. But the mental parts of the soccer can get more interesting and challenging. My over-30 team coach worked us hard physically, yes, but always armed us with a strategy. He'd get us to develop the best sense of when-to-use-what, and how to work best in our team's formations. It was a more mental rhythm than this ultra-athletic universe of younger players who could still be searching for brand new strength. Besides, maybe some of them were still growing.

I felt like a superball-gone-flat, amongst a world of brand new bouncy athletes.

I hoped to God the coach would tell me I shouldn't come back. My legs didn't want to, but maybe I shouldn't have been running that day at lunch. I decided never to run again before going to a strange team's practice. In the meantime, I was wishing for a ticket not-to-come back. Yum. I was tired and beat. Please, couldn't playing on my own team be enough?

I opted out of the latter-workout sprints and went over to tell the coach I'd already ran earlier that day, and my legs were shot. I told him thanks for letting me come. I was trying to give him a perfect moment to ask me not to come back. No one else was standing around us, and it would have been so easy.

But the coach was smiling at me, he was happy to have me at his practice. He shook my hand and told me, "Be sure and come back next week."

Pray for me. And pass the Ben-Gay.

No Fear of Flying:
Those Daring Young Women on Their Flyin' Trapeze

by Evelyn McDonnell

Sarah Steben hangs from a steel bar swinging thirty-three feet in the air. Her hands are curled around the trapeze; her shins wrap around the shins of her twin sister, feet gripping knees. Karyne is upside-down, her arms reaching for the audience, her eighteen-year-old body flying free, back and forth under the yellow and blue plastic of the Cirque du Soleil tent. It seems like the only things preventing her from continuing the trajectory of the arc up into the tent top, over the bleachers, then down, three stories, to the floor, are her sister's ankles. Limbs that were made for walking, running, standing, climbing, kicking, dancing, but not for grasping, hang on tight.

In Saltimbanco, Cirque du Soleil's touring production, surreally costumed acrobats catapult off a Russian swing while a rock band blows Andrew Lloyd Webber-esque blues. A double-jointed Russian family slithers through each other's limbs in a survivalist ballet. And in the midst of the gymnastic, Chagallian opera, the Stebens perform a dizzying display of daredeviltry. Balanced on the trapeze's proscenium fulcrum, bodies symmetrically and gracefully poised, the twins, quite literally, support girl love.

Before girls get tits and boys get chest hair, people don't care so much what they do. Life

can seem physically limitless to healthy kids growing up in American suburbs. I remember the first time I fell out of a tree. The bushes below caught me, and the whole experience was so funny and exciting that I climbed back up and fell again and again. In the moments I was airborne, the earth's magnetic pull had me giddy. That same desire to defy gravity drove the Wright brothers' propeller inventions and guides the Steben sisters' trapeze tricks. "As kids, we always go on a tree, or a roof," Sarah says in the fractured English these Quebecois teens speak. Once, they held on to an umbrella together and jumped off their house.

"One day, we would like to jump from airplane with parachute."

Acts that challenge our notions of movement are at Saltimbanco's core. Contortionists, acrobats, muscle men, and tightrope walkers defy death and dare the air. In a circus devoted to the aesthetics of danger, the Stebens seem particularly fearless. "We don't want to scare the people," Sarah says, "we just want to have fun."

For two Montreal schoolgirls tired of the torturous, tedious gymnastics they had practiced for three years, trapeze offered an adventurous and artistic—and healthy—alternative. The point in Cirque isn't to abuse the human body, but to marvel at the extremes to which it can be stretched and pushed. It's a far cry from the Stebens' lithe forms and joyful swings to the emaciated physiques and pained faces of last summer's Olympic gymnasts. "Gymnastics is not emotion; it's just technical," says Karyne. "You saw the Olympic, the little girl cry, because she have so pressure. One day if I'm coach, I don't want to have students whose parents push them. I want them to have fun. And maybe if they see the Cirque, they can understand the emotion. It's really important, because it help the movement to be stronger and beautiful."

You would have to be even more cynical than a New York *Village Voice* writer not to be charmed and captivated by the Stebens. They are petite and pretty, but strong and well-muscled. In conversation, they frequently reach across the table to hold hands. "We have complicity together," they somewhat awkwardly explain, using a word more common in French than English.

"We move together," Karyne says.

"Like a mirror," Sarah adds.

"We are like one together, just one people. We dance on the trapeze."

The Stebens are fraternal twins, but they're almost impossible to tell apart. Sarah is slightly larger; Karyne, thinner in the face. A stranger can detect only a subtle, tonal difference between the two, even after a couple meetings. But the twins are not trying to confuse their identities. Karyne and Sarah readily delineate their differences.

"She's left-handed, I'm right," Karyne says. "I prefer to fly. But she don't like to fly."

"I prefer to be catching," Sarah says.

"But we do both things in the show because it's fun to try to do both."

Leg grips are the Stebens' calling card. According to their on-site trainer, Warren Conley, they are one of only two groups in the world to catch leg to leg. Cirque aerial trainer Basil Schoutz and Saltimbanco artistic director Andrew Watson developed the act. Conley credits their training for the twins' early success. The Stebens agree. While performing, they sometimes whisper "Basil Schoutz" to each other, to remind them of his encouragement "to fly."

Such confidence is crucial—trapeze can be dangerous. In the *fixe* part (the first half of the act, when the trapeze doesn't move), the sisters have nothing but each other to keep them from hitting the ground. Although they use safety ropes attached to belts while they are swinging, there is still a possibility of injury. Trapeze is a demanding physical sport: The twins constantly have shin splints, and rope burns form lines on their arms.

Their worst accident occurred one night last fall, when both were nervous. The anxiety threw them off, and when Sarah felt herself sliding out of Karyne's hold, she panicked and tried to catch the bar with one hand. Two ribs popped out of place, and she lost consciousness for a moment. "I didn't know she was injured," Karyne recalls. "I say, Stop? She say yes. Then I feel like I'm hurt too." Sarah pulled muscles and ligaments that took six months to heal. "I'm always in a little pain," she says.

Less than three years ago, Sarah and Karyne Steben had never been on a trapeze. They were planning to go to college: Karyne to study physical education, maybe to become a choreographer or gymnastics instructor. Sarah wanted to go into the performing arts, maybe to be an artistic director. Then they went to see the Montreal-based Cirque du Soleil.

Like a million dreamers intoxicated by the promise of fantastic escape—from the confines of a fixed life, a small town, or the limits placed on the body—the Stebens immediately wanted to join the circus. They walked into Cirque's offices and, after two months of auditions, were given the job as Cirque du Soleil's new trapeze act. Less than one year later, the twins tested their performance at the Festival Mondial du Cirque de Demain, an international circus tournament in Paris. In a field where acts often take four years to develop, the novice Steben sisters returned to Canada with a gold medal.

Cirque has helped the twins develop their independence and ambitions. Indeed, they are already outgrowing its fold. "We want to go to Europe, to Paris, and do the trapeze together in cabarets," Karyne says. "Because we want to learn a little bit more. Here, it's too easy. Here

we can't learn how to put my trapeze, how to work for pay and receive the money. We have no choice. Maybe I will think about the money and the business, and she will think about the costumes. That's why we are strong together."

The Stebens' togetherness fuels their independence. Their sweet, feminine looks may make them attractive to the family audiences Cirque draws. But alongside their graceful beauty there's a bravery and a bravado to their act. As Erica Jong has pointed out, feeling free to fly is no small feminist victory.

Like many people, I have dreams where I fly. I leap into the air and don't come down, gliding over people's heads like Baryshnikov on acid. In my sleep, flying feels wholly natural, as if I'd been airborne all my life. Karyne had the same kind of dreams, until she swung from a trapeze. "Before, sometimes I dreamed I run, and I fly. And now I never dream about it," she says. Of course, you don't have to dream about something when you're doing it every day.

Women Swimmin':
Marathoning's Not Just for Runners Anymore
by Maria Vetrano

Driven woman-on-a-mission, goal-oriented, disciplined disciple of marathon swimming—that's Cheryl Elinsky, the woman whose name will go down in the record book with women like Gertrude Ederle when she achieves her dream of swimming the English Channel.

While training in the gym, the pool, or on the track for a competition is something I've always understood, training by yourself hour-after-hour, day-after-day to reach an event where you'll spend hours and hours by yourself has always made me wonder. For swimming the English Channel is nothing like a hockey game or a swim meet. Fans do not cheer you along the way. There are no teammates jointly responsible for the outcome of the game. Such an accomplishment is not a stepping stone to the Olympics or to potentially lucrative endorsements. It's a bit like *The Grinch Who Stole Christmas*: Marathon swimming is much more than presents and trimming. It has a soul of its very own, a soul which only the initiated can truly understand.

If you've marveled or wondered about marathon swimming, read on. Cheryl Elinsky reveals the life she leads as a marathon swimmer. She is now just eighteen months away from swimming the Channel.

A competitive swimmer since elementary school days, Cheryl Elinksy is a Vermont resi-dent who lived in eight different states by the time she was in high school. Her lifelong love of sports inspired her career choice—athletic training, and later, physical therapy, which she now practices and teaches. Swimming led to triathlons; triathlons led back to swimming. Prior to her current incarnation as a marathon swimmer, one of Cheryl's greatest thrills was placing sixth in the triathlon at the Vancouver Gay Games in 1990. For the past two years, she has altered her focus. Her primary goal has become swimming the English Channel, notorious for its cold, rough water and funky tidal activity.

When I met Cheryl in Provincetown last fall, she told me of her dream to do the Channel. I almost said, "Cheryl, take the *Chunnel* if you want to go from England to France! Not only will it be infinitely quicker, but your hair will still look fabulous and you'll be able to shop upon arrival!" But I didn't. There are one or two things that are more important to Cheryl's life than her hair—like her goggles, for example.

MV: *What were you thinking, getting into marathon swimming?*
CE: I have always had a passion for long open-water swims. When I see a body of water, I have an incredible urge to swim across it. There's something overpowering about it—

MARATHON MAVEN KATE GOODALE TALKS ABOUT THE CHANNEL

In August of 1989, Kate Goodale completed the English Channel swim in eleven hours and fifty-three minutes, finishing in the top one-third of those who have accomplished this feat. Kate shared some of her memories with *Girljock*.

Kate dreamed of swimming the Channel thirteen years before she actually did it: "I had the feeling I could pull it off. But first, I had to overcome emotional and physical obstacles in the way." Coached by her partner Karen Fortoul, herself a Masters Swimmer, Kate prepared for the big one by doing eight swims over eight hours each. Kate told *Girljock* she never questioned that she would complete the swim. In fact, she was in such good shape, she felt strong enough to turn around and swim back to England.

Kate recalls experiencing mixed emotions upon finishing the swim: "I was very tired and cranky and deep-down very satisfied—and I wasn't that surprised because I knew that I could do it and I knew that I could make it." The question is, would she do it again? "The only thing that I would contemplate now is going for the oldest women's record. Some years ago, a woman in her fifties did the Channel. If I were to get into my sixties, I would try to go."

for some people it's like seeing a piece of chocolate cake and wanting to dive into it. When Diana Nyad was in her prime, she came to a local college to speak, and I bee-lined to see her. It was thrilling to see her talk—I remember her chomping on a pickle and drinking a Perrier.

MV: *Confess, Cheryl, how long have you been swimming?*

CE: I had a passion for open-water swimming when I lived in Puerto Rico, from two to six years old. The ocean was my playground. When I was in first grade, we moved to Rhode Island, where I started swimming competitively with the Barrington YMCA. I've always been grateful to my parents for getting us into the water at such an early age.

MV: *What's your earliest memory of water?*

CE: My brother and I used to put our hands up to try and stop the waves in the ocean. I used to think that I could do anything—even stopping waves. Now I'm thirty-three, and with some grace, I'm learning that it's not possible to stop the waves anymore.

MV: *Even if you can't stop the waves, your goals are bigger than many people's.*

CE: I work hard in a lot of different parts of my life and I like that. Being very focused on my swimming and working hard in the pool—I can't help think that it overflows in my job and my teaching. I'm teaching anatomy at Springfield College [MA], which has a graduate physical therapy program. This year, I'm teaching two two-hour cadaver anatomy classes.

MV: *So, not much makes you squeamish?*

CE: You can get weirded-out looking into dark water for long distances. You see little shadows.

MV: *What kinds of aquatic life have you seen on your swims?*

CE: Lots of jelly fish—I once got stung by a Portuguese Man of War. I had just gone swimming after a twelve-hour car ride to the Florida Keys. I saw a thin blue line, which I thought was a fishing line. I ran out of the water into a hut, where they gave me Milk of Magnesia and meat tenderizer to put on the cut. And sometimes it seems like there's little insects in the water—like little mosquito bites. On my twelve-mile swim in the Keys, I got stung by something. I also saw sand sharks and nurse sharks, but they leave you alone.

MV: *What's lined up for this summer?*

CE: June 1st, I'll do the Potomac River swim, a 7.5-mile swim from Maryland to Virginia—it's a benefit for the environment and they only take twelve swimmers. Next, I'll do Against the Tide. Then I'll do the Boston Lighthouse swim, ten miles. Then, I'll do the P-town swim and I'll go down and back twice with a kayak. And I'll go around Spofford Lake (in southwest New Hampshire) at least twice this year, so that's two six-mile swims in the low sixties.

MV: *What kind of personality do you have to have to be a marathon swimmer?*

CE: You have to have a lot of discipline to get in the water day after day after day after day. And you have to be focused to stay in the water for a long chunk of time. Right now, I'm in the water at least an hour a day at least five days a week. It's important to stay a well-balanced kind of healthy. I have to be very well rested and I have to eat very well. I'm very disciplined with both of those things. At different times in my life, especially at harder times in my life, it's hard to stay in the water for a long time because I was thinking about hard things in my life and I'd get out. Now when I'm in the water, I'm focused on being in the water and it's just that. I think that I really have to want this. I'm sacrificing other things. I used to be very active socially. I had a lot of acquaintances. A lot of things have to go when you go to bed at 8:30, work full-time as a PT

and teach part-time. I'm in the water from 6 until 7 A.M. at least five days a week. I take one or two days off a week from swimming because I'm trying to be strategic. I average 3,600 yards per workout, about two miles. I mostly train on my own, but in January and February, I'll train with a Masters Swim program in Brattleboro two days a week. It breaks the monotony. I also get together with other swimmers, like Kate Goodale and Karen Fortoul. They're very encouraging. I have a little collection of articles about people who have swum something, that usually gets me back in the swing of wanting to swim. The other thing that might sound a little bit funny, but it's a big love of mine, is classical music and choral singing. To me, classical musicians have to have an unbelievable discipline to do what they do. Sometimes, when I'm in the water, I take a break from thinking about stroke after stroke and some Bach piece will be going through my head while I'm swimming.

MV: *Do you cross-train?*

CE: I lift light weights three days a week. I'm doing six different lifts, which I feel great about. During the summer, I do a lot of mountain biking and running. I try to keep running up year round, although it can be tricky in the winter. Hopefully, I'll do cross-country skiing if we get enough snow. The more fit I am, the better I think I'm going to do.

MV: *Is it going to be hard to put on weight when you're training?*

CE: It won't be exclusively ice cream and bonbons. I will have to put on fifteen pounds, and I'll try to do it in as healthy a way as I can. I don't want to do it with foods with a lot of fat. Tofu has a lot of fat, and so does olive oil. I'm sure that I'll have at least a couple of oatmeal chocolate cookies a day. All the reading I've done says, be good to your heart when you're gaining the weight. It's going to be hard to put extra weight on, but I'll get over that.

MV: *Who are your sports heroes?*

CE: Diana Nyad. My very first sports hero was Carlton Fiske. He's probably the only male—he's a professional and an excellent athlete. Other than him, there's Billie Jean King; she was the first woman. Did you ever read *This Life I've Led*, by Babe Didrickson Zaharias? It's a great, great book.

MV: *Have you ever read* Water Dancer? *The character is a marathon swimmer and she eats raw meat and things. The Jennifer Levin thing is that catharsis comes through intensity and pain in sports. Can you relate to that?*

CE: I always get like two or three chapters into it and I put it down. There is something about long grueling challenges that does something for me. One of the most physically challenging things I've done is an 8,300-foot mountain climb in the North Cascades—it was a four-day climb with a forty-pound pack. It was grueling, but I would do it again in a second.

MV: *What do you do for fun?*

CE: Run up a mountain twice a week—up and down. Takes about an hour and a half.

MV: *Do you ever* veg *and just watch videos?*

CE: I don't have a TV. I read books and listen to music. There's something about pushing yourself physically as hard and as long as you can that just moves me.

MV: *What do you dine on?*

CE: I don't eat meat or fish. I do eat lots of oats and fruits and veggies and herbal teas and plenty of rice and Japanese noodles with a lot of garlic and ginger. Also, at least one hit of coffee and chocolate daily.

ME: *Why the Channel? Is it because you finally get to wear petroleum-based jelly?*

CE: Why not? It's the thing that marathon swimmers try to go for. It's the thing that we do. I think that with the cold and the current it's probably one of the tougher known swims to do.

MV: *Lynn Cox did the Bering Strait, will you?*

CE: It surely is appealing to me—definitely. I prefer cold water swims. I think that I'm a cold water fish. I do better in the cold.

MV: *If you could encourage a marathon swimmer, what would you say to them?*

CE: If you have it in you, go for it. It's an incredible thing to do. Just the movement in the water—to do it around an island or from one piece of land to another. Once I was flying away from Key West, realizing what I'd just done. I had swum completely around it—it was amazing.

MV: *It's 8:30 P.M. Sweet dreams, Cheryl!*

KATE'S ADVICE TO THOSE WHO DREAM OF THE CHANNEL

"Get a coach and/or whatever support emotionally and physically that you need, give yourself enough time to train, reserve a good boat pilot in advance, and be sure to be the number one swimmer on the tide that you go on. And do cold water training—train between 55 and 65 degrees, preferably 57 to 62 degrees."

What kind of mentality does it take? "You have to have a strong will—you can't be someone who gives up. You have to have physical and mental endurance. And it's very helpful to visualize the ending of the swim."

If you're thinking of doing the Channel, remember that you have to have completed a ten-hour open-water swim before the Channel Association will let you make any attempts. And you'll have to endure cold water temperatures wearing just one swimsuit and one cap. Most swimmers prepare for the swim by increasing their body fat (adding an extra layer of insulation can help keep you warm)—and they develop an affinity for greasing up. What the marathon swimmer has more than anything, including a love of Vaseline, is desire, focus, and a will that will not falter.

SWIMS YOU CAN DO WITHOUT BEING A MARATHONER

You don't have to be a marathoner to participate in open-water swimming. While U.S. Master Swimming lists some of the competitive open-water swims, there are open-water events for fitness swimmers, as well. There are swims to fight AIDS, such as Provincetown's Swim for Life. There's also a swim to fight breast cancer. It's called Against the Tide and it's now a fourth year event, which will be held again on Saturday, June 27, 1998, at Hopkinton State Park in Hopkinton, Massachusetts, home of the Boston Marathon. Against the Tide offers both a low-key one-mile open-water swim for fitness and recreational swimmers and an old-fashioned race for those with a competitive spirit. The focus of the event is on raising money to fight breast cancer—and having a good time. Former Olympians, marathon swimmers, and triathletes join mother-daughter teams, lesbian couples, and nuclear families for a morning of empowerment and celebration. A postevent breakfast and awards ceremony add to the overall feel-good atmosphere. For more information on Against the Tide, call (617) 484-4458.

GIRLJOCK TIP FOR ARMCHAIR SWIMMERS

Jennifer Levin's *The Sea of Light* follows former all-American, sure-to-go-to-the-Olympics hunkette Babe Delgado through a journey from tragedy to recovery in this engrossing novel about swimming. Swimming is life, says Levin, and Babe swims for hers on a number of levels. As one might expect from Levin, there is pathos and passion. When Babe sheds the shell of her old self and embraces life again, she finds a great love—with a woman on her college swim team. You'll be panting from the anticipation and the exercise when you read this one. It's well worth the price of a hardcover, but you can get it in paperback, too.

Baseball's New Open Season for Women

by Roxxie

And on the morning of whatever day it was, God rewrote the Book of Baseball, which had greatly influenced many men. And Coors Brewing Company decided to sponsor a team of women, a team formed after tryouts were held in twelve different cities across the Land. Women no longer had to file court injunctions to get into the sport of baseball, and were instead left with the ongoing dilemma: How to get the masses to believe that they— women, with only one rib—could compete in a sport against men.

Perhaps a better title of this article would be "Baseball's Previously Unwanted Children Asked Back," because major-league baseball is now courting American women. On December 10, 1993, at a meeting of the National Association of Professional Baseball Leagues, the all-female Colorado Silver Bullets were approved to play Class-A ball in the men's Independent Northern League this summer. Ex-major-league pitcher (and future Hall of Famer) Phil Niekro will manage the club, and the players' salary for the first season will be $20,000 (slightly higher than the norm for that level of the minor leagues), plus endorsements. Louisville Slugger will be producing bats for each Bullet, according to Silver Bullets president Bob Hope (not *the* Bob Hope), and Reebok is working on a silver shoe.

"I'm not a libber," said Greg Orr, a scout with the New York Yankees who was among those assisting with the Silver Bullets' Sacramento tryouts, "but I think it's long overdue. I think women should have equal rights. If they have the physical abilities to play, they should do so."

The implications of this gender-bending are enormous. Why, it could lead to the destruction of a deeply etched part of Americana: the common insult, "You throw like a girl." Once we see that women throw as well as men, will we replace this expression with, "You throw like a person who doesn't know how to throw"? (Too long, is my vote. Possibly: "You throw like a soccer player." But since a soccer-based insult may cause further havoc in a sport damaged by hooligans, thugs, and fan violence, I propose: "You throw like an amoeba.")

And what about baseball cards? The world of card prices may well go berserk. After all, goaltender Manon Rheaume's hockey card, following her first appearance in minor-league hockey, was worth as much as (or more than) a Gretzky. And, finally, will women abandon fast-pitch softball, with its college scholarships, its Olympic Games status and the possibility of a professional league?

In February, having placed a call to the Silver Bullet's 1-800-ASTARSB hot line, I attended the Sacramento tryouts in an attempt to answer these questions and to, well, try out. Some fifty women, in a predominantly Bay Area rainbow mix of races, sizes, and ages, converged on Sacramento City College's diamond. The baseball drag was sublime: Converse cleats in white on black (or black on white) and some of those unbiodegradable polyester softball pants—the kind that go below the knee and the shorts kind—with the back pockets stuffed with Franklin batting gloves. Jackets, the athletic scalp-system symbols, were especially prominent. COLLEGE WORLD SERIES 1992 said one, GGC CHAMPS 1980, 1982, 1993, said another. I tried not to stare too much for fear of gawking.

Most of the women attendees were softball veterans—recent college grads, coaches from local schools—trying to make the adjustment from the softball to baseball. "I haven't hit a baseball in ten years," said San Francisco State assistant softball coach Rachelle McCann. "I'm afraid the ball will get lost in my mitt," said Kendra Hanes, a twenty-three-year-old former Oklahoma State player who's now an assistant softball coach at Chabot College.

Others were like me: athletes in our thirties who still play in adult recreation leagues. We were easily identifiable; we were the ones shaking our heads and saying, "Ten years ago . . ." Saundra Ardito was eager to try out because baseball wasn't available to her when she was younger. "Going back and doing this makes me feel like I'm an eighteen-year-old again," said the thirty-two-year-old San Francisco accountant.

After some initial instructions, Shereen Samonds, the Silver Bullets' G.M. (and Rawlings' 1993 Female Executive of the Year in Baseball and, with the Orlando Cubs, the only female general manager in Double-A baseball last year), welcomed the group and turned the proceedings over to Tommy Jones, the tryout manager. He explained the drill to us. "Our job is to project," he said, motioning to a small gang of maroon-clothed and-capped Sacramento City College coaches who were assisting him. "Do you have the athletic skills that could transfer into baseball in the future?"

Jones was originally hired to run each tryout. But after the one in Chicago, he decided to quit his job as manager of the minor-league Orlando Cubs, telling Bob Hope, "You've got to find a job for me. I could field half a Class-A team just from what I saw in Chicago." His workout? "We'll all take a lap around the field and have a forty-yard dash. Then you can loosen up your arm, and we'll have a shortstop drill. We are looking for arm strength and accuracy. Then we'll be hitting balls off tees, just looking for mechanics. There will be no live pitching until tomorrow. Just give us a sense of some athleticism."

The drills began. Some of the women had vacuum-cleaner mitts that sucked up every ball in the area; some delivered lightning throws; others almost whacked balls out of the stadium. As for me, I tried to heed Hanes's advice on fielding grounders: "Relax. Don't try and pressure yourself. It isn't a life-threatening thing."

But I experienced deep internal confusion when the poker-faced coach hit one to my left side. I placed myself in position in front of the ball, only to feel my body asking me what to use—the big glove or my foot? As I wondered, the ball flew by. I was upset, but then, I've played soccer for the last four years.

At the end of the three-hour tryout, Tommy Jones told the assembled group, "If this is your dream, don't give up. You can try out as many times as you want to." Then he read off the short list of those women invited back for the second, more grueling day of workouts. (In March, about fifty women accompanied Jones to Orlando, Florida, for the final tryouts.)

Even though I'm sure I zipped through the sprint faster than many of the lankier athletes, my name was not called. But, as many athletes have told me, excuses are unathletic. Unfortunately, I seem to have an imaginative knack for them—they're an art form for writers.

Forty-two years after the official banishment of women from baseball's minor leagues—and one week after Ila Borders pitched a complete-game victory for the Southern California College men's baseball team—it appears that the long-slammed-shut gates to baseball are beginning to open for women. "This is the first time baseball has ever been a reality," said Sue Jacquez, who played shortstop for UC Berkeley. "My brother is going to UCLA this year to play baseball, and he has a lot of opportunity ahead of him that I never would have thought of. I feel lucky to even get my education paid for—that was a big deal. But I think it's great that we're being given more opportunities as women."

"A reporter asked me if baseball was my dream," said Hanes, who was invited later to Florida for the Silver Bullets' spring training sessions. "Well, 'no,' I answered. Why would I dream about baseball when it's been closed [to women]? [Now] it's like a door for the little ones opening up."

Lifestyle Questions in the Nation of Jogbras

PART THREE

3

The *top* **13** *most highly* **unlikely** **matchbook** *covers*

by Jackie Weltman

AMAZE YOUR FRIENDS!
Levitate your kitty!
CAT LEVITATION
$10 kit explains it all
De-luxe Set $25 teaches
cat to levitate self

Not everybody has a
chance to climb Everest;
But YOU can learn –
BALANCING ON ROCKS!
One, Two, Three Rocks!

Los Angeles Chamber of
Commerce
COME TO L.A.
"Half the Person at Twice
the Speed"

In Your Spare Time Learn
To Be An
Edible Flower Consultant!
Details inside!

THANKS FOR COMING to
the
Dan Quayle Memorial Spelling Bee
Poughkeepsie, NY

30-Week Certification-Midwest Vocational University
Tongue or Iris Reader
Thought-Generating Couch
Potato • Knife Sharpening
Technician • "Spoken Word"
Performer • "NY Style"
Performance Artist • Duck
Decoy and Hat Block Carving
Artisan – OR – Household Mold
Biologist and Eliminator!

Learn **Small Hat and Glove Repair**
Become a maestro with
hats and gloves under 10"
in length
B.J.'s Dollhouse and
Snuffbox Emporium

Special Enzyme Turns Toenails into Valuable Protein Source!

Tired of speaking in tongues?
(Rather be learning English?)
Drinking strychnine ruin your
love life?
One too many scary bites?
WE CAN HELP
PENTECOSTAL SERPENT HANDLERS ANONYMOUS
1-800-NO-SNAKE

GET RICH THROUGH SOIL SCIENCE!
Money from DIRT!
MOUNDS of cash! EARTH-
MOVING riches can be
yours with our simple min-
eral and soil-test kits !

WIN A FREE ROCK AND ROLL TOUR OF ISRAEL!
Free Drawing when you purchase
"JEWISH ROCK" by K-YEL
Featuring:
"In Haggadah Da Vida"
"The Immigrant Song"
"Master of Prophets"=more=Charge
by Phone!

DISAPPEAR
Immediately and Painlessly
24-hour Wedding Escape
Hotline

LEARN to be GAY!
Interior Decor and Fashion
Training • Personal Political
Tutor • Simple Sex Training
Method makes you an
EXPERT in HOURS!!
Parents! Friends! They'll
never believe that you're
NOW GAY!

How Girljock Are You?

by Nancy Boutilier

How *Girljock* are you? Here's a way to get in touch with your Inner Athlete. We've devised this little test for personal assessment and self-reflection. Because *Girljock* is a state of mind, it doesn't matter whether or not you've ever actually been in any of the scenarios described. What matters is how you see yourself responding to these situations were they to arise.

So, to find out where you stand on the *Girljock* Scale, circle the letter that best reflects your Inner Athlete.

1. If you lost a tooth in a field hockey game

a) you would invest in a mouth guard

b) you would invest in a gold cap engraved with your girlfriend's initials

c) you would learn to whistle through the gap

d) it couldn't happen since you take your teeth out before play begins

2. In your code of ethics

a) pulling hair is a nasty foul

b) pulling hair is just part of the game

c) pulling hair is a strategy for winning

d) pulling hair is a come-on

3. To relax during the game,

a) you chew gum

b) you chew tobacco

c) you chew flesh (your own)

d) you chew flesh (someone else's)

4. Which nickname comes closest to yours?

a) Sun blossom

b) Feather

c) Mommy Sir

d) Hairball

e) Meat

5. Safe sex means

a) a latex barrier

b) you've showered after practice

c) you're hundreds of miles from nuclear reactors

d) you're hundreds of miles from your girlfriend

e) no sharp objects

6. The last time a teammate put the moves on you

a) you said you were straight

b) you quit the team

c) you invented a girlfriend

d) you sidelined her with a killer hip check

Photo © Pollyanna Whittier

7. You complain of pain

a) when you break a nail

b) when you have cramps

c) when you are fouled

d) when you break a bone

e) what's pain?

8. Your role is best described as

a) mascot

b) bench warmer

c) cheerleader

d) all-star

9. A training meal

a) is complex carbohydrates

b) is decaf and oatcakes

c) is Pop Tarts and Diet Coke

d) is your girlfriend

10. When your line drive hits the pitcher in the face

a) you run to your teammates for support

b) you call "time out" and run to the mound

c) you sprint to first base and apologize to the first base coach

d) you run around the bases, laughing

11. For a floor burn

b) you ignore it

c) you pick the scab

d) you tattoo around it

12. In romance, you assume she's yours

a) when she comes to your games

b) when she comes to your practices

c) when she comes

13. An easy workout

a) is an oxymoron

b) is a sprint to the fridge for beer

c) is rhythmic stretching

d) is a swim to Alcatraz and back followed by a run to Fresno

14. When your nose is clogged

a) you take yourself out of the game to go to the restroom

b) you discretely blow your nose while pretending to wipe the sweat from your face with your jersey

c) wait till nobody's looking and shotgun*

d) wait till everyone's looking and shotgun*

15. When a referee misses a call

a) you never notice, you don't know the rules

b) you scream it out to your teammate loudly so that the ref can't possibly not hear you

c) you pout

d) you scream at the ref to open her eyes

e) you shoot to kill

16. Aerobic exercise

a) is doing the dishes

b) is walking your dog

c) is picking your scabs

d) is smoking

17. When choosing sides

a) you are last chosen

b) you want to be on Shirts

c) you want to be on Skins

d) you do all the picking

*clearing one nostril by sealing the other and forcefully blowing the snot out of your open nostril!

18. In a food fight

a) you encourage everyone to be more mature
b) you run away
c) you dive for the ice cream
d) you throw unripe fruit with your throwing arm
e) you chew first, then spit

19.Your game jewelry includes

a) long, dangling earrings
b) a knee brace
c) nipple rings
d) handcuffs

20. Your hair is best described as

a) big hair
b) dreadlocks
c) lesbian haircut #3
d) what's hair?

21. Your favorite cologne is

a) Passion
b) Brut
c) sweat
d) Old Spice
e) panty moisture

22. When on the bench

a) you feel a sense of relief
b) you cheer enthusiastically for your teammates
c) you hate it
d) you poison the water

23. When you score a goal

a) you faint in shock
b) you squeal with delight
c) you act as if it was nothing
d) you swear, because you were aiming a little
further to the left
e) you give the goalie the finger and smile

24. When your inner child cries

a) you cry with her
b) you go to therapy
c) you slap it silly
d) what's an inner child?

25. When your opponent throws a dirty elbow

a) you apologize for getting in the way
b) you give her a dirty look
c) you call her a dirty name
d) you call her a dirty name, and then ask for her
phone number

115

SCORING

Give yourself **0** points for every question you did not understand, **5** points for every A response, **10** points for every B response, **15** for every C response, **20** for every D response, and **25** points for every E response.

If you score under 100, you can consider yourself a Good Sport.

Being a Good Sport is lots like being a Gemini, only different. Frankly, we think you must have mistaken this magazine for *Better Homes and Gardens*.

If your score falls between 100 and 199, you are an Encounter Athlete.

You join the game, not to compete, but to join in the cosmic exchange of energy. You may even recall that matter can be neither created nor destroyed, and so you are simply engaging in the natural process of motion.

If you score anywhere from 200 to 299, you are a Challenger.

You don't play to win, you're just in the game for show. You want to flounce around in a T-shirt and shorts . . . you want to meet babes. Winning isn't everything, but getting her number is. You don't aim high, but you often hit your target. Others enjoy being on your team.

A score between 300 and 399 means you are a Competitor.

What you lack in raw talent, you make up for with your hustle and perseverance. An asset to any team, and a scrapper in every sense of the word. The word "quit" isn't in your vocabulary.

Scoring between 400 and 499 suggests that you don't compete, you win. You are an MVP. And you win big, or else you don't play at all. We think you should be writing for *Girljock*, so please have your manuscript in to us soon.

Over 500 and you're a Champ.

We think you should consider joining the American Gladiators or challenging Martina to a little one-on-one. You have trouble separating foreplay from after play—it's all play to you. Your motto should be: Just do it—out of earshot.

Take Back Tonight:
A Coping Guide for Softball Wives

by Nancy Boutilier, writing as Nomial Nomenclature

Photo © Nancy Boutilier

What two words can destroy a passionate, committed relationship faster than the words "I do"?

If you answered "play ball!" then you are already on your road to recovery from softball widowhood.

You already know the magnetism of the diamond because you've been forced to acknowledge its power over someone you love. Perhaps you've watched as a friend fell deeply under the spell of that seamy sphere. Or maybe you've lost a lover to that leather fetish that stops short at cleats and a glove. Some of you may have even found yourselves drawn to the madness centered around the pitching mound. But not enough to take the plunge, so you find yourself married to the stands, a lover and fan of one of the players.

Help is on the way. Here are a few simple tricks I've developed over the innings . . . I mean years . . . that have helped me save my sanity when softball has stolen my sweetie away from me.

COMMUNICATION

First, maintaining effective communication through the long season is important for a lasting relationship. Learn to nod and echo. You don't have to know anything about the game—not the rules, not the strategies, not even the lingo—but when your girlfriend starts to talk softball just nod and echo.

For instance, here's a sample dialogue:

Her: We didn't get a runner on until the bottom of the sixth when Alice doubled to left and Monica sacrificed to move her to third.

You (nodding): Alice doubled, Monica moved her. (Note: It helps to look off into the distance, suggesting you are imagining this on a ball field in your mind.)

Her: Then after two walks, with bases loaded, Dara hits a shot. The throw from the outfield is on the money, but the catcher drops the ball, and that's the game.

You: Catcher drops the ball.

Her: Yup, and that's the game (hugging you with excitement). We win another one.

You: That's the game, honey (hugging back), you won another one.

DURING THE GAME

Just like misery, abandonment to softball loves company. The worst thing you can do when your girlfriend is at the ball park is stay home alone. Some softball wives will prefer to avoid softball altogether, but I believe that the long-term effects of such a strategy are fatal to the relationship. Therefore, I suggest you face the music. And the song is "Take Me Out to the Ball Game." So, on game day, head for the bleachers.

The sidelines can feel like a lonely place, but you should never feel alone. Remember, where there is one softball widow, there are at least nine others. And what fun it is to spend the afternoon looking sporty in the sunshine and gathering gossip! Ten times out of ten, the other softball widows won't pay any more attention to the game than you will, but collectively you who have the common goal of tending to your cleated companion will find that you have kept track just enough so that when the teams are shaking hands—evidence that the game is finally over—you will know who won.

At this point, most of your comrades-in-lawnchairs will be focusing their attention on their own partners. It's well worth listening to the observations at this time, as the comments can be very telling. "Uh-oh, Lindy just told Spike to go to hell," "No one looks cheery, do they?", "Is that Annabel who just punched your girlfriend?"

As you can see, knowing which team wins is only half the battle of knowing how to greet your girlfriend after the game. Greetings depend not only on which team wins, but also on your girlfriend's performance, the number of bruises sustained, the field conditions, the umpire's calls, the other team's record, the league standings, as well as the moon's tilt, and the coach's zodiac sign.

In other words, even when you think you know exactly what your girlfriend wants to hear, you still only have a fifty-fifty chance of being right.

For instance, if your girlfriend plays well, but her team loses, she will need to publicly display disappointment with the loss. Generally, it is not a good idea to run up to her yelling "great catch" for a spectacular play she made in the second inning of a 10–2 loss. You threaten her relationship with her teammates who could not care less about that catch. However, if it happened that a backup pitcher had resentfully yelled to your girlfriend in the middle of the sixth inning, "Hey, does your girlfriend hate softball or what? She never watches the game," then, you would do well to publicly show some interest in the events of the game in any form.

Regardless of my girlfriend's needs, experience has taught me to wait in my lawnchair—the low, fold-up ones are my preference—until my girlfriend greets me first. This way she and her teammates can process the game—what one fellow widow calls "doing that team thing"—without feeling my presence. And without putting me in the position of having to interpret any exchanges. The last thing you want to do is have to have her try to explain her teammates' actions to you.

It has helped me to develop a repertoire of

these four postgame greetings: celebration, congratulations, comfort, and the nongreeting, which approximates invisibility for those times when she wants most to be alone, but I am, for better or for worse, there.

AFTER THE GAME

Celebration is the easiest, but the rarest, postgame activity. Like all at-the-field interactions with your girlfriend, follow her lead. Feel free to celebrate with other widows whenever you like, but celebration with a girlfriend in uniform requires her initiation of such a display. Only championship games or major upsets will provide an opportunity for celebration on the field with your girlfriend.

In the case of celebration, the off-the-field activities are usually well worth attending. Everyone's in good cheer, and you can expect your girlfriend to be just as eager to return home to celebrate, one-on-one, as you are.

Generally, however, not all postgame socializing is good for your relationship. Individual couples need to work out arrangements, but the compromise that has worked for me is my "Take Back the Night" campaign.

This campaign relies on our ability to maintain what I call, a "ménage à twilight." The trick is, of course, learning to share your girlfriend with her team during the early evening and daylight hours. During the game, she belongs to softball, but in the later evening hours, I expect her to be fully mine. It's only fair.

LAST DITCH SAVE

The key to maintaining balance in this convoluted configuration is by having my own Dugout.

Rather than competing with softball for attention, I simply shift mine elsewhere while at the ball park. On days when I don't feel like watching softball, I rationalize my time at the park as an extended walk with Dugout—my trusty, non-softball-playing but, nonetheless, quite fetching canine date.

Not only are they wonderful companions for the ups and downs of the game, but dogs have a remarkable sense of smell that seems to tip them off to the postgame moods of players. And that sure can be handy for the softball widow. Dugout is particularly useful in those moments when my girlfriend wants to stew. I can focus on Dugout without feeling the intensity of my girlfriend's wish to be alone.

Then, when she finally comes over to me for comfort or commiseration, I can show her I haven't gone through the wild flux of the game she has. Why, I'm having my own well-invested day at the ball park, and what is it she could possibly need from me?

The flipside of our "ménage à twilight" is, of course, that my girlfriend shares me with my dog Dugout during the early evening hours. But, later in the evening, she can expect me to be fully hers. It's only fair.

Grand Island Assist

©1993 Joan Hilty

Girl Sloth

by Laura Miller

"To be frank," I said idly to *Girljock*'s charming and talented editrix, Roxxie, at a Mission District lunch spot, "The concept of *Girljock* does not lie close to my heart. If I were to publish a 'zine, it would be called 'Girl Sloth.'"

"Really?" queried Roxxie, trying to appear casual, but with visions of copy blocks dancing before her eyes. "Perhaps you'd care to explain the mysteries of Girl Sloths to my legions of avid readers?"

Such requests are usually met with a scornful, indolent laugh, but never underestimate the persuasive powers of an insomniac who leaves clever messages on answering machines. I have committed myself.

We might first ask: What is a Girl Sloth? Leaving aside the question of nature versus nurture, a Girl Sloth is guided by a simple mandate that can be expressed in two words: energy conservation. Let's face it, we are on the verge of destroying ourselves and our planet with our insatiable energy consumption—Girl Sloths are on the cutting edge of reform. To pursue a truly slothful way of life ("deep sloth," as we call it) one must adhere to the following principles:

1. Leave your apartment as seldom as possible, which means you should
2. Work part time, if at all, which means you must

3. Spend very little money, all of which demands that you
4. Maintain fetchingness.

Ignorance leads many in mainstream culture to stereotype Girl Sloths as lazy. Nothing could be further from the truth. Girl Sloths eschew physical activity in favor of intellectual exertion. Slothfulness, above all, requires planning and organization. A Girl Sloth, for example, carefully studies television schedules so she can program her VCR to record movies from broadcast in order to avoid unnecessary and exhausting trips to video rental shops (see principle 1).

Principle 4 requires some elaboration. "So, Girl Sloth is lying in bed eating potato chips and oogling female athletes on TV, right," suggested Roxxie.

"She is *not*," I replied testily. "Girl Sloths find spectator sports draining. And Girl Sloths do *not* eat potato chips. They must keep their figures, a significant part of maintaining fetchingness, which is the fourth principle."

"Oh, okay . . . Why?"

"Because being fetching is one of the best ways to get somebody else to perform unpleasant tasks for you without charging you a lot of money. It gets you rides so that you don't have to own a car or take taxis. People will install your stereo and give you copies of

124

their software. Girl Sloths have even been known to exercise regularly on the understanding that this saves money in the long run."

"Whatever you say, but I think Girl Sloth should be really horny and have a power strip with six different kinds of vibrators plugged into it, so she doesn't have to get up to change the plugs."

"Girl Sloth could get into that. But they should be vibrators that ex-girlfriends left at her house."

Girl Sloths must come to accept that educating the public is one of their few responsibilities. In a dominant culture that values the industrious above all, the slothful are often rendered invisible. The truth about sloths' lives and the reality of sloth voices has been silenced. Even our symbols have been devalued. Think about it: In all the public zoos in this country—zoos that exhibit exotic and shy animals like the koala or the kiwi and even endangered creatures like the Tasmanian Devil or the California condor—have you ever seen a sloth—two *or* three-toed? How can we claim to have truly representative zoos when such major influences on sloth culture are systematically excluded?

Some sloths have resorted to organizing to combat their marginalization, leading to the formation of Sloth Nation—patterned after such grassroots groups as Lion Nation (see *Girljock* #5). This group foundered, however, when the membership realized that they have serious issues around the concept of "actions." Rather than accommodating activityist straight culture by adopting its excessively fatiguing methodology, sloths have decided to return to what we do best: getting other people to do our work for us.

How can you help? We're so glad you asked. If you frequent conferences and panels, then by all means raise your hand during the question-and-answer session and earnestly inquire: "But how does all this affect the issues of women of sloth?" Do, however, refrain from tartly noting that you "see very few sloth faces on the panel today," as this may brand you as hopelessly ignorant of the very people you wish to defend (see principle 1).

GIRL JOCK EATS FOOD...

© Joan Hilty 1990

As a rower, I was not necessarily subject to a strict dietary regimen.

KICK IT IN! I WANNA FEEL IT AT TH' CATCH! LET'S TAKE A MONDO POWER 10!

GRR UNK

ERGGH UGGH

UNHK

Crew's basic requirements -- brute strength and endurance -- left a lot of leeway for weird food theories.

For instance, our coach John had a thing about...

ICEBERG LETTUCE!

DON'T EAT THAT STUFF!

99 PERCENT WATER!

NO NUTRIENTS WHATSOEVER!

OKAY, JOHN, OKAY.

Of course, he also drank too much.....

HOW'RE YA FEELING THIS MORNING, JOHN?

FINE!

MUST YOU YELL?

And he had no butt.

FAVORITE SUBJECT OF ANNUAL TEAM DINNER SKITS

...WHICH WE PROMPTLY ADDED TO OUR PASTA.

[THIS WAS THE ANNUAL SCENE AT THE PRINCETON, N.J., RAMADA INN, PRE-RACE....]

BUT THE COXSWAINS HAD IT THE WORST, FOOD-WISE. IF YOU DON'T BELIEVE THAT, IMAGINE BEING SANTA CLAUS AND HAVING YOUR JOB SECURITY HINGE ON HOW TOUGH IT IS TO PULL THE SLED......

SUPPERTIME, SUE!

YIPPEE.

NO NO, JUST SALAD FOR ME, THANKS......

MOCHA CHIP PECAN CREAM AND SUGAR BBQ TORTILLA CHIPS CHOCOLATE COVERED SHORTCAKE WITH FROOT LOOPS AND NGE TAFFY WITH TRIPLE DE FUDGE

UH... YOU'RE SURE?

WHAT I MEAN IS THAT COXES HAD TO MAINTAIN A CERTAIN WEIGHT TO RACE. UNDERWEIGHT COXES HAD TO SIT ON SANDBAGS TO RACE, AND THE REST OF THEM HAD TO DIET CONSTANTLY WHILE WORKING AND SOCIALIZING WITH WOMEN WHO COULD EAT CIRCLES AROUND ARNOLD SCHWARZENEGGER.

ISN'T IT WONDERFUL HOW WOMEN CAN BE MADE TO WORRY IRRATIONALLY OVER THEIR WEIGHT NO MATTER WHAT THEY DO? AT LEAST THE COXES HAD THE LAST LAUGH AFTER THE FINAL RACE OF THE SEASON.

HEY SUE, WHERE DOES THIS BOAT GO?

SUE?

The End

Long-Haired Lesbians

by Roxxie

"When you have long hair, people think you must be straight," explained a long-haired lesbian girljock, "they'll come up and offer to braid your hair, or run their fingers through it, but often will not think you are a dyke." Even the most aware and politically conscious lesbian sports spectators will state in front of a whole crowd of spectators, that "Number 9 out there with the long hair, she's got to be straight."

Girljock magazine explores the often misunderstood world of the long-haired lesbian in the following interview with Rita Tit, a long-haired lesbian soccer player and member of the fabulous Bay Area soccer club, the Follies.

Roxxie: *Have you always had long hair?*
Rita Tit: Well, when I was six or seven, my mother got sick of brushing out the rats' nests in the back of my long hair. She said, "C'mon out here, we're going to cut your hair."

It was quite a shock, but I was tired of the pain of her trying to brush the rat's nest out. She (Mom) took me in the back yard and cut my hair into a pageboy cut. Then I'd get mistaken for a little boy sometimes. I liked my short hair, but it looked awful.
Roxxie: *Those rat's nests can really be painful.*
Rita Tit: Yes, they are. If you (a) don't brush your hair everyday, it mats up, or (b) go driving

in a convertible and then have sex all night and still don't brush your hair, then it can be terrifying. Then you can get big rats' nests.

I couldn't brush out the last rat's nest I had. I had to go in the shower and put lots of conditioner on it, and then brush it out. It was so painful, I vowed not to go longer than a day without brushing.

Roxxie: *Is that advice you'd pass on to other lesbians who want to grow their hair out?*

Rita Tit: Yes. To long-haired lesbian wannabes, brush your hair at least once a day. And always tie your hair back when you play sports or are horsing around. Once, when I was playing soccer in my bedroom, goofing around, I almost choked on my hair. It went down my throat. I thought to myself, this is dangerous. And then attackers could grab it, or it can be dangerous around large machinery. But my girlfriends really like my long hair. . . . It can be very sexy, too.

Roxxie: *Rita, I've heard you mention that some Bay Area lesbian establishments are not friendly to "long-haired lezzies." What is it like, being a long-haired lesbian? Do you ever get called names?*

Rita Tit: Well, I used to belong to a U.C. Berkeley support group for lesbians, but all the short-haired dykes felt I wasn't a "real lesbian." It was isolating. The women thought I must be a bisexual because I had such long hair.

I relieved that trauma by realizing that those types shouldn't be my friends. If they can't handle my hair, they can't handle me.

I used to have a long-haired dyke best friend, but then she cut off her long hair. I like her hair short—she looks better. Right after her haircut, we went into a supermarket and a woman recognized her as a sister and gave her a little smile. Then, whenever I'd go places with her, and all the dykes would turn and look at her (short hair).

That moment of instant recognition makes me want to cut my hair. Even though times are changing now and we are starting to see lesbians in all shapes and sizes and colors, greater opportunity and acknowledgment exists for the short-haired lesbians. But, short hair does make a rebellious statement against the stereotypically feminine.

Roxxie: *If you could say something to the short-haired sisters who don't acknowledge you unless you are wearing a gay pin or a gay T-shirt, what would it be?*

Rita Tit: Coming out and cutting your hair are not synonymous, even though they both begin with a C. I'd like to tell people to loosen up. Don't think in stereotypes. All lesbians are not the same.

It's even worse to be blond too, because of the stereotype of being blond, stupid, and a sexpot. And I'm not stupid.

Shaved Glory

by Paisley Braddock

In the Play-Doh beauty world, it's so easy. You pump the hair dough through the plastic sieve on top of the plastic neck and simply shave it off when the urge hits. It's instant gratification—and the doll retains its perfectly molded self-respect in the meantime. There are no awkward moments with the barber, grocer, friends, or family.

But when you try this game at home, the results are much more confounding. A friend, who'd just gotten her hair cut and shaved by six laughing dykes in a kitchen, went into her corner store and the clerk had decided she was now dangerous—"I always thought you were sweet and quiet."

Maybe she was all three. But the one thing she was for sure during that particular Snapple transaction was bald—which suddenly made her a traveling inkblot test.

Photo © Chloe Atkins

STRANGE COMPANY

Sinead O'Connor didn't invent the shaved head, though the many stunned interviewers never seemed to catch on. In fact, in many ways, she suffers from it—accidentally filed as a feminist in many rock critics' computers—more for what's not on her head than what's in it (though, in the *Rolling Stone* interview, she set the record straight on the subject of feminism when she dissed Desiree Washington).

It's not good cultural policy to assume: If we divided the world by hair length, we'd have one group with punks, Nazis, fashionable bald lipstick lesbians, Sinead O'Connor, the pope, and Sigourney Weaver. In another group would be career politicians and sensibly closed-cropped women; in still another there'd be Kurt Cobain, Tammy Wynette—and much dissonance.

But, as cross-dressers Ru Paul and Phranc could tell you, assuming is actually the radical part.

At XTC Lounge, a lesbian sex club in San Francisco where my friend made a pre-Thanksgiving appearance, I watched as she became one of the pages in *Sex*: "These girls came on to me like I was some kind of big, learned, hard-assed dyke." And even though she might have enjoyed the attention, she didn't exactly feel like she had done enough time on the docks to deserve it: "They were grabbing me . . . as if, just because I have no hair, that that must be the sort of life I had lead."

With the inkblot factor, however, you also have to weather the less-flattering interpretations. When she traveled up to Ukiah, it turned out, she was seen as a menace: "They made me turn in my groceries to go to the bathroom." In her apartment at water-meter time, she had become a mutation: "They stare, don't know what to think."

But the truth is, even she doesn't really know what to think. Is she butch, femme, punk, an ascetic, or just bored with the shampoo aisle?

It's making her reconsider herself in relation to haircuts past. She's lived through mistakes— one Florence Henderson cut in college, when she thought the bi-levels created sisterhood.

But now, with a seeming successful nonhairdo, she says, "Everything has changed because my hair is gone: looking in the mirror, walking down the street and seeing my reflection."

Through the looking glass, she says, again, having no hair is an improvement: "The way people talk to me, the way I appreciate my own sense of independence and self-direction and inventiveness is better. It's interesting how when you shave off the most prominent feature of your feminine identity, people don't know how to interact with you anymore. But also it's been extremely feminizing to have no hair. It makes the things that are feminine about me stand out much much more."

Is it "free your hair, your mind will follow?" I'll have to check-in in three months, when the newly grown-in-Play-Doh is getting stale.

Is Writing a Sport?

by Laz-Y-Girl (Sara Miles)

Is writing a sport? Are female writers girljocks? (Note: For purposes of emotional and political clarity, this writer distinguishes between "macho" and "jock." Thus Hemingway isn't a jock just because he writes about bullfights; Blanche Boyd isn't a sportsman just because she can outbutch Norman Mailer.)

Let's look at a checklist for writers and jocks. A "yes" answer indicates that the activity in question is a genuine sport:

- *Is there a significant injury potential?* Yes. And I'm not talking about writer's cramp. Try Repetitive Stress Syndrome, for starters. I wound up with my wrists in splints for six weeks from pounding away at a Macintosh keyboard.
- *Is the level of competition truly crazed?* Are you kidding? Have you ever heard one writer say anything nice about another? In comparison, most pro athletes knock themselves out trying to be gracious.
- *Are there activity-specific bonding rituals incomprehensible to outsiders?* The Algonquin Round Table, maybe. But in general, we're weak here: Writers are an antisocial bunch.
- *Do you get better at it over time?* Always. (Except for men. It must be hormonal.) Think of M. F. K. Fisher, or Jessica Mitford, or Gwendolyn Brooks, or . . .

how many seventy-year-old competition runners have you heard of?
- *Can participants aspire to product endorsement?* Yes, though writers generally get alcohol ads instead of hydraulic-lift shoes. See next question.
- *Are participants role models for America's youth?* Yes, and the particular strength of writers is that when we become drug-addicted (which we do, as frequently as athletes) and recover (which we do, as frequently as athletes), we almost never tell kids we turned our lives around by finding Christ.
- *Do girls swoon at your feet when you perform particularly well?* I've never been so much as pecked on the cheek for the way I caught a ball. I broke up someone else's home, ran away with a beautiful woman, and had a year-long torrid affair on the basis of a single poem.

So there it is: Writing, the perfect sport. Train hard (drink lots of coffee, sharpen your pencils, and get moody); play hard (don't forget pacing the floor on deadline, an aerobic activity if there ever was one) and *write!* Best of all, you don't even have to buy new shoes.

Am I Stuck-Up? The Test

PREPARED BY THE FOLLOWING SOCIAL RESEARCHERS: CAITLIN GROOM, KATE SORENSEN, PAMELA AUGUST RUSSELL, DAPHNE GOTTLIEB, ROXXIE, AND KAREN MILLER, AND COMPILED BY ROXXIE

Ask These Important Questions of Yourself and Your Loved Ones:

1. Do you only talk to your special friends on your team?
2. Do you ignore people for no apparent reason?
3. Do you pretend to be in the Bahamas when you are only at the neighborhood bar?
4. Do you correct other people's grammar at the drop of a pen?
5. Do you refuse to play if you aren't on the starting lineup?
6. Do you throw parties and not invite anyone because nobody else is good enough?
7. Do you think that everyone wants to go out with you?
8. Do you lie about athletic successes?
9. Have you ever impersonated a famous athlete, besides in a crank phone call to your best friend(s)?
10. Do you start all your sentences, when you are speaking with other people, like this, "And, hmm, you are?"?
11. Do you pretend you are Bette Davis?
12. Do you pretend you are Bette Davis when you are alone?

If you have answered yes to any of the above questions, you may be stuck-up. We have created the following test to discern the stuck-up from the temporarily deranged, dehydrated, or others. Take our test to evaluate your stuck-up quotient. It is an easy test if you read through it carefully. It is a multiple choice test, and you may select more than one answer if appropriate. Instructions for scoring are at the end of the test.

1. Whenever you can drop the name of a famous person, you

a) mention their first name only so they are unrecognizable and you don't have to be embarrassed, because, gee, well, some of your pals are famous

b) say their full name followed by "and she's so cool"

c) say their full name and mention the time they tried to pick you up and you declined

d) talk about what they look like naked

e) say, "Between you and me, we're seeing each other"

f) say their full name followed by, "Can I just say two words to describe them? BREATH MINTS"

2. When you wake up in the morning, you

a) want to make out with yourself when you look in the mirror

b) you think about coffee and a shower

c) you turn to the other person in bed and say, "You have to leave"

d) don't get up in the morning.

3. If someone was wearing a really bad hat, and was just starting to talk with you, maybe even flirt with you, would you

a) not talk to them?

b) make them take the hat off first before you talk to them?

c) talk to them and just not look at the hat?

d) give them a new hat for their birthday?

e) meditate on the variety of fashion styles available in the universe and how wonderful the universe is, while talking to them?

f) mock punch their face and miss and knock off their hat?

g) sprint away?

4. You critique your teammates' playing skills

a) to your friends later, in a bar

b) behind their back to the coach

c) to their faces, but also tell them how they can become better players, and find something else good to tell them about their playing

d) to their faces, without saying anything constructive about their playing to keep them motivated to improve even if they aren't as good as you are and you wish the coach had never added them to the team roster

e) or are you too busy yelling at them and swearing about any mistake ever on the field to say anything in a normal tone of voice to them at all?

5. When you describe your ex-lovers, do you ever say they are

a) better lovers since they've been with you

b) good lovers just because they've been with you

c) attached to your forearms

d) expensive because of the string of names you had to get tattooed and de-tattooed from your left buttock

e) Let me just say two words: "BREATH MINTS."

6. If someone who plays on a really bad team, way worse than your team, walks over to talk with you while you are standing around with your teammates and you just finished a game or a match or a competition of sorts, would you

a) talk to them and introduce them to your teammates

b) say something mean and snooty so they go away quickly

c) make fun of their clothes

d) make a nasty joke about their team

e) talk to them about computers and hope they will ask you on a date because even though you are a much better jock than they are, they are way smarter than you and have a major job with a computer company somewhere, and you heard they were really swell to their last girlfriend

f) tell them they have something in their nose and walk away

134

7. When there is a mistake by your team in a game, it is always

 a) the rookie on the team's fault, so you yell at them first

 b) the coach's fault

 c) all the players' faults besides yours

 d) your fault when it is your fault

 e) fate . . . it was supposed to happen

8. If someone comes to practice dressed like a punk rocker, a suburban housewife, a go-go dancer, Hillary Clinton, or anything else, would you

 a) offer to do her nails if she's a suburban housewife

 b) tell the punk rocker you could do her nails too because you still have some black nail polish left from the time you went out Goth-rocking

 c) make snide comments about them to your teammates behind their backs

 d) make snide comments about them to their faces

 e) ask them to teach you a few steps of their latest go-go routine

 f) ask them out on a date immediately because they are such an amazing individual and different than all the others

9. You critique other people's outfits

 a) behind their back

 b) to their face

 c) later when you write a letter to your mother

 d) by sending them an anonymous letter

 e) I could never critique someone else's outfits, because I am a devoted girljock and all outfits beyond sports gear are drag, and I am not an expert in drag.

SCORING

Question 1—the name-dropping question: If your answers were A, C, D, E, F—score one attitude point for each of these answers.

Question 2—the morning wakening question: If your answer was A—score one attitude point. If your answer was C, "You have to leave," and you don't have a drinking problem, score one attitude point.

Question 3—the bad hat question: If your answer was A or G, score one attitude point. If your answer was B, you may be a top.

Question 4—the playing skills critique question: If your answer was A, B, or D, score one attitude point. If your answer was E, score three attitude points.

Question 5—the ex-lover question: If your answer was A or B, score one attitude point. If your answer was E, consider anonymously sending mouthwash to your ex-lovers instead of dishing them to your friends.

Question 6—the social pecking order of goodness-in-the-sports-world question: If you answered B, C, or D, score one attitude point, you creep. If you answered F, score one attitude point and beware of the ugly booger karma coming your way, you nasal fixation queen.

Question 7—the team mistake question: If you answer A, B, or C, score one attitude point. If you answer E, you must have been going at the tarot cards again lately.

Question 8—the alternative outfit question:

If you answered C or D, score one attitude point.

Question 9—the outfit critique question: If you answer A or B, score one attitude point. If you answer D, go to therapy, OK? If you answer E, you are a real girljock, and your heart is in the right place, so get on back to the sports world, baby, and rock out!

NOW, ADD YOUR POINTS TOGETHER

If you have 1 attitude point, you have a tendency to be stuck-up; 2–3 attitude points, you may be stuck up; 3–5 attitude points, you are stuck up; 5–7 attitude points, you may be a creep. More than 7 attitude points, you need to get a life, badly, and the peanut gallery somewhere may be watching when karma rears its ugly head on you, babe.

If you are stuck-up, there is hope for you. First you'll just have to get over yourself, and learn there are other people in the world too. It's kind of like going to an observatory and watching all the other solar systems through a telescope, and remembering there's something else out there beyond planet Earth.

You still can help yourself and all the people who have to be around you, before you either drive all the people in your life away, and/or before a professional has to help you.

Our research has shown that most people who are stuck up are secretly extremely insecure, and only feel better after they've made someone else feel bad. So if you are stuck up, look in the mirror and tell yourself you no longer have to be pathetically insecure, that you are beautiful exactly how you are, without having to make anyone else feel less. Say that every morning when you wake up for the next three years, and immediately see page 137 for a special self-help guide we have prepared: "How to Be Friendly."

How to Be Friendly

TWENTY-TWO HANDY SUGGESTIONS OFFERED BY THE FOLLOWING CAST: CAITLIN GROOM, KATE SORENSEN, PAMELA AUGUST RUSSELL, DAPHNE GOTTLIEB, ROXXIE, AND KAREN MILLER. SUGGESTIONS COMPILED BY FAITHFUL NOTE TAKER ROXXIE

1. Say "Hi!"
2. Be sensitive. If you weren't wearing your glasses or contacts and made a face at someone you know by squinting and contorting your face awfully in order to discern them. Like, apologize for making a face at your friend, and do blame it on not wearing your contacts or glasses.
3. Make eye contact a lot.
4. Smile.
5. Try not to smile at people if you have just been to the dentist and are eating soup in a public place, and your mouth is half asleep, because your sleepy mouth will spill your soup in an uncontrollable direction. Be careful.
6. Start conversations with strangers.
7. Get other people to talk about themselves.
8. Remember other people's birthdays, even if you have yet to get them a present.
9. Offer to share.
10. Offer rides.
11. Offer licks of your lollipop.
12. Talk to all of your teammates instead of just the ones you know.
13. Invite the whole team out for beers or Cokes after practice instead of just your pals.
14. Be nice to the rookies and the shy players on the team. Just because you don't know them doesn't mean you won't need them, since you are teammates, after all. Besides, you might like them. You never know what may happen on any given day in any given sport, which is one of the things we like about sports. Besides, you never know who may grow up to become what. . . .
15. Return phone calls.
16. Remember your breath mints.
17. Remember to shower.
18. If you don't have anything nice to say, even if you think it would be really funny right now to say it, try not saying anything.
19. Search for the positive.
20. Be considerate.
21. Don't worry about being a spaz. The dork factor is very charming, our experts have found.
22. Take your clothes off in public. *What's that doing in here? Hey, who said that one?*

How to Pick Up a Cyclist, or . . . If You Like Lycra

by Lucy Jane Bledsoe

Okay, so like you see this woman strapped to a piece of machinery. She's panting and shiny with sweat. You enjoy the way she's hurdling herself and that machine across the hard, gray pavement. You really like the sensual pumping rhythm to her movement. No ungainly slapping sounds, or pounding, or splashing, just smooth, round pedal strokes.

Seconds later, though, she's a speck on the horizon. Then she's way gone. Out of sight.

If you had your own bike, you could mount it and pursue. But these cycling girls are wild, reckless, and fast. They're damn hard to snare. But don't despair. Here's a few tips on how to track down that dreamjock in Lycra.

It's okay if you want to take up cycling, you know, to familiarize yourself with the sport. Cyclists tend to be very friendly, rather than snobby, toward newcomers. However, here are a few lines you should know not to cross.

Whatever you do, don't go to a club or out to breakfast in your spandex biking shorts. To a cyclist, that's like wearing cleats in bed, or your best fuck-me pumps to a basketball game.

(Ditto on those little round mirrors that people attach to their biking helmets. A definite fashion travesty. Do not do it.)

And please don't wear five shades of day-glow, wrap-around shades, and designer biking socks; these are the sure signs of an amateur. I mean, some of those outfits cost as much as a good bike.

Get yourself some cleats, a couple of pairs of shorts, and maybe a tasteful jersey or two. T-shirts, though, are just fine. Avoid wearing product endorsements unless you are being paid to do so. And relax on the outrageous color schemes, girls.

There are some gray areas in biking coolness. Like stopping during your bike ride at a café to munch on a croissant and slurp down a coffee.

While eating a lot is definitely something cyclists brag about, there is a time and a place. Like, how hard and far can you ride with grease and acid sloshing around in your gut?

I say, finish your ride, go home, have a shower, pull on some comfortable jeans, then go out for your *latte*. I mean, those biking muscles will show very nicely through your jeans. And subtle is sexy. Especially to cool bikers who, for the most part, are not into superficial body display. As for what to do when you're actually out riding, just let the sweat and endorphins flow. Keep your eye out for other cyclists (i.e., dyklists). Definitely do draft women you see and like on the road. Pull right on up on her back wheel—you don't have to say anything, just enjoy her thighs. Just be sure you take your turn pulling at the front, since that's where most of the work is done.

Unless, of course, you're a total bottom. Finally, if you do snare that big-legged girl, beware. Bikers are often loners, insisting on their hours alone in the hills. Get used to it, or get another flame.

On the other hand, by the time you get your crush's attention, you may already have been seduced by your own bike, leaving her pining for your attention. Because once you allow yourself to glimpse the underbelly of cycling, that dark, shadowy, seductive force, there's no turning back. It feels so good.

The Cyclist's Vocabulary

Animal: A very tough biker.

Carbos: A long-standing point of contention among cyclists questions whether we ride to eat carbos or eat carbos to ride.

Drafting: A form of sex that involves riding a few inches behind the wheel of a cycling buddy, so close that her sweat flies off onto your skin and you feel her throbbing muscles like your own.

Mountain bikes: What road bikers disdain.

Road bikes: What mountain bikers disdain.

RPM: Stands for "really pretty macho" and is a unit that measures how tough a cyclist is.

Sweat: A cycling goddess.

Wheelsucking: Another word for drafting.

Learning to Brace Yourself Against Tackles and Nonbelievers:

An Inside Look at New Zealand Women's Rugby

by Ming Nagel

Living legends line the walls of the Auckland Marist Old Boys clubhouse at Liston Park. Only a visitor to the country would fail to recognize winger John Kirwan's snarl as he fends off an opponent; only a foreigner would see the number 8 jersey, frozen in celluloid, without thinking of Zinzan Brooke. Framed behind glass, Pat Lam buries his head in a scrum. Bernie McCahill flips a ball out wide.

Many of the Marist rugby players are current or former representatives for the All Blacks, New Zealand's fabled international team, but even those who are not enjoy privileged status. In New Zealand, rugby football is more than recreation. It is more than a sport as we in the United States often define the term. For these two remote islands in the South Pacific, rugby is the undisputed obsession and a way of life. Here, it is an honor to play for one's province and a common dream to represent one's country, but the nature of the game and the size of the nation ensure that even those who make it to the top do not forget their roots. The rugby life—so universal that it seems more destiny than choice for some—begins and ends with loyalty to the clubs.

The evening after the Auckland senior men's club final August 21, the Liston Park room waits under a thin layer of cigarette haze and conversation for the return of its heroes. Marist has defeated Suburbs 18–13 to bring "home" the coveted Gallaher Shield. The game has ended around four o'clock, and the club begins to fill by six o'clock, but the team has not yet arrived. First, they must endure laudatory postmatch speeches, buffered by the option of free drinks from the bar at test-venue Eden Park.

But at Liston Park, someone has already recorded the victory on the Marist club scoreboard: Written in sprawling hand next to the senior side's schedule is the giddy declaration, GALLAHER SHIELD CHAMPIONS! The board also lists scores for the other Marist teams—senior reserves, under-twenty-ones, under-nineteens, junior boys. The last item on the list, written in chalk instead of the plastic lettering used for the others, has an air of impermanence. It says, "Women's," and, almost as a fading afterthought, "Club Champions 1994."

The Marist women's rugby team, in fact, has completed its season with a dazzling 12–0 record, having scored a total of 682 points against its opposition. In club competition, the other Auckland teams tallied only 20 points against the Marist players. Four women were selected out of the club to represent New Zealand in the impending tour of Australia—the first women's tour to be fully sanctioned and funded by the powerful NZ Rugby Football Union. Yet last week, when the women's finals took place, there was no grand reception at Liston Park. The clubhouse did not welcome back its victorious daughters with drinks and a live band. Following the after-match function at Otahuhu, the team celebrated in solitary fashion at one of its sponsors, the Tainui Pub.

Perhaps because of the number of celebrity players on the men's team, and doubtless due in part to the attitude held by many of the older members in particular, the women's team lingers on the fringes of the club community. Field priority at the club is inevitably given to the men, as is recognition for the fruits of rugby labor. Some regard the female players as snobs because they rarely socialize with the men, but this does not take into account the different schedules for the teams (men play and celebrate on Saturdays while the women's games are relegated to Sundays) nor the fact that many of the women have children and family responsibilities to return home to. In addition, other obstacles bar the Marist doors: the unwelcoming personalities of several male players, for example; and the underlying sentiment that, ideally, women at the club—if not relatives, "partners," or groupies—should be participants in the more "feminine" sport of netball. The women's rugby team is seen as a nuisance by some, a novelty by others, and, by the more staunch traditionalists, an atrocity. Still other Marist members do not realize that it exists at all.

This night being that of the Gallaher Shield final, however, five of the women's team members have shown up at the club. They sip beers quietly in a back corner, waiting to congratulate their male counterparts and talking amongst themselves of the match they played the afternoon before in Putaruru. To those who have seen them on the field, sporting mouthguards and mud-caked jerseys, they look oddly clean and slightly out of place. When the men's team finally arrives, they rise on tip-toes to see over the heads of the crowd, and clap against their bottles while the clubhouse fills with a hearty cheer.

After the speeches are made, the festivities can begin in unbridled earnest. The bartenders are kept busy as the senior players mingle with the multitudes, flirting capriciously in a sea of supporters and peers. Amidst the preeminent company, women's rugby is only a temporary conversation piece. An older woman appears bemused. She is holding a beer for one of the All Blacks, a responsibility she is thrilled to have. "Why would girls want to play the sport?" she asks. "It's so violent." Behind her, a male player chats with one female admirer while surreptitiously groping the backside of another. A drink is spilled, but no one notices.

John Kirwan, the number 14 who has become an All Black institution—"the best winger in the world," some say—approaches a young American woman who has joined

141

Marist during her two-month stay in New Zealand. He towers over her. He, too, wants to know why she plays rugby. "And don't give me any of that feminist bullshit," he adds curtly over the noise of the hired band. She seems puzzled by the question. "I love the game," she answers. Her reason is almost depressingly logical—why else would women subject themselves to such an underappreciated role?—but Kirwan refuses to accept this response and insists on further justification. "I don't believe in women's rugby," he says. "Why don't you leave something to us?"

The request sounds absurd, given the status of male rugby players, and surely it is meant to be ironic. John Kirwan, after all, claims to meet up to a thousand people in one day. For him, the constant ego trip and public adoration are an enticing combination. And one can see that the allure of the rugby culture's glory is not lost on those of a more "innocent" age: an under-twenty-one Marist "colt," the son of legendary ex–All Black Joe Stanley, has taken a young female under his wing. "Who do you want to meet?" he offers importantly. "I can introduce you to anyone here." He suggests that she pursue one of the players. "I think he likes you." He reminds her how famous the man is. "He's married and has a kid," she replies.

"That's all right," he says. "His wife's not here."

Perhaps to avoid such complications, Monique Hirovanaa and Davida White, also NZ national team reps, are the first women's players to leave. On the way out, a male club member approaches Hirovanaa and lewdly offers her a ride. She curls her lip at him in a patented sneer and goes home alone.

The band is soon replaced by someone's CD collection, and Marvin Gaye's "Sexual Healing" comes on during the fraternizing and flirtation. Meanwhile, the American (an alum of Amherst College) is having an animated conversation with a New Zealander who is also the former coach of the Dartmouth College women's rugby team. "I was skeptical at first too," he is explaining. "I was like a lot of the guys here. I couldn't stand the idea of smart, attractive girls going out on the field to rough up their faces and bodies." The coach seems delighted to have fallen upon someone who can relate to his overseas experience and will appreciate his change of heart. "Isn't it great," he raves a bit drunkenly but with admirable intentions, "that you and I can have an intelligent conversation about the game, and I can ask you things like do you use your outside shoulder on a tackle and how do you run your lines, without bringing sex into it?"

But once he disappears, Kirwan is there again, grinning with devilish charm. "Hey, Breast Cancer," he says. He thinks this is the medical fate of women's rugby players because of all the knocks they receive in the chest area. "Joe doesn't think women should play rugby either, do you Joe?" Joe Stanley shakes his head solemnly.

It's difficult to tell how serious they are. In their powerful positions, the line between teasing and contempt can be a fine one. But maybe that is not the point. Even in jest, such comments reflect a lack of appreciation for women's "un-feminine" goals and ambitions. Two of the well-known men's seniors are talking with a woman who has political aspirations. She is dressed modestly in a pale brown sweater; the players straddle barstools with casual ease and tell her coolly that she'll never be elected Prime Minister because her breasts are too big. "Nobody'll be listening to you. They'll be too busy looking at your tits," they tell her. She tries to debate the point, but her protestations fail under their taunting appraisal.

Still others perceive nontraditional women as a real threat and are openly hostile toward them. Off to the side, one of the Marist "old boys" grabs a female rugby player's arm in a less than friendly manner. He has been watching her and seems to feel that she was disrespectful toward one of the All Blacks. "You're a little fish in a big pool," he hisses. "Settle down." She stares at him incredulously. "Settle down," he insists, his blue eyes bloodshot and venomous. "That's why no one likes having your team here."

"I wanted to clock the old bugger," the player admits to a friend later. "Then I thought he might kick me out of the club. Then I thought he might kick the whole team out of the club. And I realized that, like it or not, for him and for most of the other men at Marist, one girl can represent the whole of women's rugby."

After all, people like the Dartmouth coach—those who have amended their stereotypical viewpoints because they have actually worked with women's teams or seen them play—exist, but they are not very visible. And even involvement with the teams does not ensure sympathy. All too typical are referees who stop play to correct foul language ("It doesn't make a good impression for the men on the sideline to hear that") and make comments like, "Frankly, I'd rather be at home with my feet up watching TV than reffing your game."

In a small country where rugby football is closer to a religion than a sport, there is little room for radical change. The power structure is clearly defined and endorses only a few images of women who want to play rugby: Either they are masculated as "big girls," too butch and coarse to be taken seriously; or they continue to be objectified and preserved as the possessions of men. (The idea of delicacy is held by males and females alike; a common response to a women's rugby player is, "Real rugby? You don't tackle, do you?")

Moreover, there is a general lack of public support for women's teams. In New Zealand, where the All Blacks dominate headlines and TV listings and the sports pages are filled with details of men's provincial matches, the media virtually ignores the presence of women's rugby. One would be hard-pressed to find a Kiwi who has not seen a rugby competition at some point, but many admit that they have never watched a women's game.

In the world of sports, women are caught up in a vicious cycle of lack of exposure and lack of respect. At a place such as the Marist clubroom, where the air is thick with tradition and testosterone, the temptation to maintain the status quo is very real. If a woman does not play by the rules, she risks being resented or dismissed. At Marist, it is a particularly wearisome battle for women's rugby players. Surely it would be easier, in some sense, to succumb to tradition, than to keep rocking the boat.

Still, there is hope.

At the beginning of the Gallaher Shield celebration, the club emcee called the men's team up to the front of the room where they were invited to squeeze onto a small platform. Here, he boisterously eulogized their performance before putting the microphone under each player's nose in turn, asking them to comment on the game. As the brews had been cracked from the moment the team re-entered the locker room after the final, many of the players were already feeling the effects of their rejoicing, and the speeches were soaked with alcohol and good humor.

This went on for quite some time before the team stepped down, but the generosity of the evening had not yet run its course. The announcer then called for everyone to listen while the senior reserves took the stage. "The senior reserves and the women's team; could we have the women's team up here please?" One wondered if he realized that only five of the women's players were present. They looked at each other, eyebrows raised by the club's first real recognition of their accomplishments. When they understood that he was serious, they shuffled as a collectively embarrassed unit toward the front of the room. One of them muttered, "I shouldn't go up there—I didn't even play in the final"; another prodded her forward. They reached the platform and reluctantly stepped up, exchanging mortified glances in the unfamiliar setting. Monique Hirovanaa, the intimidatingly compact half-back/fullback for the team, has proven her skills at the highest levels of rugby and touch rugby. She is arguably the best player on the Marist team, known for her superior handling and tactics and explosive running. On the

rugby pitch, she is anything but reserved; yet on stage, suddenly shy, she turned her back to the audience.

The men's senior reserves were given a few words. Then the announcer acknowledged the women's week-old championship and handed the microphone to Davida White, the team's openside flanker and captain. She cleared her throat and, tactfully ignoring the hypocrisy of the moment, began a matter-of-fact thank you to the club; but by now the crowd was getting restless and it was difficult to hear what she was saying. When the women finally received their scattered applause, they rushed down from the platform with an air of palpable relief—relief, one would guess, as much for having survived the limelight free from catcalls or scorn as for stepping out of it.

But at least one member of the crowd was paying close attention. Later in the evening, one of the female Marist players was standing near the bar when she heard a hesitant, "Excuse me." Thinking that someone needed to get by, she moved aside, but the woman who had spoken was still looking at her. She was attractive, probably in her early twenties, with shiny, walnut-colored hair. "I was wondering," she began slowly, "I was just wondering, what do you have to do to join the team?"

The rugby player was instantly attentive. "You want to play for Marist?" she asked.

"Yes, well," the stranger leaned in conspiratorially, glancing over her shoulder as if she thought there might be a sexist spy nearby, "I used to play when I was little, but they kicked me out when I got older because I was a girl." The other nodded. It is a common story in New Zealand, the story that, on the rugby

144

pitch, boys and girls are created equal—up until a certain age. Then the girls are expected to relinquish their football rights without a word.

What do you have to do to join the team? There are two responses: one for the athlete, and one for the female. As a woman on the Marist team, you must toughen your skin. You must accept that the real hurt comes not only from the blows on the field, the real frustration not only from dropped ball. You must learn to brace yourself against the tackles and, more significantly, the nonbelievers.

But the Marist rugger spoke to her as a player.

"Just show up at training," she said.

"Excuse Me, Were You Born in a Barn?"

by *Girljock*'s Born-in-a-Barn Correspondents

Photo © Roxxie

I was approaching the Central Park softball field with some trepidation because I was expecting to see a woman who had recently dumped me when I was signaled by a blond, possibly heterosexual, woman who was in the process of zipping up her Louis Vuitton bat bag.

"Could you answer this if it rings?" the blond woman asked, holding out the cute little folded up telephone she had pulled from the pocket of her navy linen blazer.

My first thoughts were, Who is this woman? Do I know this woman? Where does one buy a Louis Vuitton bat bag?

After a moment of bewilderment, not only at this complete stranger's brazen request but also at the fact she was wearing a blazer with spandex shorts and cleats, I said, "Why are you expecting a call from a barn you undoubtedly call home?"

Overheard at a Navaho reservation craft center and scenic viewpoint (on private Navajo land):

Old Caucasian Male Fart: [on the lack of park service style spoon-fed explanatory plac-ards and signs] They sure don't tell you much, do they?

Old Caucasian Female Fart: [looking over the edge of the canyon] I'm too old for this.

Old Caucasian Male Fart: [speaking to a Navaho craft seller] What's this made out of?

Navaho Craft Seller: Sterling silver.

Old Caucasian Male Fart: What? Stolen silver? [laughs at his own "joke."]

Navaho Craft Seller: [Laughs politely, rolls eyes.]

Girljock Magazine's suggested response: If that old fart wandered into our backyards and bitched about there being no explanatory placards, we'd suggest he quickly sod off by saying, "Do you need a placard to get out of your barn stall?"

Girljock correspondent, receiving the latest book sacrifice from the supplicant publisher hoping to appease the *Girljock* correspondent's inner review goddess. "Imagine my surprise to discover I was expected to review this particular book," the correspondent wrote us, adding, "When I suddenly found myself inside the very book they'd sent me." Indeed, it turned out that our correspondent's own character, although in fictional effigy, had been completely character assassinated in the text of the book. The *Girljock* correspondent had had enough. She reached deep into the postcard file until she found the correct Midwestern barn photo, and addressed to the book's publicist and author: "Excuse me, but were you both born in a barn?"

Girljock correspondent on a soccer field, suddenly discovered her female opponent's body pressing extremely closely into her butt, as if they were in that phase of body contact known as "joined at the hip." Our correspondent, an out lesbian, thinking that the woman pressing into her so deeply might be trying to distract her from the soccer activity, decided she'd try to fake back on the woman pressing so closely into her.

While this may have been a good opportunity to ask if the hip-presser was born in a barn, our soccer player said, aiming below the belt, "You must really like me!"

"Oh, yes, I do," said the opponent, still pressing deeply into our correspondent's behind. After the game, our *Girljock* correspondent took it a step farther: "How can you like me so much when I don't even know you?" she asked the hip-presser.

"Because of your odor," the hip-presser responded.

This dominant butch dyke friend of mine called me to tell me she just got her tongue pierced.

"Your tongue pierced!" I exclaimed, "You must feel extra holy now."

"Do you think doing such a submissive act as bowing down before a piercer to be totally humiliated is going to make you more of a butch thing? Excuse me, were you born in a barn?"

Girljock correspondent was presenting a special talk on a subject she had great familiarity with—even to the point of having a national reputation in that particular subject under discussion. Immediately following the presentation, an unnamed person approached the *Girljock* correspondent, asking her if she was an expert in the subject matter. Our correspondent was in shock and was stunned. Hadn't she just given a speech on the subject? Her only explanation for the unnamed person's question: Was she a bozo?

Our suggested response: Excuse me, were you born in a barn?

Girljock correspondent was playing soccer in the wilds of Sacramento, California, at a soccer tournament. An opposing player brutal-

147

ly body-slammed her, tackling her and causing her to fall on the ground. "Hey, don't do that again! You don't need to body-slam me," said our *Girljock* correspondent. The opposing player came right up to our correspondent and stood about eight inches away from her and said, "Fuck you!"

Our suggested response: "Excuse me, were you born in a barn?"

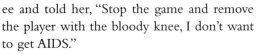

Girljock correspondent was innocently attending a "literary salon." A friend, known for her gregarious social introductions, sat down next our *Girljock* correspondent. Then a young, shorthaired, trendo baby-dyke, known for her descriptive verbose, self-absorbed narratives, joined them.

"Oh, hello," said our *Girljock* correspondent.

Mutual socially gregarious friend interjected, "Oh, [giggle] do you two know each other?"

Young trendo, self-absorbed baby dyke said, "No."

Girljock correspondent, appalled by trendo's disclaimer, responded, "You've been sleeping with my roommate for the last three weeks. *Excuse me, were you born in a barn, honey?* We don't all look alike."

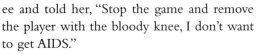

Friend of a *Girljock* correspondent was playing a regular women's indoor soccer match, when a young woman brutally tackled her, causing her to get her knee bloodied on the Astro Turf floor. *Girljock* correspondent with bloodied knee continued playing until a player on the other team waltzed up to the refer-

ee and told her, "Stop the game and remove the player with the bloody knee, I don't want to get AIDS."

Our *Girljock* had to leave the field and wipe off the now dried blood on her knee.

Our suggested response: *"Excuse me, were you born in a barn?"*

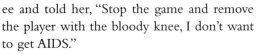

Strange man on the soccer field starts talking to a woman player. The woman player, our correspondent, is warming up for her game.

"Is this an all-women's team?" asks the strange man, who, incidentally, was dressed like a runner.

"Yes, it is," answers our correspondent.

"Well," asks the strange man, "are you in this because you don't like men?"

Our correspondent was bothered for a minute, remembering all the years she had spent training with men. She had a flash of insight and queried him back, "Are you a long-distance runner because you live in a bad neighborhood?"

Our call on the play: He was born in a barn.

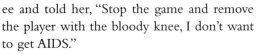

Girljock correspondent was busy eating lunch with her boss in popular luncheon establishment, when approached by two women, whom she knew from "around town."

They approached her loudly crying out, "Hey, honey! Why didn't you come to the women-only sex club last weekend. We missed you! Your best girlfriend was there having a good old time."

Suggested response: "Excuse me, but were you born in a *barn*?"

Our least fashionable (by her own admittance) *Girljock* correspondent was hanging out with some sporty babes when a more trendily dressed creature appeared, with her Nose-in-the-Air.

Our fashionable Trendmonster looked directly at our least fashionable correspondent and said, "Hey you, I just wanna know what on earth *you* could possibly ever wear to work at your job! Ha! Ha!"

Logical response: "Excuse me, but were you born in a barn?"

A friend of a *Girljock* correspondent, playing in a local soccer tournament, and having a very nice time to boot, was approached by an acquaintance.

The acquaintance eagerly said, "Hey! Honey!

I heard your sister's team just won the National Championship! You know, you could have made that team! Why didn't you go play on your sister's team? That was really dumb of you!"

Natural response: "Excuse me, but were you born in a *barn?*"

Situation: Our *Girljock* correspondent played a very difficult soccer game against a very aggressive team, and played such tight babe-to-babe defense against the opposing player, she took away all of her scoring opportunities, and blocked all of her shots on the goal.

Conflict: After the game, the opposing aggressive player came up to our *Girljock* correspondent to say, "You played pretty fuckin' tough, you ugly cunt," and she turned around and walked away.

Suggested Response: "EXCUSE ME, BUT WERE YOU BORN IN A *BARN!!!?*"

Actual Response: Our correspondent, rendered speechless momentarily, thought as hard as she possibly could. By the time the opposing player was twenty paces away, our correspondent turned and yelled at the top of her lungs, "How do you know what my cunt looks like?"

MAJOR FUN!

UNREPENTANT CONFESSIONS OF A BATON TWIRLER by Angela Bocage ©1991

JUST OUTTA THE GATE—YOU GO, GO, GO! THEN YOU'RE ELEVEN, TWELVE, OR SO

(TENNIS O.K.)

STOP!

DALLAS. 8th GRADE. A GIRL WITH GLASSES & SHIRTTAILS OUT, I DAYDREAMED ABOUT WHICH GIRLS WOULD I BE BEST FRIENDS WITH, AND WORRIED ABOUT *SILENT SPRING*, AND WHY SUCH GOOD ARTISTS ENDED UP DRAWING FASHION ADS FOR NEIMAN'S OR TITCHE'S. *REBELLION* WAS SQUASHED BY PEER GROUP CO-OPTATION: 8th GRADE WAS THE GRADE WHERE YOU HAD TO GET IN LINE FOR THE GOODIES. LIKE THE FUTURE DEPENDED ON IT, AT LEAST THE NEXT FOUR YEARS. THEY MADE IT THE *TRYOUTS* YEAR...

ANGELA! GET IN HERE!!

JUMP!

FOR CHEERLEADERS, DRILL TEAM, PEP CLUB OFFICERS, MARCHING BAND, HONORS SOCIETIES, & WHO KNEW WHAT ELSE? NOT ME. BUT I HAD TWO BEST FRIENDS NAMED SHARON, & THE ONE WHO PLAYED CLARINET IN BAND WITH ME SAID I OUGHT TO TRAIN WITH HER FOR SPRING'S MAJORETTE TRYOUTS.

OW!

O.K.

WE PRACTICED, MADE UP TRYOUT ROUTINES (MINE WAS TO "AGE OF AQUARIUS") AND WERE PROUD TO BE TRYING OUT FOR THE MOST *SKILLED* (YOU EVEN HAD TO BE A GOOD ENOUGH MUSICIAN TO MAKE MARCHING BAND!) AND PERHAPS MOST *ATHLETIC*—

(THOUGH THE CHEERLEADERS DID *JUMP* MORE) FEMALE ROLE IN THE SANCTIONED LIFE OF BENJAMIN FRANKLIN JUNIOR HIGH. FROM BEGINNER IN OCTOBER, I TURNED OUT TO BE QUITE GOOD AT TWIRLING BY TRYOUT TIME. IT WAS EXHILARATING! SOMETIMES EVEN DANGEROUS!

AND I COULD SHOW OFF MY NATURAL FLEXI-BILITY IN A MORE APPROPRIATE VENUE THAN MY BORING MATH CLASS

YAWN. DO A SPLITS, ANGELA

YEP—SHE KIN DO IT IN A SECOND.

YET ANOTHER THANG GIRLS KIN DO BETTER, HUH, JEFFREY?

WELL, MA DON'T EXPECT US TO, DO MA?

AND WHAT WAS THE SIGNIFICANCE OF THE COOLNESS HIERARCHY AMONG DIFFERENT TYPES OF BATON? THE BEST WAS SILVER, ABSTRACT "FOILING" ON MINI-SHAFT, NEXT A PLAIN MINI SHAFT. BUT *WORSE* THAN A PLAIN STANDARD SHAFT WAS ONE *WITH DIMPLY* FOILING.

DOES SOMEBODY, SOMEWHERE THINK GIRLS WOULD *SMASH* THE CAPITALIST *PATRIARCHY* IF WE DIDN'T HAVE STUFF LIKE THIS TO THINK ABOUT??

...AND WEAR BOOTS, ONCE I MADE IT, WITH A STUNNING RANGE OF PSYCHOSEXUAL MEANING

panel 7 dedicated to Larry-Bob of *Holy Tit Clamps*

"THE MAGIC OF CARTOON TELEKINESIS"

Femme Jock Corner:
Girljock's Answerwoman
by Amy Cheney, our revered Femme Jock

Dear Femme Jock:

I'm just an intellectual kind of girljock with dark hair who plays soccer, softball, runs, and lifts my laundry basket on a regular basis. I've got an awfully embarrassing problem. I know how to fly through the air and catch a softball, but I have no fashion sense at all. My soccer team has complained that all they see me in is sweatpants, Jogbra, T-shirt. I know I've got to wear something else to the next soccer-girljock party, but I don't know what to do. Please help me. Please please please please please please. What color jeans are in? Should T-shirts be baggy or tight? Are polo shirts out now? Are suspenders in or out? What about polyester?

Girljock in
Trouble in Berkeley

Dear GJiTiB:

Honey, you sound just adorable to me. I can spot a butch a mile away, and the good thing is that you aren't expected to know these things. So just relax! There's something appealing to every femme jock about a butch in polyester. Of course polyester is out! It was never in. But never you mind, just wear what you will and you'll soon have girls flocking to you, wanting to move in and take you shopping. Obviously your soccer team either (a) doesn't appreciate you laundry-basket lifting (I assume you follow through like you do on the soccer field and actually wash what's in your basket and wear the clean items to your parties), or (b) are simply too shy to make the first move. But until they shape up, in more subtle ways than their physical appearance, FJ suggests you stick to dark-colored jeans (please, no pink for you, that would truly be an embarrassment), a nice tight T-shirt to show off your biceps, or a button-down shirt discreetly open at the neck. We would like to see your girljock bod, so just keep that in mind the next time you want to wear sweatpants to a party. FJ likes it when you beg and is glad to help anytime.

Femme Jock

FEMME JOCK LOCKER ROOM TALK

The *Girljock* Editrix asked me to write something about "How to keep your girlfriend once you've got her," and "locker rooms." I wasn't sure exactly what the connection was, and since *my* girlfriend just split . . . well, I went to the local women's gym.

My friend Ann J. calls this gym the

"Girlfriend Shop." Really! There were plenty of sweaty butches in scant clothing in dark corners. Now as most femmes who enjoy butches know, these lovely creatures are few and far between. It was difficult to even pay attention to all the questions they asked me as I cycled on the Lifecycle. Did I want hills or a random workout? How many minutes did I want? What level did I want? *Who cares—Who was that girljock?*

Other traumas followed. The communal shower and hot tub brought up the daily and important dilemma over whether or not to shave my legs. Somehow I've reached peace with my underarms.

I do wish my underarm hair was a bit curlier, yet many women have complimented me on the hair itself, as well as the way it parts. So, I try to appreciate it. Personally, I like a girl with underarm hair. I like to stick my face (and nose, and mouth, and tongue) in there. This is getting a bit personal here.

Back to my legs. Yes, they are for running, kicking a soccer ball, and fancy double-backs on the racquetball court, but, I must confess, uh, well, uh . . . I enjoy their display purposes more. Okay, okay. So I should shave my legs. But, geez, what a hassle. I've heard from various femme sources that electric razors don't work. While I'm coordinated enough to move a pen across the page, I'm not coordinated enough to move the razor across my legs. So it's back to the old scratch and slice. Okay, okay. So I shouldn't shave.

Does Hairfree equal Carefree?

Dear Femme Jock:

For some time now my girlfriend has been fretting over the fact that I head the ball a lot playing soccer and she's afraid I'm going to get brain damage. I never paid much attention to her until I played in a tournament this summer, hit the ball with the wrong part of my head—you know, on top where you had a soft spot as a baby—and got a headache the size of Jonathan Winters. It got me thinking: Is she right? Have you heard of girljocks losing brain cells over a long period of soccer involvement? I know I could do worse as an amateur boxer, but is this worth worrying about?

Girljock with Soccer Hangover

Dear GJ with SH:

FJ has done extensive research about your compelling and frightening question. Yes GJ, (and GJs) there is evidence of soccer players suffering from too much soccer ball heading. The question next seems to be, What is "too much"? Just remember, the brain is the biggest sex organ. (I found this out from a pamphlet included in a safe-sex kit. I had forgotten, if in fact I had ever known. This is an encouraging reminder to all of you who may suffer from dildo-size anxiety.) Oh, but I digress! What is too much? FJ suggests you use your own best judgment along with other selective body parts. How about improving your chest traps? Stomach traps? Or my favorite—thigh traps? FJ is just getting excited thinking about it. I also suggest you pay more attention to your girlfriend. When was the last time you gave head to her clit? Yes, keep your hands and soft parts off the balls and you'll be fine.

Femme Jock

Dear FJ:

I am distraught. Perhaps you can help. At a recent party, some lout spilled beer on my only favorite lizard skin pumps. These are a thrift store find that will never happen again. The skins are starting to separate and shred. It is tragic. But I can't locate a shoe repair store that knows how to fix them What can I do?

Piqued and Pumpless

Dear PP:

Femme Jock is distraught as well. Lizard skin pumps?! Oh, the poor darlings. I admit, it's difficult for FJ to determine where her alliance lies: with femmes, or with lizards. Truthfully, the answer probably is with the lizards, or with femmes who don't wear them. On the other hand, I do know about those thrift store finds: luscious items in hot pink or glitter fur that turn out to be baby kangaroo, or what have you, that you've just got to have. And hey, they've already been maimed, killed, separated into bits, made into shoes or whatever else, bought and worn and are now sitting on a shelf in front of you just waiting to be put on so you can wear them to pick up your girlfriend at the pizza parlor party scene. So maybe the way to look at it is, even if they didn't have a long life, they've at least had a long and, hopefully, enjoyable death-after-life that you can most certainly add to. And perhaps this will put the whole thing in perspective: your lizard skin pumps have had a long, varied, and sordid history, only one small part of which is an encounter with a beer-spilling lout. I admit, Femme Jock is being a bit harsh. Are there any dyke (do you like butches, dear?) shoe repairers out there who can rescue this distraught femme and keep her pumping?

Femme Jock

ARE YOU THERE GOD/DESS? IT'S ME, FEMME JOCK . . .

It happened. I mean, I did it. I shaved my legs.

They broke out in a rash. They itched. Occasionally, I drew blood. Hair nubs appeared the very next day.

When I went away for the weekend, I forgot to bring a razor. I went to the supermarket and went to the personal hygiene aisle.

There weren't any femme jocks there. There was something called Nair that sounded good but smelled awful and reminded me of oven cleaner. I thought maybe shaving cream might help. There wasn't any shaving cream for femmes. There was Barbasol with a spice or menthol fragrance. I'm going to put something called Barbasol on my legs? No, God/dess, I couldn't.

I went to the local bathhouse. Girls had cute little twats and had shaved their hair into cute little triangles. No loose hair down their thighs. Soft hairless creases where their legs joined together.

I started to feel insecure. I started to question if I was really a femme. I started worrying about my time scheduling, if I'd have time to include a shower before hot tubbing, a shave before showering in the gym, and shave before pulling on my leopard sport shorts for running and black lace shorts for softball practice. A shave before every bike ride, soccer match and team picnic? Basically, I figured I'd have to figure on a shave in at least one area of my body at least once a day.

Are you there, God/dess? Is the idea of hairless legs, underarms, and other personal areas a patriarchal plot to undermine our precious team and sports playing time in exchange for being a babe?

Are patriarchal plots irrelevant considering we're dykes and play on all-women's teams?

It's me, Femme Jock: shaved legs, hair armpits, and a cunt of curls. I'm all for choices, I just wish the decisions were a little easier.

Dear Femme Jock:

I recently moved to a small town in the Tampa Bay area. I walk every day and have a great route here—over a long bridge to the neighboring town and overlooking the river and bay—it's beautiful! The best part, though, is all the women I see—usually running. Many of them look like true girljocks to me, but my dilemma is this: How can I get beyond a smile and (exaggerated breathless) hello when these cute women are running the opposite way I'm walking? I've thought of tripping one or two but am afraid that won't endear me to them. Should I feign a pulled muscle and ask for a hand (or massage)?

I'm ordering a Girljock T-shirt in hopes that will help. I don't know what to do unless I start walking backward.

I need your expert advice, Femme Jock.

Trying to Bridge More Than the Distance

Dear Trying to BMT the D,

Such a dilemma. How to meet girls. Especially girls who are running, seemingly, away from you. Darling, are you sure you want to? You've considered the possible heartache, not to mention the shin splints? The mud kicked up, seemingly in pursuit of physical well being and harmony? You've considered the difference in pacing, rhythm, and breathing styles? You've checked out books from the library on *Women Who Love Women Who Are Running (Away)*? You've looked into, deeply

into, your childhood and past-life experiences where you were, indeed, a bridge? You're sure you're not repeating a painful pattern? Yes? No? Well, then.

I'm sure that my editrix would encourage me to assure you that a *Girljock* T-shirt is the answer. Walking backwards does do wonders for the gluteus maximus. And possibly for your perspective on life. But, truly, I suggest finding (and, yes, I have faith they exist) women who are walking the same direction.

Femme Jock

Dear Femme Jock:

I am a scuba diver, and have about decided to replace my old pair of black "jet fins" with a new, improved set in a fashion color. However, my girlfriend says that my "big feet," as she calls them, are a real turn-on for her—she gets excited whenever she sees them drying in the bathroom after a dive. I offered to get her a pair of her own for our upcoming Caribbean trip, but she says that it's the fact that they are mine that gets her going.

Now I can't decide whether to risk getting a new set, because they might not have the same effect. What do you think?

Diver Wanting to Keep Things Wet

Dear D Wanting to KTW:

What are some of the things we femmes like about butches? One of them is your earnest bafflement at being loved for who you are. Darling, the key to your dilemma is simply what your girlfriend has already told you: Your big feet turn her on. Yours. Whether they're old and funky or new and groovy. Granted, some of us find irresistible a lack of fashion sense, or that old comfortable clothing look.

But we're flexible. So, Miss Diver, dive away. Dive into her and see if you can reach that spot that will tell you—really, really tell you on every inch of your epidermis-without-a-wetsuit—what she's already told you. Baby, she loves it when you're doing what you love best: diving. There, in the bathroom, is one physical reminder of your pleasure and hence hers—your big wet feet. This is, I assure you, normal: many of us have foot fetishes.

In case your loved one really is into the old worn-out comfortable and familiar dyke daddy look, come up, so to speak, with some alternatives, until you get your new feet fitting and feeling the way you like. I suggest you get her to help by making her show you how much she loves your new, groovy, and fashionable feet by performing various acts with them, one of which might be fellatio.

Femme Jock

FEMME JOCK TRUE CONFESSIONS

I am not really a jock. I don't even like sports much. I just like the accessories. I like watching groups of girls flex their muscles and sweat. I like cheerleading. Pom-poms and miniskirts. High-stepping it in boots. Displaying my legs and ass amid yells, growls, and grunts.

Speaking of legs, I thought all of the girls on the East Coast shaved their legs. (Not so! According to the coordinator of the Yale Women's Center Feminist Reading Group and summer student, *half* of the girls in her reading group don't shave, and she doesn't *either.*)

While we're on the subject of shaving (have we ever really gotten off it?) GJ with SH writes: "P.S. About the shaving thing: All I know is I like underarm hair on my girlfriend but not on myself. She thinks my shaved pits look like a plucked chicken, but obsesses about the hair on her inner thighs, which I think is sexy. We both shave our legs. Go figure." I figure, hairfree does not equal carefree.

For the parade-day display of *Girljock*, I had shaved my legs; now they are hairy in all their glory. These are a few of the advantages of hairs on my legs as I feel them:

The breeze teases them.

Your tender tongue, fingertips, and breath can do the same.

Tugging on them provides alternate sensations.

When I get out of the pool, beads of water glisten and highlight—a sort of femme au naturel glitter.

I have time for more important pursuits now that I am not all alone in my bathroom with my leg up on the sink with a razor.

Speaking of more important pursuits, I decided to give up on team sports (true—I've never partaken in them much anyway—I've always been a soloist) and get into group sex. This is what I did several weekends ago with Ms. Betty Ann Dodson, BAD for short. What a fantasy! A room full of straight girls and Lezzbians (some of whom shaved their legs, some of whom did not), individually displaying and looking at each other's cunts one day and masturbating (mistress-baiting?) the next. Sweating, flexing their muscles, breathing hard and cheering each other on—yes—there's a lot to be said for aerobic activities.

Dear Femme Jock:

This is a very simple question, but no one seems to know the answer. Thus, I turn to my Girljock guru. What should I do when I see a beautiful goddess while driving down the road? Assuming we're both in cars, and we make eye contact. Thanks! Keep up the good work!

Babyjock

Dear Babyjock:

Darling, babyjocks are my favorite kind. My editrix, in the flurry of her busy and important life, has lost, misplaced, or perhaps confiscated the photo you sent, so I am unable to respond, so to speak, on that level.

And, in answer to your question. First, darling, don't get into a car crash. This would never do. Babyjocks are much needed in this world. Let me reassure you that you've done the right thing. When you're turned-on yet thwarted—yes—turn on to yours truly, femme jock (Miss Femme Jock, to you). Because, babyjock, she may look good in a car, bar, train, or plane but be lacking in some essential ingredient such as kindness or even personality.

As is often the case, I know from first-hand experience. Allow me to elaborate.

Once there was this butchly babe with beautiful bulging biceps that I would see around town with a glamorous femme in tow. Each time I saw her cut-out T-shirt, my breath would catch in my throat and I was speechless with her butchly beauty. One day as I

was zooming up in my sporty sports car to the stop sign, there she was! Alone! Walking across the street, right in front of me. My breath caught, my mouth opened, my salivatory and other juices began to flow and my muscles relax. As my senses melted into fantasies of her hard arms around my soft femmely body, my foot slowly slid off the brake pedal and my sporty car was rolling into the intersection at my bicep babe's body!

Luckily, I came to my senses in more ways than one. First, I slammed on the brakes, and second, I did some research. Alas, the bicep babe may have had biceps (oh, and she did!) but she didn't have brains.

The other experience I've had with babes in cars (separate cars—I've had many memorable experiences with babes in the same car) was horrifyingly heart stopping. It was rush-hour traffic (i.e., stopped cars) and I was in the far lane. Across the center divide, going the opposite direction also in rush hour (i.e., stopped traffic), was the ex-girlfriend who'd had an affair. And there we were, eye-to-eye.

So darling, leave the driving to Greyhound. Get on it with some babes going the same direction, where you can make more than eye contact. Why limit yourself?

Wishing you the best of full body contact,

Femme Jock

Dear Femme Jock:

My girlfriend has recently taken up basketball, softball, and soccer. I think it means she doesn't want to be around me as much and I feel rejected. I've thought of getting a blow-up doll for a companion, but I don't know what size or kind to get. Do you think she'll get the hint if I get a blow-up doll? I've even found myself getting absent-minded crushes on

Photo © Roxxie

other women, and thinking during the slow hours of the afternoon about their dresses and skirts, and how lovely women's bodies are. I miss having one next to me, and I miss touching female skin.

Should I get a doll? Should I hide my girlfriend's athletic gear? Should I go out for all the sports that she does? Should I go to sex parties I get invited to? Whatever should I do?

My Girlfriend Is Lost in Sports

Dear Lost in Sports:

On the one hand, blow-up dolls have really bad hairdos, the same expression on their face all of the time, and certainly are no substitution for female skin, particularly the kind that is toned and solid from basketball, softball, and soccer.

On the other hand, a blow-up doll may rekindle your desire for your girlfriend so much that you won't care if she's on the basketball court, softball or soccer field—you'll simply throw your clothes off, throw her down (wherever she is), and get yours next to hers, using both of your hands so that you no longer have to use them to debate the pros and cons of blow-up doll companions.

Femme Jock

Dear Femme Jock:

Here's the story of a lovely lesbian. She was busy raising hopes of dating three lovely lesbians of her own. All of them had hair of gold, like Michelle Pfeiffer, the youngest one in pearls.

Until one day when this lovely lady met this straight girljock, and they knew it was much more than a hunch that one day they would do more than lunch.

But before they could become a lesbians bunch,

there was the little problem of model-bot behavior the straight girljock came to show when hanging out with her own!

Oh, Femme Jock, please tell me true, why do one day straight girljocks flirt and sweat and tell us what to do one day and then giggle, sigh, and blink blankly at three hairy little boys of their own the next?

Have I, a lovely lesbian, become a girljoke?

Pitifully Yours,
Too Much Arizona Sun

Dear Too Much Sun:

1. Yes
2. Forget about the bunch . . . go for Alice.
3. Study metaphor and the inappropriateness of mixed metaphor. Mixed metaphor is like mixed messages: passive aggressive. Femme Jock and others would prefer you, simply, aggressive.
4. You have provoked Femme Jock's unusually harsh nature by signing your letter "Pitifully Yours."
5. Pulease.

Femme Jock

Dear Femme Jock:

Recently I had cause to attend a party, complete with a large box of stuff. Upon leaving, I was escorted out by two women, one of whom told me I was carrying the box incorrectly, and then took the box from my arms and hoisted it on her shoulder. I asked her if this was like when you carry someone's books home from school; she said yes, exactly. I told her then I was supposed to bring her an apple or chocolate or something else to school the next day, only, I'm not in school: Neither is she, and it was only a metaphor for something. What should I do now? Do

you think she likes me? What next? Unfortunately, I am very shy and when I like a girl, my wits often fail me, and I stumble verbally. I don't know how to bring up the subject, any subject, and I don't know how to ask her out at all.

She-who-trips-over-her-words

Dear She-who-tohw:

Dear. You don't need to do anything. Just stand in her path, being as awestruck as you are. Many girljocks enjoy being worshipped while tying other girljock's tongues. Suffer. She'll respond, eventually, and put you out of your misery. If she doesn't, she's obviously not the girl for you.

Femme Jock

Dear Femme Jockiest:

I'm writing to tell you of an old problem I am having. I happen to like two women who are roommates, and I don't know what to do. One of them said a few nasty things to me recently, and I don't mean nasty as in bitchy. I mean nasty, as in raunchy/ sexy/dirty/sexy nasty. At the time, I didn't know what to say back to her. So I didn't do anything. So now, I'm starting to like her roommate also. She is so completely cool. One is a redhead, which I find very sexy, and the other is a brunette. I find them both sexy, and they live together. That means: I can't go out with both of them. When will the answer be clear? I like talking to both of them. Am I just badly horny right now, and starting to like anyone who will talk to me for longer than two seconds, or should I go for one of these babes? What should a girljock like myself do? What if I blow it with them, and they talk to each other about it, or make fun of what I like to do on dates with each other?

Multi-directional Confusion

Dear Multi-DC:

Confusion, or the aura of, can be very sexy in both baby butches and femmes. For the former or the latter I suggest glasses and/or an uncombed or slept-upon hairdo to add to the confusion appeal.

Now, dear, you are suffering from tunnel vision, trapped in survival mode, where you can only see one or possibly two solutions to a problem. An example of this is the common dilemma: Should we move in together or break up? Don't panic, darling. I'm digressing. I know you're suggesting dating, not marriage. You are seeing two women who are roommates as limiting your sexual horizons, but as the Doublemint commercial puts it, it's "double the pleasure, double the fun." Or in your case, triple. Yes. Femme Jock is advocating a ménage à trois. And dear, you can't "blow it with them" until you start to blow. Which I suggest you do: in their ears to begin with, continuing to explore other orifices other than the nose. You might want to alternate with small nibbles or small appendages. But don't worry. Let your instincts take over. Theirs will, and then you'll all be in the same boat, so to speak.

Femme Jock

Dear Femme Jock:

I've got a really bad problem these days. Everyone keeps asking me if I'm butch or femme! I have serious issues with being one or the other. Why can't I embrace aspects of both of them? Or neither? I'm so confused.

To top it all off, my mother doesn't want me to ever ever ever identify as "butch." She thinks that butchness is the ultimate negative stereotype for a modern lesbian. Yet all the women I know who say they are "femme" complain about the lack of butches in San Francisco. And then I get attracted to both butch and femme women. What am I? Why aren't more lesbians into androgyny? Am I the only confused one?

If I am butch, must I always open car doors? May I never wear makeup? Must I learn how to change spark plugs? Must I know how to set up a tent?

Already people think I'm butch because I am a jock, but I like to wear dresses also. My friends have decided that this is a form of "cross-dressing" for me. I'm equally happy in softball sliding pants or tight black dresses. What am I? Who am I?

Lesbian in Search of a Post-Butch/Femme
Identity

Dear L in Search of a PBFI:

A serious series of questions that make me laugh. Darling. Everyone goes through this. No, you are not alone. This is a normal developmental stage of being a lesbian. You feel awkward. You look for a cure. A way out of the inevitable. The pimple has emerged, so to speak. Your voice is changing. Yes, even the way you view the world. The confusing thing about this developmental stage is that it doesn't happen at a certain age. It just happens. And honey, it's happening to you. Now. Of course, you have "issues" with one or the other. If you didn't have "issues," you might wonder if you were a lesbian. The question, as you probably do know somewhere in your lesbian body, is which issues do you have?

What kind of makeup would you like to wear? Personally, FJ loves it when butches open car doors for her, change her spark plugs,

and pitch tents; makeup is not out of the question. A little eyeliner, or whatever else suits her butchly face, works fine. And, my dear, there are many femmes who enjoy nothing more than getting under their car and squirming around. Darling, continue on.

"Top it off" with your mother by letting her know that in Femme Jock's opinion, the modern butch lesbian, whether she is a spark plug changer or a hairstylist, is one of the more glamorous creatures on the planet. Yes, FJ's harsher nature is emerging, as she is irritated by mothers and others who continue in this automatic lesbophobic autocratic attitude.

Femme Jock

THE FEMME JOCK ABCs

A is for aerobics, B is for Butches, C is for Country Western Dancing, D is for . . .

Okay, so I went to aerobics. Of course I am attracted to skin-tight fashion attire, hair do-wa-dads, bright colors, endless opportunities for accessories and strip tease possibilities as the workout progresses.

Several things happened when I went to aerobics. First, whatever muscle it is that you use when you are laughing got a terrific workout, along with my PC muscle. I was laughing hysterically at the fembot instructor with her high-tied ponytail and bizarre instructions and didn't want to pee all over my tight-fitting shiny emerald-green body suit. Second, when I wasn't laughing, I was crying—this stuff is a killer. I could barely lift my thigh a-one and a-two, not to mention a-three and a-four and a-more.

Third, and of course, most importantly—where were all of the butches? There *was* one gorgeous gal with her gray sweatpants resting on her hips and her bandana tied around her head, but I've seen her jogging around Stow Lake and when I've moseyed on into the Y on occasion. I'd much rather be jogging and moseying than suffering in aerobics. And let's face it—aerobics is for femmes.

So, I've accepted that my athletic workout consists of, yes, country-western dancing. And let me tell you about the advantages. First, you can wear a skirt. Skirts, lacy bras, lacy under-garments that are conveniently displayed when you are twirled, cowgal boots—good-bye to those clunky high-tops and squash-them Jogbras. You can even be cool and wear black. (This, to me, is a disadvantage; I do love those bright colors those girlie-girls wear in aerobics, although a friend cautioned me the other day that she saw a bumper sticker that said, FRIENDS DON'T LET FRIENDS WEAR NEON. But again I digress.)

Secondly, there are many, many butches. They are slinking around the sidelines, being shy in the corners and striking on the dance floor. Not only that, they take your hand and lead you around. You get to mingle, sweat, and sometimes get close enough to breathe in their lovely ears.

Oh, yes, so D is for—you guessed it, gals—dating. And when can you combine your exercise of choice with a date? Unless we begin to classify dating in and of itself as an aerobic activity, one of the answers to this question is when your exercise of choice is country-western dancing. But back to dating . . .

She left a vegan-no white sugar or honey-chocolate-raspberry truffle on my doorstep wrapped in pink paper with a shiny card just like I like. I wondered if this meant she was monogamous and capable of emotional depth and expression. Sure I care about what color your handkerchief is and what side it's on, but now there are so many other things to consider.

The trick is how to find out if she's monogamous and capable of—or at least will-ing to—express her feelings and be with yours without suggesting marriage or creating a traumatic experience on the third date. A truf-fle code might take care of this awkwardness.

The other code that simply has to develop is code for the percentages that Joann Loulan brought to us courtesy of some butch she met in a bar. Are you 100 percent (like to do it 100 percent of the time?), or are you 90, 80, 70, 60, 50 percent? Conversely, are you 0 percent (never want to do it to your lover, but get it done to you?), or do you like it done to you 90 percent of the time and like to do it 10 per-cent of the time? In which case you'd be a 10 percent. Or are you a 20, 30, 40, 50 percent?

Knowing these things from the beginning would certainly make life that much easier . . . then again, it'd certainly slow down the old heart rate and take the aerobics out of dating. After all (I keep forgetting), it isn't about the race to the finish line but about toning your muscles and changing your outfits as you go along.

The Big-Monster Cycles of Life:
This One's for Sara Deerheart Woolery

by Roxxie

Once, somewhere back in the hazy field of memories, in that time before all the Kiss-ins, the die-ins, and the Queer Nation and ACT-UP protests, but maybe right before these things started, I went to what might have looked like a bowl-in, a female invasion of a bowling alley, but it was just a birthday party. We crashed the El Cerrito, California, bowling lanes, some kind of "Bowl-o-rama." Bowl-o-ramas: bowling's soul food—tall, diluted Cokes in wax paper cups with a waxy taste, cheesy empty nachos, fluorescent hot dogs. Bowling balls of all different colors, some speckly and some not. People wearing shoes of all different numerologies on the shoe-backs.

The mysterious numerology of shoe sizes. When Tucker, the greatest Casanova ladies' man from my college days, went out he'd wear bowling shoes with number 10 on the back, although they were too big—he just liked the number. It had that Bo Derek magic, that feeling of sexual affluence: Tucker was a demigod of sex appeal. Women bedded him like he was Tom Jones in the sixties. We hated him for it because it was sexual affluence the rest of us didn't have: We also revered him for it because he was so amazing.

Every time I enter a bowling alley I fantasize boasting a number 10 on the back of my shoes like Tucker's. But my fate is always sevens, and sevens and sevens. It was from this state of 10-envy, from my deep wishes to be able to be something of that person that Tucker was, that when I entered this bowling party I allowed my friend Mabel Maney to sign up my: "Hello, my name is_____" tag with the name Roxxie. That was how I became Roxxie. I was sure that it was this sexual-affluence-shoe-numerology or something which had been keeping me dateless for a while, and "Roxxie" was my attempt at having some kind of equivalent to Tucker's 10; it was my stab in the dark recesses of my singlified existence.

We'd been a little late, but when we walked in to the birthday party/bowl-o-rama, Sara Deerheart Woolery's party, it was full of wild and freaky women, and they were having a really good time. Sara had a million friends. She had frequented the Michigan Women's Music Festival for years. There were lots of other "festies," and Mabel and I didn't really know many people there, but then, there were so many women that not many people knew all the people there. The party filled up most of the bowling lanes and you needed the "Hello my name is_____."

Mabel looked at me and said, "I know, let's be Mitzi and Roxxie, and that way I can tell my friends Mitzi and Roxxie that I took them bowling."

We slapped the name tags on our newly-pressed-shirt-covered chests, and eased into an

166

open lane at the back of the alley. We started a game. Some other women also popped in late, and our birthday girl, Sara, the quintessential hostess, I guess this was her thirty-fifth birthday, she guided these women to our lane. These women were festies too, and had very short hair, and were sort of fun to bowl with. They called me "Roxxie," and they called Mabel "Mitzi." We didn't tell them our real names, I think, and much to my surprise, at the end of the night, one of the festie bowlers we'd been playing with asked me to go out with her. She later called me on the phone asking for Roxxie, and I don't think I told her my real name for a while. I felt sorry for her because I don't think she liked San Francisco very much, she was visiting here for a year on an academic sabbatical from a Midwestern university. So I decided to go out with her and I was very surprised because I didn't really think I'd like dating her, and she kept calling me Roxxie. I liked dating her more than I thought I would. When I told my female art-support group about it, one awesome cartoonist named Cheela Smith decided that this was a great omen: My new meaning in life was to channel Roxxie's adventures.

Roxxie was to signify a certain part of our lives that was missing, that leftover from the seventies sexual-instinct-gone-wild, a woman with confidence beyond any of ours, that woman who could not ever get turned down for a date. In short, Roxxie was to be everything we were not, and I became her channeler. I have faithfully brought Roxxie's adventures to you, my dear readers, and she was born at Sara Woolery's birthday party in the winter of 1989–1990.

Sara Woolery was someone I'd known since I was twenty-two, and she was a massage therapist in Kansas City, Missouri. She and I met at the Midwest Wimmin's Festival at the Lake of the Ozarks, in Missouri, a really small women's camping festival about two hundred women attend every summer.

If you were a city gal like me, and couldn't stand the stillness of the country, you'd end up mysteriously drawn to the kitchen every day where you could chop a zillion carrots for the luncheon. You'd sort of freak. No phones were ringing, it was hard to sit still in an inner tube on the lake all day, and it was hot too.

I don't know how I signed up for a massage, or why. It was one of those for-some-reason things, it was because I was so agitated at the country stillness. But that was how I met Sara Woolery. She gave me a nighttime massage that lasted for an eternity because I can still remember it today, an outdoors massage table set under tall tree branches covering the dark star-speckled sky. How beautiful her hands felt as they rubbed on my face: She could find the deepest knots and work them out. After that summer I would send postcards at regular intervals to her house in Kansas City, always hoping to get closer to the enigma she had become to me: the beautiful woman with magic hands.

The summer I met Sara Woolery I'd graduated from college, my best friends decided that I should move to California with my girlfriend; and at the Midwest Wimmin's Festival we played a raucous shirtless country-dyke softball game. I know I tried to show off as hard as I could in that game, little twenty-two-something girljock me, shirtless (course, you always had a bandanna around your neck), and then you'd get chiggers from playing in the outfield. They'd itch for days and days, a true reminder of the essence of country softball, and the sunburn would make your skin dry.

Five years after I moved to California, Sara moved here too, and I got to know her as a friend. She had the kind of laughter that would light up a whole room. She had a knack for making friends, and bringing people together.

I was trying to write an essay, or an editorial, or some story, but really this whole thing I am writing to you is about the big monster cycles of life. Sara Woolery was a great friend to so many people: I just found out two days ago as I am about to write this awful thing— she died of cancer on the twenty-first of July. I think that was the date, and tears are rolling down my eyes as I write this. I think it started out as breast cancer, but it ended up all over her body.

After Sara Woolery moved to the Bay Area, I rediscovered her in a new way. We'd both been party-friends in the past who then opted for a drug and alcohol free life, or rather, we both had no more choices other than to give up our party-fiendness, and take another lifestyle. She was the first person from my "before" days: before I moved to California, before I quit partying and got myself together.

Most of us ex–party fiend types get afraid of people we knew before we got out of that lifestyle. Sometimes I've been afraid that the people I've known from before will make me want to drink or do drugs with them again. Sometimes I'm afraid I won't be able to relate to those people. Sometimes I've been afraid

that they might dislike me as much as I disliked myself during my drug-and-alcohol-filled time period. When I got to know Sara Woolery, I realized that these were my fears, and that was all they were. What a great person she was to know.

She was so nice, she had a crazy laugh, she worked on cool projects and cool women's music and helped produce alternative cultural stuff, she had more friends than you could ever count, and she wasn't judgmental.

Oh, her loss—how quickly time flies. Just a second ago in my life I was a young woman in St. Louis, Missouri (which you can mispronounce easily into Misery), and today I can only barely believe that the entire life of Sara Woolery is over. She didn't want to die. She had so many things she still wanted to do. Some of her friends told me she wanted to go back to the Michigan Women's Music Festival again. She didn't get to go back, she had to let go and die because her body lost the battle. I keep crying as I think about this. Was it a horrible death? How much pain was she in? Was she scared? Was she angry? Was it fair? What is fair?

"Please touch your breasts," the Lyon-Martin Women's clinic brochure said to me just this afternoon. Touch your breasts: After I found out Sara died I went in the bathroom and decided to become friends with my breasts and I felt every little texture of them as if they were some other woman's. I am a lesbian, after all, and I live for those moments of touching other women's breasts—that is, when I am so lucky. I touched my breasts like they were a typewriter and I was writing a new story. I touched my breasts with fear of mortality. I touched my breasts as far as I could reach into them and begged them to tell me any of their deep secrets. I touched my breasts like they were another country and I was a long-lost expatriate looking for my roots. I touched my breasts knowing how suddenly and deeply a body can betray: I was desperately ill for part of the summer, and dangerous possibilities haunted me for a while. A series of nasty and violent stomachaches this summer foiled three different doctors until, as a last ditch effort, an ultrasound showed that I had appendicitis. How happy I was—appendicitis, the curable. Appendicitis, the trouble with an end. Appendicitis, the bringer of a new scar to my stomach. Appendicitis: not cancer. Lucky me.

While I was recovering from my own surgery, I didn't even know Sara was dying. I missed her memorial service too, but I found out that her friends had selected two charities to donate stuff to: The Charlotte Maxwell Clinic, 5349 College Avenue, Oakland, CA 94618, and the Women and Cancer Project, 3543 18th Street, San Francisco, CA 94110.

I'd called her ex-girlfriend Allison and told her that I wanted to write about Sara in *Girljock* but I was afraid to do it.

Allison absolved my hesitancy by telling me, "There was one rule we followed, those of us who arranged the memorial service and who were close to her at the end, and this is the rule. Everything is okay."

"Should I write, then, about her party where Roxxie was born?" I asked Allison, who doesn't call me Roxxie, she calls me by my real name.

"Yes," she said, "she'll like that very much, she always likes to be at the beginnings of things."

Sara's memories are now haunting me with every touch of the keyboard. They have become, like a once-upon-a-time children's story, enchanted with all the sing-songiness and lulling qualities of some faraway imaginary land. Once upon a time I felt so young I didn't even know what, and I met a woman that I've known for what seems like an eternity and now she's gone. This now is my memory, those branches, those trees; the postcards I'd sent her; the peacefulness inside I had gained from being her friend, that massage, our friendship, everything she ever told me, hearing her laugh that noisy laugh, that infectious laugh. Just a feeling, just a story, just a bunch of letters on this page I write to you. I missed her memorial service, but maybe this small collection of words will do.

Products
for
Girljocks

PART FOUR

4

Nation of Jogbras

by Romy Kozak

Several years ago, before jogbras were just coming out, I went into an athletic store and asked a sales clerk if he carried the "jogbra." He answered with "I don't think we carry that kind of sneaker."
—*Jeanne, writing in America Online's* Girljock *folder*

Why is it that the most essential elements in life get the least attention? On a given day, within fifteen minutes of turning on the radio, you can find out exactly how much is in that lottery jackpot you have a one in bizillion chance of winning (less, really, since being against regressive taxation you never buy a ticket, though since the latest Nicholas Cage/Bridget Fonda movie you have considered it as a way of finally getting a date with a gorgeous femme); you will hear what the weather is like in Livermore, California (as though you ever go there, except maybe for an occasional soccer tournament); and you can learn the exact terms of leasing a Lexus, with monthly payments that are larger than your gross monthly income.

But where are those really necessary soundbites, informing you as to who currently has the best deal on dental dams (or whether anyone but Good Vibrations or your friendly neighborhood medical equipment supply warehouse actually stocks them) or what one should really look out for in selecting a roll of Saran Wrap (regular or microwaveable)? I could go on, but let us stop and explore but one stellar example of such a neglected girljock essential: the jogbra. Admittedly, there are a few among us for whom the jogbra is as indispensable as, say, a jockstrap. Perhaps even less so. But most of us are profoundly beholden to the jogbra; whether we are aware of it or not it is the *sine qua non* of our athletic existence.

Think about it. You're out on a postnightclub Sunday morning ramble, having pulled on jeans, a sweatshirt, and your Docs, the laces of which you still haven't managed to tie up, and stumbled out the door in instinctive need of finding material evidence that smoke-free air still exists somewhere in the city. "Oops," you suddenly realize, waking up slightly after a speeding Miata makes your flattop start to curl involuntarily, "forgot the chest harness thing." Oh well, just keep shuffling along—the "I don't wanna face the day let's just have a good look at this pavement" stoop is working well for you too. But then, you see it. Actually, you've been hearing it for a few blocks now, the inimitable thunk of a perfectly arched chip, the staccato commands of a beautifully executed impromptu give-and-go. But it isn't until you turn the corner that the sounds begin to resonate in your mind and fall into that endearingly familiar pattern. You look up, and there it is: ye auld Sunday morning pick-up soccer game.

Suddenly, you're alive. Excitement courses through your veins; you've been given an energy transfusion that makes a space shuttle lift-off look like the beginning of a banana slug race. You gallop over to the touch line, and eagerly start to count the number of players: seven on that side, and yes! six on the other. Somebody notices you eyeing the pitch: "Hey," she beckons, "Wanna play?"

Photo © Nancy Boutilier

just took off for the hospital with a broken leg, but she forgot her cleats. If they fit you can use 'em." Undaunted by this explanation of your good fortune at finding the teams lopsided, you rummage through the equipment pile until you find your treasure. Old Adidas Copa Mundiales Teams: "Too bad about the leg," you reflect, "cuz she sure knew her soccer shoes." You slip them on; magic! They fit. Now then, your jeans. At least they're loose-fit; if those guys in that Levi's commercial can do bicycle kicks in jeans, then so can you. As for the grass stains? "I can always call my mom,"

You nod back, grinning, and then begin to survey the state of your attire. Even for the notoriously minimalist sport of soccer, you're not in great shape. The Docs? The leather's so scuffed it might well belong to a pair of soccer shoes that have been to Flushing Meadow (site of the New York Gay Games soccer tournament—it was covered in stones) and back, but let's face it, twelve-eyes and corner kicks just don't go together. You call out to your future teammate, "Any extra cleats?"

"Sure," she replies, after clearing a cross out of the box with such consummate skill your toes begin to tingle in anticipation, "Someone

you decide. She spent sixteen years erasing the signs of baby-dykehood from your wardrobe; the attempt was futile, admittedly, but she still gets excited at the thought of subjecting impossible stains to violent deaths. The sweatshirt is the one you wear to soccer practice anyway, and if you get too hot you can always . . .

Oh no. There it is. Or rather, isn't. That lack you've always known would creep back in upon you at the most inopportune moment; that mark-under-erasure, *pace* Luce Irigaray, of what being female is all about. The absence of a jogbra dashes all your nascent hopes of playing soccer that beautiful sunny morning. No goal is worth suffering that graceless, painful *boom-boom* (okay, I'm exaggerating; personally, it is more of a *wunk-wunk* while most of my soccer teammates have agreed upon *wing-wing*) of vagabond boobs caught up in their own syncopated battle with gravity and behaving like two uninvited, squabbling extra passengers on your attempted flight down the wing. No amount of dribbling glory is worth the back and shoulder aches of tomorrow morning, afternoon, and evening, assuming, that is, that you make it through the game without being sidelined by an ill-advised and poorly timed chest trap. Feeling naked, exposed, violated, you flop down (all three of you) onto the pile of equipment bags and dejectedly begin unlacing the Copas. Ms. Thing calls over to you from the field. "Don't they fit?"

"Yeah, they're perfect," you reply, "but I forgot my jogbra." Her answering look is sympathetic but helpless: a sweet shrug that says, "I've done all I could." "Thanks anyway," you mumble, stuffing your feet into your boots and skulking away.

Yes, the jogbra is indispensable. But how many of us ever stop to think of how indebted we are? How many of us really take care of our jogbras in a way that reflects their position at the fulcrum of our girljock universe? How many of us possess a systematic mental inventory of jogbra styles, sources, and prices that is anything close to our knowledge of, say, soccer shoes, tennis rackets, or softball bats? Granted, the fault is not all ours. In general, even the best sporting goods meccas have but a paltry selection of jogbras, most of which are made from scrap fabric by exploited workers in Central America or Southeast Asia for like-ly pennies a bra. No two are quite alike; in fact, you're often in luck if you can find even one with two straps of matching length. Continuing the traditionally Neanderthal ignorance of the commercial sports world toward women athletes, single sport stores, or suppliers, such as those catering to soccer, don't bother carrying jogbras at all; predictably, they seem happy to have us buy into whatever men want, but they offer no recognition of any specific needs women might have (other than, of course, the requisite hot pink trim that makes the "women's version" of even the best running shoes look hopelessly dorky).

Despite this generic obliviousness, however, a small but thriving subculture has begun to emerge around the jogbra. Some jogbra historians note the coincidence of this phenomenon with the development of the uniboob jogbra (also known as the "pullover" style) in the late 1970s. Exactly how women athletes managed before then is an issue crying out for Ph.D. treatment, but the surge in jogbra awareness around and since the discovery of the uniboob is indisputable. Suddenly, scurrying off to the washroom to change into one's uniform has become unnecessary; even the most modest among us can blithely tear off one T-shirt and slip on another, irregardless of our position on the field, confident that everything is properly tucked away, flat as can be. ("Is there anything in there?" we are sometimes even moved to wonder of each other.) Furtive glances at one's teammates in the changing room have given way to exclamations of delight and admiration: "Lisa, *where* did you get that gorgeous jogbra? It's absolutely divine!" According to Missy Park, founder of Title IX Women's Sports Equipment, women are buying jogbras at an unprecedented rate: "Seventy-five to eighty percent of all our orders have bras on them," she said (really, she did), and "of our ten top-selling items, four are bras." In the midst of this boom, an impressive *bricolage* of jogbra lore has taken shape.

"To dry or not to dry" is, for instance, one major source of dispute. Throwing your jogbra in the dryer, predictably, significantly shortens its lifespan: the cotton thread shrinks, the Lycra fluffs into little balls, and the dry, brittle elastic twists and breaks. Living in a neighborhood fairly well populated with girljocks, I frequently participate in minutes of silence at the local laundromat for old faithfuls who "just didn't make it this time"; how well we know that feeling of irreparable loss. Yet who among us would willingly single out a jogbra from an immense pile of dripping laundry, only to carry it home, soaking wet, and let it hang for days over the shower rod, where it never really does get completely dry? A similar argument holds for the merits of bleaching. "One bad bleach can ruin your whole bra," I once read on a bumper sticker (okay, I didn't really, but it's true). Yet your jogbra is perpetually stationed on the front lines of battle against sweat and B.O. Is it possible to get rid of the indescribable stench of an aging but well-loved jogbra, without killing the patient in the process? Baking soda seems to the latest solution to all postnuclear hygiene quandaries; does it have anything to offer jogbras? Every team, of course, has at least one ultrafemme who stares, wide-eyed, lips pursed, and silent through a discussion on any of these issues.

Having never sweated or stunk, being always freshly aglow, she answers inquiries as to how long she wears a single jogbra with an incredulous, "Shouldn't jogbras last forever?"

Perhaps the most enduring subject of jogbra deliberation, though, is the decades-long debate between the merits of uniboob ("smushed like a pancake" re: Park), versus Playtex styling ("lifted and separated" re: Jane Wyman). Park notes that Title IX's best-selling jogbra is the classic uniboob model known as the "Frogbra": "It lets you leap," she explains, "but not bounce." Another favorite is simply the JogBra by JBI, which Park affectionately calls "the bomber": "It gives you the best of both worlds; you can wear it from work to the workout." But Park adds, another probable reason the JB is such a good seller is "the model shot is really great." The trend in current jogbra design, she continues, is toward treating each breast separately. For many women, such as those who have had a masectomy and/or wear a breast prosthesis, the uniboob style is simply not an option. Others merely don't want the uniboob look, and opt instead for underwire models.

I feel, personally, the advent of the uniboob has decreased by a factor of about a thousand the likelihood that my own boobs will be neighboring my knees when I hit fifty. Even as a twelve-year-old I knew I was resolutely odd in a world where all women had breasts of no more and no less than an even number of inches between thirty-two and forty-four (I also thought then that all women got their periods on the first of each calendar month, thus setting me up for a tremendous shock when mine arrived promptly one July 16). I felt I would never fit in, nor did I want to; I didn't even want breasts, and, like many baby dykes, wore the baggiest sweaters I could find lying about my brother's closet to conceal their embarrassing presence. When I did finally find a bra style that was marginally bearable, it was naturally instantly discontinued. But then came the uniboob, and suddenly, the world was mine again. Sure, there was absolutely no consistency among sizings: S, M, and L often seemed to mean So-so, Massive, and Little as often as Small, Medium, and Large. But it didn't matter. No poking, no pinching, no fiddly hooks, no see-through lace to stop me from taking off my shirt on a miserably hot day; I could even play skins in the pickup soccer game on the esplanade down by the pier. At last I had found myself; never again would I feel such an outcast—I was home.

Indisputable evidence as to the superiority of the uniboob/pullover style presented itself, in my view, to the general public a few years ago at a Stanford Women's basketball game. Halfway through the second half, as Stanford was about to put the ball in from an out-of-bounds turnover, All-American forward Val Whiting suddenly started to stumble off the court, hunching over slightly and clutching her elbow. Coach Tara Vanderveer stood up in alarm and a murmur rose through the crowd: "Is she hurt? What happened? Did we miss something? Is she going to be all right?" Reaching the bench, Val muttered something to an assistant coach, who followed her into the locker room, barely stifling a grin. With oracular certainty, one of the numerous gray-haired dykes standing two rows in front of us revealed the mystery: "It's just her jogbra. It

came undone." The crowd sat down again, chortling but truly relieved, and the game resumed. "Poor Val," I reflected. "If only she'd worn a uniboob."

And yet, as Missy Park observes, there is no single ultimate jogbra that will be all things for all women. In her words, "It simply doesn't exist. There are different bras for different needs." Indeed, girljocks have been accommodating jogbras to their individual requirements for years. Those in the throes of physiological reproduction, for instance, have discovered wearing two and three jogbras at a time to be a useful antidote to their ever-increasing mammary mass. Types of preferred jogbras also differ according to what sports one plays, with low versus high impact being the key differentiating factor. In all fairness, too, there are times when any type of jogbra seems not to be the best choice, in strategic terms. A uniboob devotee on my soccer team recently switched to wearing black lace underwire, about the same time, the rest of us couldn't help but notice, she started dating another woman on the team. It's a sacrifice I couldn't make under any circumstances, but I must admit, it seems to be working.

Jogbra diversity has been even more in evidence since its all-important crossover into the realm of staple nightclub attire. Fashion mavens such as *Girljock*'s own Femme Jock recommend keeping your sporting and slutting jogbras separate, at least between washes, but in a pinch, and especially during a particularly notorious San Francisco soccer festival "For lesbians and any woman willing to be mistaken for one," a few drops of cologne can take you direct from pitch to party. Some hardcore femmes, of course, allow nothing to come between them and their silk and lace underwires, but many others happily compromise between comfort and style, opting for the shirred divide, wide lace strap and teardrop back opening of a stylish spandex-Lycra number. Far from the exclusive property of femmes, moreover, the jogbra is arguably the most crucial individual element in recent renaissance of the bulldagger swagger (a.k.a., the return of the butch to lesbian communities throughout the continent). Finally, the considerable time investment required for a firm and secure breast-binding has been reduced to the simple maneuver of "stretch and stuff" familiar to all uniboob disciples.

So what lies ahead for the trusty jogbra? Is it to remain the unacknowledged heroine of our athletic lives, the paradoxical nexus of an essentially oxymoronic girljock worldview? A noble fate, perhaps, but Park and her colleagues at Title IX have different ideas, namely, market research. "It's unbelievable the number of comments and questions we get," says Park. Something *had* to be organized, she explains, to figure out what women want and need in a jogbra, and "somehow, we ended up with this van. . . ." Thus, as *Girljock* goes to press, the Title IX Bra Recycling Van is on its maiden voyage to a 10K road race in Sacramento, where the "bra experts" it will be transporting will endeavor to talk with partic-ipating (and visiting) women athletes about their personal jogbra needs. The "experts" will examine old jogbras to find out what women are wearing, what they like and don't like, and what they would like to see in jogbra design. They'll also offer a free fitting for a new bra, and five dollars off an order for turning in an old one. To learn about future Van voyages, call Title IX at (510) 549-2592. Exactly what is Park & Co. planning to do with all the recycled jogbras they collect? "If they're still wearable, we'll probably give them to a homeless women's shelter," she offers. And if they're not? "Well, we were looking for a way to sound-proof my office." Truly, we live in a nation— and who knows, perhaps we even work in an insulated office complex—of jogbras.

Ode to a Jogbra

(sung to the tune of
"You Are My Sunshine")
My trusty jogbra,
my smelly jogbra
You save my boobs from
that dread "wing wing"
You crush my chest in—
To a big flat pancake
Oh please don't take
my jogbra away.

Loving and Leaving Your Jogbras

by Stacey Foss

Those excitable breasts! Thinking of holding them as close to your body as possible, and gaining more maximal streamlining! Defying Gravity! Helping you conquer the unconquerable! Here are some critical jogbra pointers from *Girljock*.

TO TOSS OR NOT TO TOSS

No one can give us a real definitive answer on when you should throw one of these away. This product, unlike a regular wired bra or a sexy, thinly strapped bra made of lace, never completely dies out. It may get a little faded out and grungy but unlike the previous bra-wearing situation where you wear the thing to the point were it starts to disintegrate, rot, or decay, the jogbra is always kind of . . . wearable. Girljocks everywhere can be found cramming these bras into the backs of their socks drawers, waiting for that day when they have misplaced all their other favorite lucky, black jogbras. Their extreme gratitude for not throwing these oldies-but-goodies away comes through the night before their rugby final. Or, when you've misplaced a bikini top: that old jogbra can come in really handy.

OLDIES BUT GOODIES

This lack of initiative in throwing things out is especially apparent with some people in their day-to-day lives. For some reason they cannot throw anything away. This also holds true in their inability to trash their worn-out, tired, bitchy girlfriends. This is where the parallel begins between jogbras and girlfriends—both never completely fall apart, they just start to smell pretty bad. Regular washings in Woolite, and not drying them in the dryer can add to the lifespan of a jogbra, yes, but this *Girljock* reporter has found this following gem of advice: Completely replace your jogbra and Girlfriend supply either once a year, or when they start to smell really bad. But don't think the sniff test will work if you sniff them after exercise: You must sniff them in their resting state following thorough washing and drying. For every new bra purchased, take one old supporter and throw it away. Although the gesture is sincere, the manners department at *Girljock* does not recommend giving these bras to the Salvation Army or your local Women's Center. Giving them to your dog as a new chew toy is an appropriate way to use up every last inch of elastic, or burning them is the next best way if you are having trouble completely giving in to the fact that your dog has taken your favorite fashion statement.

Only financially struggling athletes are allowed to bend these rules.

SIZING

Sizing a jogbra can be a very tricky subject.

It is true that some packages come with those charts on the back, but they are freaky charts: They don't always work, and every different model of jogbra is a little different in how it holds your boobs. The biggest questions facing the future potential purchaser: Is it O.K. to try jogbras on in the dressing room? If you put them that close to your skin, aren't they more like bathing suits? And are you supposed to try them on with underwear underneath? Go figure: No jock we have asked about store jogbra procedures knows the answer! After calling various stores, almost no salesperson can illuminate us on this pressing question.

What the hell does small, medium, and large really mean? It is sort of like real sizes in department stores: One minute you're a size six and the next minute you are size eight, for ten minutes you get to enjoy yourself as a lithe six and the next time you look in the mirror fitting into the eight your belly, unnoticeable before is now pouching out all over and your once toned, flat stomach is now round and limp.

After many unsuccessful tries, our most useful information was delivered by a very nice salesman from Koenings Sporting Goods store who, although first admitting his embarrassment discussing the topic, did later admit that he intimately knew the jogbra product line. This salesman, who knew more than any of the other salespeople we talked to, informed me that if you are a 34–36 C D, you must wear medium- to large-size jogbras. He also said there is even a bra for cool weather called the *cool max*. It somehow keeps the wetness off of your body as it magically disappears into the fabric.

Finding stores where jogbras are sold can be very difficult, and many of the most common-sense obvious places do not have them. Oftentimes, when calling a department store and asking for the right department, they often mislead you. Many don't know where they could be found and very few even carry them. Many of these stores send you to the lingerie department when they should be sending you to women's athletic wear. Nordstroms may not carry jogbras, but I did get some very, very helpful information from the saleswoman in the San Francisco store lingerie department. She herself was a 34 DD and has found that wearing two jogbras did not even support her like the Vanity Fair Super Bra. Vanity Fair Super Bra is complete with an underwire and a cup so supportive that our 34 DD salesperson says it is the best athletic bra out there. She next countered, like any good salesperson, by telling me "This bra is on sale right now for $15.90."

The most successful line selling these products was Champion. Also, if you are looking for many exciting, bright colors, Champion's seasonal line will give you that added fashion-forward edge. Since we heretofore never knew that Champion made anything other than men's toys, weights, and equipment, we decided to call this company and find out the secret to their success.

The idea that they made something for women that was as successful as their men's products made me extremely excited. Suzette, a customer service representative who has been working for Champion for over ten years, struck me as very East-coast and completely pro-Champion.

She also loved the jogbra that Champion put out and gave me some background history on the first women's chest supporter.

Champion, the originator of the jogbra fifteen years ago, has its original hanging in the Smithsonian today. She also told me at that time it was created by jogbra before it became Champion, but they had the same parent company. When I questioned Suzette on how these jogbras were made, she pointed out that there were two types of bras: the panel type which minimizes the chest area by pressing the chest against the wall in an even motion. These are mostly designed for the small to medium chest sizes. However, with heftier cups the panel type is not nearly as effective, and there is a more gripping cup, known as the "cut and sewn" cup. You, dear jogbra wearers, do not need to cut and sew them, the company does it for you: But these are extra strong.

How much does the average jogbra compress the bustiness of the chest?

According to Suzette at Champion, this bra minimizes chest size by 25 to 50 percent. *Girljock* magazine wanted to challenge this figure for the truth. So we got together some of our own jocks to do the chest measurement test. This, by the way, was the best part of doing this article. Depending on the types of breasts we measured for compression, we found that breasts are certainly, um, compressed by jogbras, and held closer to the chest. The 50 percent figure was not one we ever reached in our studies, at least, not yet.

ETIQUETTE-OLOGY OF THE JOGBRA

jogbra etiquette is very important, especially when it comes to the dating scene. Should you wear a black jogbra under a white T-shirt and go out to a club like this?

My answer is no. Please, if you are dating, and feel you must go out in a jogbra and T-shirt combination, wear a non-see-through top. If you do not follow my advice, you will just look like a jock that cannot dress herself for doodleysquat. We only recommend this jogbra-only dance floor style for either: post-tournament parties, or parties where the heat and humidity is so very high that you have had to strip it all way down and you got to the jogbra very naturally.

Still, hear my advice: You can show off your hunky body with a sleeveless, low cut, navel-exposing sexy top. This is not a hard thing to find at the stores and it is even easier to take one of your favorite shirts and cut it for purposes of style.

Looking for Ms. Goodbar

by Laura Miller

Workout videos are my beat, but I can't say I was sorry when our editrix, Roxxie, suggested a change. I was trembling on the brink, contemplating a foray into the dark continent of the Richard Simmons weight loss subculture (Realm of late night infomercials, Bill Haley aerobics, and the morbidly obese) when the call came.

"Wanna do a review of those sports candy bars? We can get a couple of people together, do a taste test, and then see if any of them make us want to exercise!"

"Listen, Roxxie, I can do a taste test, but not even three double *lattes* can make me want to exercise."

Later that week a brave handful of women gathered in a Mission District café to face one of the greatest challenges of their lives: eating at least a small amount of thirteen different "energy bars." Our adventuresses included soccer stars Kathleen Bonnet and Jodi Fechner, militantly sedentary photographer Phyllis Christopher, a karate practitioner who insisted on being referred to only as "Natalia," our editrix, and yours slothfully.

The playing field was far from level. Roxxie rashly spoiled her metabolism on a cinnamon-

raisin bagel while Phyllis announced that she had "fasted for hours beforehand." I elected to begin with the least-appealing looking item and slowly work up to the most appetizing. It was going to be a long night, and even the waitress paled when she realized what we proposed to do.

By the end of the evening more than one of us was making a face like a cat coughing up a hairball, and there was a grisly pile of sticky brownish energy bar fragments at one end of the table. Someone had done something unsavory to a baguette with another scrap. No one was happy. But we had our results, and here they are:

Spirutein High Protein Energy Meal (1.4 oz., 159 cal.): Only hubris could dub this fairly typical specimen a "meal." Like most of the bars, its initial flavor is innocuous, but a gustatory downturn soon sets in. Our tasters' comments: "Smells like instant breakfast or chocolate covered vitamins." "Good, but a little gritty." "Sweetly cardboard." "Horrible." "It makes me want to run—to the bathroom."

Twin Lab Ultra Fuel High Energy Sports Bar (4.87 oz., 490 cal.): Roxxie suggested that one hundred curls with this hefty entry would whip any girljock into shape. Inexplicably mammoth and excessively named, the TLUFHESB comes in a package that reminded Jodi of hair dye: "It doesn't look like a food." Other remarks: "Looks like twenty-year-old baby food." "Taffylike and flavorless. Sort of like caulking." "You can use it to fix your shoes. It has a bad aftertaste that kicks in later. Really bad." Kathleen suggested sending a box to the other team. "They'd die before the game."

Stoker High Performance Energy Bar (2.6 oz., 252 cal.): This item, while pronounced "grainy looking," proved to be popular with the more hardcore athletes. Some of us liked its dude-alacious name, while others approved of the "sexy, androgynous" figure on the package. Jodi found it "gives you some room to chew." The Stoker gave Roxxie "a feeling of hope" for some reason; she took a second bite and claimed to "feel like jumping." Others dubbed it "Paste made with sawdust."

Bee Pollen Sunrise (1.5 oz., no nutritional info): Feelings ran high on this, the hippie entry. "Tastes like athlete's foot powder," said Jodi, while Roxxie shrieked "Bummer!" afterwards elaborating, "That was a bad experience." "They fool you. The aftertaste hits like a ton of bricks like a bee sting!" quoth Kathleen. Phyllis kind of liked it.

Hoffman's Energy Bar Club Sandwich (2 oz., 296 cal.): "This isn't an energy bar; it's a s'more," announced Roxxie of this graham cracker–based item. Nevertheless, she said it made her feel like "dancing really fast." Phyllis declared Hoffman's her "favorite so far," while Kathleen dismissed it as "a crowd pleaser, a candy, not a health bar."

Tiger Milk Bars, Peanut Butter and Honey and "Protein" Flavor (1.25 oz., 160 cal.): This bar sparked unsettling ruminations on what "protein flavor" could be. "Oh no, this one tastes vitaminy!" warned Roxxie, although Jodi disagreed. "Ever eaten a tire?" Kathleen queried. The peanut butter and honey flavor was even less popular; Roxxie spit it out, proclaiming it a "nightmare." Tiger Milk bars remind me of old-fashioned health food stores, the kind that never seemed to have any food in them, just shelves and shelves of bottles, pills, and powders. It tastes like it belongs there, too.

Power Bar: Apple Cinnamon, Wild Berry, Malt Nut and Chocolate flavors (all 2.25 oz and 225 cal.): Power Bars turned out to be a product some of our panelists consume regularly. Kathleen in particular was prone to discussing their merits and proper usage at length. She was elated by the appearance of the new Apple Cinnamon bar since "We've had to suffer with just three flavors," and declared the new product "yummy and crunchy." A schism appeared when Roxxie spit out a sample of the same bar, exclaiming "BAD!" The Wild Berry flavor was likened, visually, to raw meat. Natalia, who had abandoned the taste test in favor of falafel, did deign to sample this one, which she said "tastes like the smell of fish bait." The Malt Nut was Roxxie's favorite, while the Chocolate reminded us of chocolate oat bran spackle. "They've got to get over this oat bran thing," said Roxxie. She then informed us that eating two Power Bars in a row "really speeds up the digestive process."

Nectar Nugget Peanut Butter Crunch (1.12 oz, 120 cal.): "This is not for sports," Kathleen said scornfully, but her objections were drowned out by exclamations of "This is goooood" and "Wait, don't take the whole thing!" Essentially a "health food" version of a Reese's Peanut Butter Cup, the Nectar Nugget hardly qualified as a full-fledged energy bar, but most of us were too eager to replace the synthetic aftertastes in our mouths with something resembling real food to complain.

Panda All Natural Licorice Bar (1⅛ oz, 110 cal.): Another ought-to-have-been disqualified contender, this entry got preferential treatment from Roxxie, a fan. "Happy, happy, happy," she beamed. "It makes me feel like doing push-ups!" Others pronounced it "an excellent antidote."

Of the "real energy bars," Kathleen and Jodi

both came out in favor of the Stoker for its "zest of oatmeal" and easy-to-open package. Jodi finds it "looser than the Power Bars. You don't feel like a big glob's going down." However, the Apple Cinnamon Power Bar still brings Kathleen "fond memories of childhood when I'd eat one and go out and kick someone's butt." (Perhaps they add testosterone to that one?)

Roxxie liked the taste of the licorice the best, but when she needs that pregame "extra reserve of energy to stay competitive with the younger, faster editions," she'll stick with the Malt Nut Power Bar, her current regular.

Natalia announced that she "used to do Power Bars when I was a jock," but remained reticent when asked if they worked. "It felt like the right thing to do," she said with characteristic inscrutability.

"They all taste bad," insisted Phyllis. "Everything that's good for you tastes bad, and I don't exercise. I still don't see why it's necessary to eat these things." That said, Ms. Christopher was the only panelist who could find anything positive in the Bee Pollen bar, or "foot power bar," as Jodi dubbed it.

As a sloth, I speak for the whole community when I question the Eurocentric impulse behind these so-called "energy bars." There's something wrong with the values of a society where people eat to exercise rather than exercise to eat. Many people don't realize that energy bars didn't even exist in Native American cultures—and we all know that they did everything right. Perhaps it's time to rethink some of our basic assumptions about food and exercise in America.

Pass the rigatoni.

Everything You Always Wanted to Know About Trading Cards but Didn't Know Who to Ask

by Winifred Simon

There are a bezillion trading cards currently in existence. Of this total overload of available cards, a teeny, tiny number feature women athletes.

This makes collecting women's cards both easier and harder. Easier, because it's very simple to focus your efforts and zero in on your target. Harder, because there are so few cards and most dealers/traders are not very interested in them.

FANS of Women's Sports is interested in them, and perhaps through sharing information with fans around the country, we can all benefit.

With that in mind, we'll get the ball rolling in this issue with the hopes that you will respond with ideas, requests, information, questions, etc.

WHY COLLECT CARDS?

As you may remember from your old chewing-gum-pack trading card days, collecting is fun. (If you're too young to remember those days, you bought the sheet of gum and got the card as a bonus.) It's exciting to find cards of your favorite players, trade for ones you are missing, and look through your collection. And today's cards are a lot more beautiful to look at!

Collecting also adds a new dimension to traveling, as you can pursue your hobby in any city you may be visiting.

HOW TO GET STARTED

The most accessible sources are friends who are collectors, card shops, and card shows. If you have any acquaintances who are interested in cards, start there.

Next step is to look up card shops in the Yellow Pages. They're probably listed under "Comics." Call up and ask if they have any cards with women athletes.

When you get to a shop that has some women's cards, pick up a copy of the latest *Beckett Magazine* for the information and price guidelines. You will probably be most interested in the Basketball, Hockey or Focus on Future Stars issues. Refer to the pricing guide to see what a fair cost would be for any cards. Cards are generally listed by the year of issue, company, set, and card number. The dealer will show you how to look up particular cards. *Beckett's* listed values will be on the high side.

Tuff Stuff is another useful publication and has listings of a lot of smaller publishers and vintage cards.

Most shops sell singles in addition to packs. Don't invest in any packs unless you have friends who might be interested in trading the

guys' cards or you are interested in collecting them yourself. There will not be enough women's cards in the packs to make it worthwhile.

Watch the local sports section to see ads for sportscard shows. In addition to dealers with shops, you will find many collectors who have become vendors. Ask at each table to see if the seller has any women's cards. Leave your name and phone number in case the vendor remembers any cards later or knows someone else who might have some.

When the word gets around that you are looking for women's cards, sellers or traders will start looking through their zillion men's cards for the one or two women's cards they may have tucked away. Be patient.

Once you get some experience, you might want to try some of the online traders' services. Collector's Direct Network is one of the many available (800-556-9113). *Tuff Stuff* is filled with ads for others.

HOW TO BUY CARDS

Remember that any price is negotiable. Also, prices go down as well as up, and since a card may be easier to find right after its issue, you might not want to wait.

The seller will have a relevant *Beckett's* price to use as a starting point. Many cards will be in the ten- to fifty-cent range. Some, including hockey player Manon Rheaume, can run up to $150 for a autographed card. You can expect a show vendor to be more willing to bargain, but the stores will also bend on price. Don't just agree to pay the first price asked for a card.

Handle and store cards carefully and pay attention to the condition of cards you are purchasing. Corners should be sharp and show little or no wear. In cards with borders, the image (front and back) should be centered for highest value. Other flaws to watch out for are surface bubbles, slanted edge-cuts, warping, and any surface damage such as scratches, stains, fading, or marks.

Keep your collection in individual sleeves, sheet holders, or specially made plastic boxes. Card shops will have all the supplies you need. Remember that humidity, sunlight, fire, and silverfish are death for cards.

WHAT'S OUT THERE?

There are so few cards with women on them that most dealers will know right away if they have any. That doesn't mean, however, that there isn't a good variety of women. The challenge is to find them.

Currently on the market are several beautiful basketball cards. Upper Deck has a set of ninety-two cards of USA Basketball. Seven of them are women: Jennifer Azzi, Daedra Charles, Lisa Leslie, Katrina McClain, Dawn Staley, Sheryl Swoopes, and Cheryl Miller. Cheryl is also pictured on brother Reggie's card #38.

Flair has a set of one hundred and twenty USA Basketball cards including six women's "legends": Carol Blazejowski, Teresa Edwards, Nancy Lieberman-Cline, Ann Meyers, Pat Summitt, and Lynette Woodard.

The woman with the most cards currently is hockey goaltender Manon Rheaume, who is the subject of thirty-nine cards, all of them by Classic. She is also featured on the cover of the October *Beckett Focus on Future Stars*.

Classic has also issued cards for two other women, Cammi Granato and Erin Whitten, and is considering sets including players from the U.S. Women's National Hockey Team.

Another 1994 Upper Deck set, the World Cup Contenders, has ten members of the U.S. women's national team: April Heinrichs, Mary Harvey, and Julie Foudy all have cards.

Tetrad has a 1994 Signature Rookies set with two women, Shannon Miller and Picabo Street.

The Ted Williams Card Company has seven women from the All-American Girls Professional Baseball League in a 1994 set.

NETPRO has issued a tennis tour stars series. The first, in 1993, had cards for forty-four women and five women's doubles cards.

Cards for women in other sports sometimes show up, and there have been many different Olympic sets over the years that include women.

College teams sometimes issue sets of cards, but these are harder to acquire unless you have a local contact. UConn and Virginia put out cards last season, Tennessee has had several over the years, and Texas Tech celebrated their national championship with a set in 1993. Most of these cards are in the hands of fans and not likely to show up from vendors.

Coors apparently put out promo cards for the Silver Bullets baseball team this summer. Although not confirmed, it is rumored that Classic will be coming out with cards for the Silver Bullets sometime soon. Keep your eyes open.

JUST DO IT

Now that you've got the basics down, there's nothing to stand in the way of getting your collection started. Make your first purchase and you'll be hooked. You will learn what you need to know as you go along. *Fans of Women's Sports* can help by running listings of cards folks are looking to find or trade. If anyone out there has the Nancy Lieberman-Cline from the 1994 Flair set, please get in touch right away. I'll make you a good trade.

All Workout Video Action

by Chief Girl Sloth Divinity, Laura Miller

An eyebrow or two may rise upon the announcement that a girl sloth has been chosen as "videotape workout" reviewer for *Girljock*; so many are still unclear on the concept of Deep Slothdom. Let me reiterate before I begin: The final and most imperative guideline for the committed girl sloth is "Maintain fetchingness." From the elegant state of fetchingness flows favors, the lifeblood of a sloth. A girl sloth must keep her figure or she'll soon find herself forced to pay someone to repair her stereo, drive her to cocktail parties, or put up kitchen shelves. She may even be forced to take on full time employment to finance these extravagances.

Workout tapes provide every girl sloth with a fitness regimen compatible with the first guideline of slothdom: "Leave your apartment as seldom as possible." However, they often suffer from two serious flaws: annoying performers and deeply stupid music. Since music and performers are pretty much all there is to such videos, the badness of a bad workout tape can be of daunting totality. Clearly, some consumer guidance is necessary.

CHERFITNESS: A NEW ATTITUDE

(CBS/FOX Video, 1991): This girl sloth's current favorite, *CherFitness* is an efficient, intensive ninety-minute workout broken into three modules: step aerobics, abdominal and

back strengthening, and a lower body workout. It's challenging without being hard on the back or knees. So much for the workout, now on to the important stuff.

The music is good; this is the only workout tape I've ever encountered with "Born to Be Wild" on the soundtrack. The few obligatory Cher songs back up segments that, due to some fancy footwork, require considerable concentration, and it's possible to make it through the tape without having to really listen to them.

The main attraction of *CherFitness* is, of course, Cher herself. A longtime favorite with girl sloths for her air of sardonic indolence, Cher is a comforting compatriot who forthrightly admits to hating exercise, wisecracking throughout. The director of the videotape cleverly casts Cher as one of the gals, rather than the workout leader. The directions (mostly "Squeeze yer butt!") are called out by one Kelli Roberts, an Australian who looks like a giant tendon with eyes and a little tuft of blonde hair on top.

The rest of the performers (all white and female, in flagrant defiance of most fitness tapes' earnest and somehow pathetic commitment to racial and gender parity), look like starlets-who-could-tell-you-a-story-or-two, rather than the bouncy secretary type. All the "bodywear" is black, and Cher gets to wear three different outfits, all pretty cute, but the ruffles on the butt of first one have got to go. A lurid Malibu Beach sunset is back-projected onto the wall behind the performers, lending a certain drama to the proceedings. The final cooldown and stretch session is done lying down, highly appreciated by this girl sloth, who always savors that delicious moment of thinking, "Well, thank God *that's* over."

KATHY SMITH'S WEIGHT LOSS WORKOUT

(Media, 1990): Smith, who used to be a gymnast, holds a special appeal for most girljocks. She comes across as a legitimate athlete and never says things like, "Come on ladies, let's work on those love handles!" Her former cuddly-butch look, so apparent in the 1984 tape *Ultimate Video Workout*, is gone. In *Weight Loss*, she's more bony and conventionally attractive, like a model in *Mademoiselle* magazine, but she's still pleasantly cheerful without ever degenerating into perkiness. Think of her as the straight sister that you genuinely like despite her suburban ways.

Kathy's into set as well as costume changes, and she's got a thing for weirdly sanitized-looking "urban" backdrops (imagine what the Osmonds would use if they performed a rap song). Director Robert Tinnell employs some flashy editing which only serves to make the routines harder to follow. My guess is that everyone making workout tapes, like people in the porn business, really wishes they were doing something else—in Tinnell's case, making music videos.

The workout itself is thorough and as fun as can be expected. The music is okay

(although they print the title of each song in the lower left hand corner of the screen, another sign of Tinnell's MTV aspirations). As with most of Smith's routines, the emphasis on precipitate lunging makes *Weight Loss* rather hard on the knees. The tape is prefaced with a pep talk by Kathy and concludes with some basic diet recommendations. Kathy is one of the few video fitness gurus who can pull off the obligatory inspirational prologue without sounding like an idiot. Cher, for instance, seems to be suffering from a dissociative personality disorder in the hyper-edited intro to her tape.

JANE FONDA

Beware any Jane Fonda tape: Don't even think about it. Jane is a truly scary person, with the creepy intensity so characteristic of compulsives. She seems to have gone hog-wild in the weight room, focusing particularly on the muscles in her shoulders and neck. In *Lean Routine*, she appears to be frozen in a perpetual shrug and moves around as though she were suspended from a stick affixed to the middle of her back, like one of those painted wooden toys made in Denmark and sold at Cost Plus Imports.

Jane hires a lot of whoopers and yellers to back her up during her routines, no doubt to counteract her own aura of grim determination. Their synthetic enthusiasm and bogus patter will make you cringe. The blonde Texan (a Fonda regular) has inspired several of my most vivid homicidal fantasies. Furthermore, instead of leaving me relaxed and invigorated, *Lean Routine* made me feel like I'd been waiting tables for hours, aching feet and all.

ALL WORKOUT VIDEO ACTION, PT.II

"You've been thinking: I love tape one so much, I wish that Cher would make tape two." . . . How often does one find oneself so accurately described on the back of a video box? It was with breathless and unqualified enthusiasm that your Girl Sloth, dear Reader, forked over twenty bucks for the brand new CherFitness workout tape, **Body Confidence**.

And the truth must be told about the sorry events that followed. Like Cher's first exercise tape, the masterpiece **CherFitness: A New Attitude, Body Confidence** consists of two workout "modules." (Actually, **A New Attitude** also featured a ten-minute abdominal and back session.) While **A New Attitude** was content with modest descriptive labelling ("Step Workout," "Abs and Back," "Buns and Thighs"), **Body Confidence** presses its self-satisfaction upon us with the titles the "Hot Dance" and "Mighty Bands." Let the record show that hyperbole is the first sign of inner decay.

The **Hot Dance** is a basic, acceptable aerobic workout, led by Cher's choreographer, Dorrie, a woman with an I Dream of Jeannie hairdo and a flat, affectless voice that suggests underlying psychopathology. Like the first video, it offers a much better than average soundtrack, featuring such **Big Chill** faves as "Dancing in the Streets" and "You've Really Got Me Now" (original artists, remixed). However, Dorrie's intermittent, poker-faced comments about how much "major fun" we're all having are neither appreciated nor confidence-inspiring. Going to the movies is fun; drinking coffee at a canal-side café in Venice is fun. Aerobics are merely necessary.

"Mighty Bands" employs giant rubber bands, an exercise gadget in current vogue. A pair of the requisite bands comes packaged with the tape; they look like very long, very thick dental dams. Mine broke immediately. You can order more from an outfit in Sherman Oaks, but I wasn't about to encourage that sort of thing, so I bought some generic rubber bands at a sporting goods store. They turned out to be all wrong, at which point I abandoned the enterprise in disgust. While the "Mighty Bands" workout features the upper body toning that was absent from Cher's first workout video, **A New Attitude**, the music is recorded so loud that you can barely hear the instructions, or Cher's inimitable wisecracks, one of CherFitness' unique charms.

I blame myself. Things were said in my review of **A New Attitude** that I now regret. Kelli Roberts, the instructrix for **A New Attitude** has vanished from the CherFitness scene, and I can only wonder if my affectionate, if admittedly gruff, description of her as looking like "a giant tendon with a tuft of blonde hair on top" had something to do with this. I also described her as Australian, although the British accent-consultant I called in had warned me that "she could be a Kiwi, and they get really mad about that sort of thing." Whatever it was: Kelli, come back. Things haven't been the same since you left.

While I was still distraught over the **Body Confidence** debacle, friends kept asking me if I was going to review Cindy Crawford's new tape, **Shape Your Body**. It takes a lot of hype to get people talking about a workout video at cocktail parties, so I felt obliged to check it out. I borrowed a copy (in the Girl Sloth tradition) from a coworker, who said, "It looks like a forty-five-minute Revlon commercial."

As everyone knows, the scandal over the potential dangers of this routine has rocked the workout video world to its very foundations ("What does she tell you to do, juggle knives?" my sedentary friend Joe asked.) The program was developed by Crawford and one Radu Teodorescu "over two years of one-on-one sessions." You wondered what the Romanian secret police have been doing since the revolution? Here's your answer. In his sinister Transylvanian accent, Radu orders Crawford to "leeft da leyg; back, frohnt, back, frohnt" with absolutely no precautions to protect ankles, knees and especially the lower back. Crawford manages to gasp out a few warnings, but considering the routine basically consists of swinging your arms and legs all over the place, this is hardly sufficient. And the routine isn't even aerobic. It appears that the former communist menace is now devoting its energies to incapacitating the cute, rich, and dumb, and I say, more power to 'em. It's time to get back to core values.

With so many disappointments on the workout front, I was consoling myself by returning to **CherFitness: A New Attitude,** when our illustrious editrix, Roxxie Rox-a-tronic, suggested that I review the new RuPaul video, "Supermodel," just out from Tommy Boy records in New York.

"But it's a music video, not a workout tape," I protested.

"Yeah, but she sings 'You better work, work, work' over and over," Roxxie offered by way of justification. "And she has the best press release! She says, 'You're born naked and all the rest is drag . . . everyone's a drag queen, even Barbara Bush. It's a look. From the ghetto to the White House, everything's a look.' "

I never argue with La Rox-a-tronic when she's laughing that hard because she might choke. Although the RuPaul video is only four minutes long (hardly enough time to work up good sweat), it is rife with such directives as "Turn to the left. Turn to right! Sashay shante! Make love to the camera!" (Although I think the "Sashay shante" part is supposed to be the supermodel's name, go ahead and sashay anyway. I haven't figure out how to execute the fourth command yet.)

You can have a pretty good time and get your heart rate up by imitating our supermodel while you watch this video, although I doubt that any workout will give you legs like RuPaul's. For that you need XY chromosomes. Despite some major glamor opportunitities, being a supermodel is clearly a high-stress profession, driving Cindy Crawford into the clutches of a former Bolshevik, and even the soignée RuPaul to pitch a Nora Desmond-esque fit of supergrimacing. At times like these, a Girl Sloth learns to pause, take a deep breath, and appreciate the wisdom of her chosen path.

Handbuilt Custom Bikes:

A Joy to Put Between Your Legs

Text and photo by Sharon Urquhart

Why would any sane person spend upwards of $1600 on a bicycle? Could a hand-built custom bike really be that different? An avid cyclist friend told me about her custom frame builder who specializes in fitting women. I went to Graton, located deep in the heart of Sonoma County, California, where Ian Reidel creates his bikes. Ian greeted me in his dirt driveway with ruffled hair wearing an "Unleash the Queen" T-shirt. He seemed unusually cheery for early on a Monday morning. The smell of daffodils in bloom was intoxicating; several cats played in the sun on top of a beat-up Oldsmobile and lambs were *baaaaing* in the distance for their mamas. The picturesque scene made me edgy. Ian led me into his worn bungalow for tea and conversation.

Ian began by explaining the many ways in which the bicycle industry, while they claim to serve women, continues to cater to the needs of men in terms of marketing, design, equipment, and accompanying products. While most bicycle companies have a "women's bicycle" (usually available in mauve), these token models are a weak offering to a strong market.

Ian went on, noting the three points of contact on a bike hands, feet, and gluteus maximus. The elements of the bike affecting fit in terms of the above are geometry, components, and the ever-elusive saddle.

Geometry is all in the frame and it is the foundation of a comfortable and healthy ride. While both men and women vary in height, women vary significantly within similar height ranges. The proportions of most six-foot men are similar, and the material world is engineered to suit them. On the other hand, the proportions of five-feet-two-inch women are more likely to vary between each other in terms of torso length, shoulder width, and hand size. Production bicycles, those that you can buy right off the shelf, are suited for "standard" sized individuals. Commonly, handle bars are too far away on production bicycles for women to reach properly. With improper fit, lower back strain, and discomfort surface. Unnecessary pain makes for a bad biking experience. Adjustments made to production bikes will ever remain an attempt to fit the person to the bicycle. Compromise is commonly the result, making for a less-than-ideal match of rider to bike.

A hand-built custom frame is built around a person, fitted to their exact proportions; akin to custom-tailored clothing. Custom geometry can accommodate the peculiarities and uniqueness of each individual. The result is a ride wherein the bicycle ceases to exist.

Though components come in standard sizes, arrangement and choice of those components will contribute significantly to com-

190

fort and performance. The crank arm length, handle bar width, and break lever size must be considered carefully. Crank arm length is selected proportional to the rider; short legs, short crank arms. Crank arms of inappropriate length may cause unnecessary knee strain. Handle bars need to be barely wider than the shoulders; hands are placed on handle bars at shoulder width. Too-wide handle bars will result in discomfort and inefficiency. Finally, small hands need small break levers for both safety and comfort.

The saddle is the most elusive element to 90 percent of all cyclists. Most women find discomfort not due to firmness, but because of saddle shape; most saddle designs suit the male

pelvic structure. It's not surprising, then, to find so many women complaining of chaffing, undue pressure, and pain. The cause is a poorly designed saddle. Ian cautiously warns that the "sheepskin-covered tractor seat" may lure buyers in with a promise of extreme comfort. Think about it. You don't want anything excessive in a saddle; it should fit like a glove. Tractor-style seats were made to sit on, not to be active on. Add a sheepskin seat cover to a hot spot with little circulation and you have a bacteriologist's dream come true!

Terry Precision, a woman-owned and-operated manufacturing company, makes saddles suited for women; they are the choice saddle for most of Ian's customers. One should keep

Photo © Sharon Urquhart

Reidel's Recommendations to Bicycle Buyers

First find a bike shop that has visible offerings to women in both clothing and hardware. Ask when their knowledgeable and experienced female employees will be available to answer your questions (if they grunt and make excuses, another shop!). Arm yourself with information and know what it is you want and what type of riding you'll be doing; bicycle buyer guides are available at many newsstands. If you don't feel comfortable with a shop or its employees, don't buy there. These are the people you will come back to time and time again with questions, problems, and for service.

If you decide to go the custom route, be sure your builder is familiar with how anatomical differences between men and women are important to the bicycle. Your builder must know the requirements of women in terms of sizing, positioning, and riding style. Ask for three or more references and follow through with contacting those customers—this may be the most important step you take!

Your builder should also be able to satisfy your every desire in terms of paint. The builder is creating an extension of your body in metal. Always trust and like your builder.

in mind that a certain degree of "rider conditioning" is necessary with any saddle. Cyclists with properly fitted bikes claim that a good saddle is so comfortable that it will disappear between your legs. Like most things, you may have to ride on a few saddles before finding the perfect match.

Fit, sizing, and saddle considered, I still questioned how much different a custom ride could be. Ian provided me with one of his shop bikes that was a close fit for my size. As we climbed the rolling hills of the wine country, Ian took note of my riding style and positioning. When possible, Ian rides with his customers so as to understand their needs better. As I rode, I became increasingly more aware of the world around me and lost a sense of time. Maybe it was the daffodils, but I even lost track of the bicycle beneath me. By the time we returned to his shop I was sold on custom. A pink, leopard-spotted road bike built to my exact measurements and specifications will be ready in a few weeks.

Girljock Paper Dolls

©Trina Robbins

Sex and the Modern Girljock

PART FIVE

5

Photo © Chloe Atkins

Notes for the Newly Single

by Roxxie and the *Girljock* Crew

Let's just say you have been in a relationship for a while, and suddenly you find yourself out there in the Brave New World of the newly single. Dating, which used to sound like fun, can up-close turn into a nightmare, because when you get out of a longish relationship, you may have lost your timing for dates.

We have discovered, in a recent informal poll, that being out of practice dating is just as serious as being out of practice in a sport and then diving head-first into a sudden major competition. The ensuing result: possible major pain, lactic acid buildups, aches, bruises, and possible sore throats from yelling too much, and most likely—not winning. So, hey—if you aren't ready yet, there's no shame in staying on the sidelines.

As the chief *Girljock* editrix's mother has long said, "All's fair in love and war." Losing one's timing can cause great problems, and your friends may quickly tire of listening to repeated verbatim scenarios, "And then she said . . . and then I said . . . can you believe that?"

It is also very easy after a long relationship breaks up to jump at the first possible involvement with someone, and while this can be fun sometimes, we have found that a little caution goes a long way. Just like diving into those lovely natural lakes that form in stone quarries; while the water is beautiful, it can be very dangerous—not to forget cold, and it is better to look before you leap. Getting the person you are dating to talk about themselves is a good thing, as long as they know when to stop. If they don't stop talking about themselves, you don't have to go out with them again.

We've been collecting these notes here, to aid the newly single in their dating ventures. After all, dating really is just like window shopping, isn't it? Or, better yet, dating is like driving around looking for a parking space, and you don't want to take one where you'll get a ticket unless you are very, very desperate.

WARNING SIGNALS

- Do you find you have a better time hanging out with people other than the person you are dating?
- Do you have to ask your friends for advice all the time about what to do about her?
- Do you screen your calls so you don't have to talk to her?
- Have you asked your friends how they would break up with her if they were you and then you don't follow their advice for various reasons?
- Does the person you are dating bother you when you are not around them?
- Does she not laugh at your jokes any-

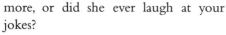
more, or did she ever laugh at your jokes?

• Has she stopped coming to watch your games, or has she refused to watch them entirely?

• If the person had repeated horrible awful breakups with every person they've dated, get the check.

HERE'S A CLOSE-UP OF WHO-NOT-TO-DATE

• Don't date women who "are confused and can't commit."

• Don't date women who break your athletic equipment intentionally.

• Don't date women who casually tell you about their multiple DUIs (Driving Under the Influence) while on a blind date.

• Don't date women you can't carry on a decent conversation with. If you do date women you can't talk with, it will be very hard to communicate later when you may need to.

• Don't date anyone who "needs time to get his/her head together." (Especially if they have to do so by spending time away from you.)

• Don't date anyone who, when talking about the future, doesn't include you or the possibility of your being together. If they don't include you, it just means they've already decided you aren't going to be together for very long, and they are just using you to have a good time (unless, of course, you are only out for a good time, in which case, don't even read this.)

• Don't date an athlete better than yourself, unless you want to get into better shape with her.

• If other people are hitting on your companion . . . well . . . don't date anyone who doesn't immediately blow off those people who are hitting on her.

• Don't date anyone who makes a pass at someone else in front of you (unless it is in a game).

• Don't date anyone who accidentally gives you Ex-Lax the night before a big game.

• Don't date women who really want to go out with your surfboard, or your skis, or your Jeep, if you know what we mean.

• Watch out for that moving truck!

This article was compiled by Roxxie following comments made by various members of the Girljock *staff, especially Mo Phalon and Stacey Foss.*

The "Don't" list in particular was courtesy of one of the Girljock *staff's brothers, who, at this point in time, has spent sixteen years listening to some of the many and various horror stories of modern dating which may have happened to assorted members of* Girljock's *staff and their friends.*

Susie Bright on Girljocks:

An Interview by Roxxie

Photo © Marguerite Lutton

When Roxxie met Susie Bright, Roxxie was intrigued—so intrigued, she propositioned Susie for an interview. Susie accepted, agreeing to become *Girljock*'s first ever "Sissy Cover Girl." Weeks later, they met in Susie's living room. The television wasn't on, but the tape recorder was. . . .

Roxxie: *Have you ever played sports?*
Susie: Only when forced to. Somebody came up with the brilliant idea in Los Angeles Public Schools that girls should be forced to play flag football. I broke my finger the first time out. Then we were forced to play basketball and I ran into the basketball pole and got a bloody nose. Then we were forced to play baseball and I swung at the pitched ball and the ball ran into my thumb and my nail came off. Then we were forced to do gymnastics, and I dived into the mat and broke my nose again.
RX: *Then did you start cutting gym class after that?*
SB: LA public schools started something called independent physical education study, which meant you could do anything off campus you wanted to so long as you could document it. I got to go off and do dance, so I was happy as a clam.
RX: *Do you have a favorite form?*
SB: My favorite form is uninhibited. Anything: It could be ballet, it could be flamenco, it could be modern dance, it could be the watusi, and I would dig it.
RX: *Country and Western?*
SB: Absolutely. Irish jigs. The thing is, I always had fantasies about being able to hit a ball really really far, being able to run so fast that everybody's mouth hung open, being able to throw this pass that would go like a rainbow across the field.

I have fantasized my whole life about being a sports superstar. But I was the daughter of nerds, a teacher and a librarian. I learned to read, read, read. It's too bad, because as you can see I'm tall and I have muscles from doing nothing but carrying groceries and my daughter in and out of the car.

RX: *The exercises of daily living.*

SB: I think the last time I actually tried any kind of sport was when bodybuilding was becoming popular. They started having women's classes at UC Santa Cruz. So I went in and there was one of those little fascist leotard numbers talking about "losing those inches from around your waist" and "getting those pounds off" and I just wanted to throw up. Any whiff of women talking about their bodies not being good enough and slenderizing just sets me into a political fury. So I happened to walk over to the coed class, which I ordinarily wouldn't have walked into because I would have been intimidated by the boys. The man who was teaching the coed class was the most laid back, most humanistic person . . . I was amazed how strong I got in six weeks. I realized there was an athlete in me someplace. It's kind of a shame it's going to waste.

RX: *But then again there's the exercises of daily living.*

SB: The exercises of daily living.

RX: *. . . laundry baskets . . .*

SB: Fucking . . .

RX: *Fucking, right, right. Which takes a lot of physical . . .*

SB: Absolutely . . .

RX: *Energy.*

SB: Gets that pulse rate up.

RX: *You use many different muscle groups.*

SB: Especially the ever important pubococous muscle, which is the muscle which goes into spasm when you have an orgasm. But you can learn to control it all on your own.

RX: *Do you have any advice about learning to control it all on your own?*

SB: I think you should flex your PC muscle at least fifty times every day. And you can do it in the car. You can do ten slow ones and ten fast ones at every red light you come to. And then if you want to make it more pleasurable, you put things inside yourself and then practice. And then when you come, try and see how many times it's contracting. It feels good, it's a little bit of a turn on, and it keeps your pussy healthy.

RX: *Have you ever had crushes on women athletes?*

SB: Oh yeah. You'll laugh if I tell you what some of my fantasies are. I always wanted to top Chris Evert real bad. I just want to grab her little pony-tails so bad, take her little tennis bracelets and string her up. She fascinates me because it seems like all her best friends are dykes. I certainly believe that she digs men, I mean I don't think she's some latent case, but she's a feminine, aggressive, tennis superstar straight girl, and I just want to pull her tennis panties off.

Who else? There are a lot of women in sports, but, like, famous women, not that many come to my attention. I admire Martina tremendously, but she doesn't do it for me. And then there were those women in the Olympics with the extraordinarily long fingernails. Those people are extraordinary, but again . . . I suppose the woman athlete who just blows my mind to this day is Patrice Donnelly, who played a woman athlete in *Personal Best*. She was the dark-haired butch. She just gives me goosebumps.

RX: *What about other sports? Golf?*

SB: Golf is pretty hot stuff, and the LPGA has gone to incredible lengths to destigmatize their dyke image. They said dyke-baiting was killing their sport and killing the tour and killing the prize money. They couldn't get any sponsorship because everyone thought they were a bunch of raving bulldaggers. So the marketing firm said, Get all your cutest golfers, put them in bathing suits, and make promotional posters.

It's one of my great regrets that I've not been to this bizarre Dinah Shore invitational. I mean, is she a dyke or not? Why does she throw an enormous dyke tournament? What does go on in Palm Springs? I think *Girljock* should go to Dinah Shore Golf Tournament and have a presence.

RX: *Do many of your friends play sports?*

SB: Yes, of course, I fall in love with athletes constantly. So yes, certain friends of mine are superb athletes and they're in charge of my daughter's sports training. I don't want her to be ignored athletically the way I was. I want her to have a decent chance in life. She's already throwing a ball and she's only fourteen months old!

RX: *That's one thing they don't write in most girl's baby books.*

SB: Right, when did she throw her first ball.

RX: *What sports do you want her to be able to play when she grows up?*

SB: The sports I'm impressed with the most? Something with strength, and grace, and speed. Basketball sometimes just approaches the otherworldly to me, because it moves so fast, it's like you're moving on instinct, there's no pause in the action. She just goes and goes. At least I was good at freethrow, because I was tall . . . I hope you'll mention I'm five foot ten.

RX: *Gladly. So dancing and sex are your favorite*

forms of exercise. What are the strongest selling points of these compared to other forms of exercise?

SB: No rules; no one blowing stupid whistles; you can stop whenever you want; immediate gratification; everyone's a winner!

RX: *Where are your favorite places to go dancing?*

SB: My living room.

RX: *Is that also your favorite place for making love?*

SB: No, I have a great squeaky bed. I like squeaky beds and water beds, beds in very expensive hotels . . . you have to have the right equipment, or you might as well not bother to play.

RX: *Do you have locker room fantasies?*

SB: I've always had locker room fantasies based on movies, not anything that's ever happened to me. Sure, I've always had fantasies of being thrown down in the shower room and fingered and fucked by five while the hot water comes pouring down and steam is going everywhere. You know, water and tile and grease and sweat . . .

RX: *Razors . . .*

SB: Well, I don't know about the razors. Oh, I see what you mean, the public shaving thing. I haven't fantasized about that.

My locker room fantasies in some ways have to do with taking the painful memories of those cheerleaders and popular girls and eroticizing it. The competition and meanness is still there, but it becomes sexual. Turning the tables on them. I'm getting it and they're not.

RX: *They could be tied up somewhere in their little cheerleading outfits, watching you . . .*

SB: Yeah, banging on the locker door, howling.

RX: *Do you have tips for how someone can pick up an athlete?*

SB: Oh sure. In many cases, the studliest, strongest, fastest, cutest, most bone-crunching athletes are totally attracted to their opposites. They no more want to go to bed with another hard body than with a two-by-four. They're looking for someone who's soft, and squishy, and curvy. The secret is that opposites attract. The perfect example, if you don't mind me using heterosexual marriage, is Arnold and Maria. I mean, Maria Shriver is no athlete. And here Arnold Schwarzenegger is in charge of the president's physical fitness, but he didn't want to be with another athlete. He wanted to be with this woman who is this zaftig, really feminine woman who probably couldn't throw a ball to save her life. So picking up athletes is really just having the confidence that they don't necessarily want to go out with someone who looks like them or has the same interest.

BEYOND *ON OUR BACKS*

RX: *What are your plans now that you're in your post–*On Our Backs *era?*
SB: I don't know what it will be called yet. I'm doing another book of my essays on sex and popular culture and politics.
RX: *The return of* Susie Sexpert?
SB: Perhaps. Perhaps that will be the name.
RX: Susie Sexpert's Lesbian Sex *universe.*
SB: Galaxy!
RX: *Solar system!*
SB: Something like that. Then there's another volume of erotica coming out that I've edited, which is an anthology of women's erotic fiction. That's been really fun to put together because when I did a book of women's erotica no one knew what I was talking about, and

trying to get submissions was like finding a needle in a haystack. This time we got lots of submissions.

The one thing I said is no coming out stories. None. I want grown-up women having grown-up sex. There's a maturity in lesbian sex after you're out and after you've been around the block a few times which makes it much . . . well, it's subjective when I say it's much hotter. I have a million fantasies about virgins myself. But I'm more interested in that experience now, in post-baby dyke, grown-up girls, their sexual thoughts and experiences.

I'm also teaching a class called Porn 101 right now at Good Vibrations, so I'm sure I'll continue teaching and writing about these subjects. I've got some new freelance assignments that I can't wait to see the reaction to. I've got a piece on masculinity in the nineties in *Esquire* this fall, and a piece on future of sex in *Elle*, of all places. So it will be interesting to see what those audiences have to say.

RX: *Do you want to say anything about* On Our Backs? *A lot of people that I know can't even conceive of* On Our Backs *existing without you; they see you as the person with the concept. I know you did it with other people, but somehow you became "lesbian sexuality" to so many women, like my friend Jackie, who says no lesbians in Boulder were having sex before you came and gave a speech there and then everybody started having sex.*
SB: [Laughter] Yes, I did bring fist fucking to Boulder and I'm proud, proud, proud. In a sense, I can't conceive of it either. I am really disappointed that I don't have a closer relationship with *On Our Backs* than I do because I feel very close to the readers. I really know who reads *On Our Backs*, because I've been all

over the country and I've met them, and so many became good friends. I had a great way to talk to a lot of people and get a lot of tremendous feedback. I met tremendous artists and it was so pleasurable to be able to give them that national kind of forum. I'm not contributing or writing for *On Our Backs* because in the wake of my decision that I wanted to write full-time, I wanted to write for books and I wanted to have a different kind of scheduled life with my daughter than I had before, my partners on the magazine were really unhappy with my decision. What started out as really constructive visionary reasons for moving on also turned into a falling out. So I've got both the pleasure of being closer with my daughter and I'm happier with that, I'm writing a lot more than I have the past few years at *On Our Backs* because I was doing more business and less writing and editing.

And on the other hand, I miss all my friends and that's . . . I can't believe it either. I think I'm still in a state of shock and some weekend when I'm not on another deadline I'm going to have the world's biggest cry about it because I can't believe it.

It's not like I don't feel appreciated, it's more . . . I was really very close with my partners and it's like getting a divorce, and you can't believe the things they say about you, and I guess she can't believe the things I say about her. And then the readers are like your kids. Like, "I want custody of ten thousand readers now." What do you do?

RX: *"I want the west, and you can have the east."*

SB: No, I want all those places. I want to be able to continue my dialogue with the kind of people who loved *On Our Backs.*

RX: *Would you ever consider doing another magazine?*

SB: I never want to edit another magazine, although I suppose these are famous last words. There's something about putting out a magazine in the same format month after month or week after week that deadens the inspiration you began with. Magazine publishing depends on becoming predictable and being able to deliver something that looks just like the thing that you delivered last time. There's a sort of ingrained end to innovation within the mainstream publishing business, that is, if you want to survive and reach a lot of people. If you're writing books, or doing plays, you really do get to say that's the end of this project and now I'm going to do something entirely different over here. You get to have some closure. So I love contributing to other peoples' magazines and I still have a million dream ideas for magazines I'd like to see. *Girljock* was one of them.

Photo © Phyllis Christopher

Georgette's Confession

by Georgette One

Late this night, I, the non-chocolate eater, felt the call of the dark lord itself. Grouchy I was, sitting on the couch, thinking of the joy of the dark stuff, and how they say the perverse chocolate sends a trigger of happiness endorphins flooding the dark recesses of the gloomiest of all organs, the brain. The torturous brain that gets me in as much trouble as it gets me out of: I, along with my body, took myself right out to Safeway, where I lamented the strange reality of lonely hearted late-night supermarket shopping.

Some fellow excused himself to me in the cracker aisle, as I roamed around looking for dark chocolate for diabetics, the kind that metabolize slower into the bloodstream so you don't get a sugar rush. Before I could wander past the fellow, he cornered me and mournfully asked if I knew "Which crackers were called Munchies."

Naturally, that sounded like every single cracker in my ex-teenage-years-pot-smoking universe, so I answered, "No," even though I was flattered he thought I was of a higher state of cracker knowledge than he was.

"Darn," said the cracker-hunting stranger boy. "My Girlfriend sent me here to find some crackers called 'Munchies,' and I can't find them."

I then felt so sorry for him, sent out late at night by his evil-but-probably-pretty-and-hungry girlfriend, who I knew was only using the young man to fulfill her late-night hunger, and had sent him on what ended up becoming some strange goose-chase. I suggested to the crackerhunter that he ask at the checkout stand, because, I explained, "I only bother to learn the names of the snacks I usually eat."

I was thinking of pretzels, those crunchy things with easy names. I never remember pretzel brands, do you? Does anybody? Off went he, to the checkout stand, grumbling that he didn't know what Girlfriend was talking about.

I sympathetically chuckled to myself, as I read the names of all the frozen desserts, looking in what I thought was vain at the time, for the diabetic section of desserts. I looked to attain slothiness and happy endorphins through the total immersion of my mouth into chocolate. At least my girlfriend hadn't sent me out to get her something to eat for her, she'd only decided not to accompany me. Girlfriends. I was on a solo search for another mental territory here.

Finally, aimlessly wandering through the coffee section in the late-night Safeway world, I stumbled upon the Weight Watchers stuff, and knew that I was close to Diabetic Chocolates.

Diabetic Chocolates are the alcohol-free beer of the candy world. They aren't noncaloric, but they don't send us sugar sensitives on a wild blood sugar ride though the emotional cosmos. Expectable aftereffects: maybe a small stomach ache the next day, and probably pimples.

I was, however, beyond sight of any internal regret-oriented or remorse-based chocolate avoidance mechanisms. And sure enough, I scored an Estee company Dark Chocolate no-sucrose bar, and a Milk Chocolate flavored bar with Crisp Rice.

I made it through the slow slow line at the checkstand, and finally got a piece of the dark stuff in my mouth as I walked into the parking lot. I drove home, even let my girlfriend have a piece, and am waiting for the endorphin/chocolate/action to hit home in my brain. I'm waiting, waiting. I changed the screen background pattern on my computer so that it would hurry up the endorphin balance change in my head.

But my girlfriend, who was out all day, returned home full of presents from her mother and a desire for cleaning. Not a desire for anything hedonistic, sinful, or anything that would be fun to me—she wanted to clean. I had escaped her mania partially, by heading for Safeway; but now, chocklified brain and all, I was doomed.

"Georgette," said my girlfriend, who is completely scary when she's in these moods, "Will you please fold your laundry now?"

I folded for a few minutes, and then begged off pleading adult responsibilities: Partially I was in shock not believing I'd wandered into as awful a nocturnal occurrence as this.

Certainly, I, like many others, including that fellow in Safeway (this was something I knew instinctively and only instinctively), have often wished our significant others could be wildly passionate at night about other activities besides cleaning, or chasing down crackers called Munchies. Five different times, and it is

12:37 now, she's walked into this room to ask me where something goes, and worse than that, she is crazed. She's obsessed. Try to get her to do anything past 11:00 usually and it is curtains time. She most frequently goes to sleep at 12:00. But tonight she is possessed by a chronic cleaning disorder. It is scaring me.

She just came into my study to ask me another question about my socks and my laundry, again. Every time she enters I hide this screen, cause I'm afraid she'll read it, and then she'll know that I'm not working on anything she can put her finger on and point to, and tell me to stop doing. I am officially pretending that I'm busy finishing some work: stuff she can't call me on, stuff she can't touch. I told her I'm finishing that issue of my magazine right now, so she'll just leave me alone. All I can think about, besides chocolate, this confession to you, and quitting my day job tomorrow, is painting pictures on white canvasses. Because the colors, the shapes, and the people alive in the paint don't bother me. The colors don't say things like, "Oh, what a nice idea—let's have sex in two days," as if one can actually wait that long if one is in the mood, or "How about switching your days off at work now," or "Why did you put such short sentences into my article you edited," or "Where do all your business letters go." My girlfriend is gone now, into the other part of the house, where she is busy making and unmaking the bed with her new sheets. She's hitting a rhythm, she's getting into a stride. But I'm safe for a while: I think the chocolate's starting to kick in. The house is getting very quiet and my hands are starting to move very quickly on the computer's keys.

True Transgressive Romances No. 25

by Jackie Weltman

I fancy myself a fag-dyke, a new breed, and I travel with my fuck-lover, Wanda—the larger and stronger of us. I took Wanda on because I liked her, because her childhood was crueler than mine and her angst and righteous queer anger were overwhelming. I respected that. I therefore allowed her to dominate me as no one else has been able to. Wanda has a peculiar trick: She likes to back me up against her huge stomach and pendulous breasts. She lashes me to her shoulders and thighs with leather thongs so that I dangle a mere half-inch above the ground. Then she walks around with me like a spare tire on a Volkswagen, making me do the housework while she finger-fucks me.

I met Wanda at a Queer Matron meeting. Queer Matron is the focus group of Queer Nation that caters to maternal, authoritarian women, lady prison guards and their admirers. I hesitantly decided to attend their gathering one night because I was becoming frustrated with the eternal passivity of my husband, Martin. Martin, that will-o'-the-wisp quantum faggot peace-worker, my slave. What's this you say, a husband? But I thought you were a lesbian, Monique. Remember, dear reader, this is a transgressive story; I am beyond the old order—free! Uninhibitedly sexual! A diesel-stomping bisexual fag-dyke! And as such, I love to torture little Martin—make him wear a French maid's dress, thread a chain through

his cock jewelry to his nipple rings while he is bound and tie the chain to a fold-out ironing board. With him helpless, ungraciously I eat Ben and Jerry's Rainforest Crunch ice cream in front of him. A whole quart.

I have thought of many novel ways to torture Martin. I bind him spread-eagled and stomach-down on the bed, his pink, adolescent-smooth ass cheeks glowing in the falling light. I find the Tupperware box full of cockroaches I have captured the night before and send them skittering madly across his bare back. While he screams like the high school cheerleader sex poodle he is, I don one of my many lifelike Stryker dildoes and prod open his screwtight asshole. I ram him again and again as sweat and hair fly everywhere. He is my little Fanny Farmer girlboyman.

My latest creation has been a sonic torture instrument. Over eight delightful months, I saved every Campbell's soup can I opened. With painstaking devotion, I washed each roll and crevice of every can and strung them closely on a length of fishline. Smacking one tin savagely with a cane sends the entire partyline clattering and banging with such horrendous din that it gives Martin a giant erection and sends him to his knees promising never again to be such an assimilationist, yuppie-scum sellout moderate bourgeoisie GAYboy (snort) again.

Yet in spite of my devoted husband and all his revolutionary prettiness, I needed a bitch like Wanda to help me vanquish all the unconquered territory of my psychopolitical life. Indeed, I lay stock still while Wanda pierced my nipples on the running dishwasher. Wanda was present at my first Queer Nation hazing and jacket-decorating ceremony. She was the first to paddle me at the Klitz Sex Club and led me like a show pony to each and every hot queer dance club in town. Wanda is rooted and silent, full of piss and vinegar when angry; and likes the simple, passionate, easy-to-digest things like "We're here, we're queer, our shopping bags are paper." I needed such a woman to break me: me, *me*, a transgressive, revolutionary, postmodern, fag bi-dyke with a drawerful of zebra-striped underwear and a tickertape heart.

The first time Wanda, Martin, and I all fucked was the most thrilling experience of my life. We had all been to an explosive demo that summer night. We were exhilarated, lithe, sweaty and in our bodies, intelligent, answering to no straight white pig! When we returned to my apartment, I hauled out three beers for us. At the refrigerator door, Wanda grabbed me and began kissing me harshly. Martin was fascinated but taken aback by Wanda and I in action, something he had never seen. Catching him in the uncouth act of eyeing us and shivering from the shock, I ordered him to strip and remain silent, and chained him to his ironing board. With Martin secure, Wanda ripped my shirt open to my waist, tore down my fly and began pinching my three erections. The jars of jam and BBQ

---

*I recommend Scotch Thick-Cut Orange Marmalade and Heinz respectively.

sauce I kept nearby for these very occasions were employed: Wanda smeared my nipples with condiments* and licked them off. Then she made me kneel on the rug and fisted me from behind. Martin was uncontrollably blissful. He chomped the aluminum leg of the ironing stand to keep from writhing in pre-orgasmic agony and taking the iron and spray starch with him. As Wanda rammed her (latex-gloved fun—action ribbed, of course) hand up my tightening pink cunt muscle, I came, hurtling Wanda halfway across the living room. Then I realized as I huffed that Martin had passed out. The excitement had been too much for him. I glanced distastefully at his limp body, but was jerked back to attention by Wanda, who seized my punk-outlaw-type hair, wrenched my head around, and forced me into her unbound and cavernous crotch. When she was satisfied, Martin began coming to. I prepared for the final onslaught.

"Martin, you were a naughty, piggy, p.c. husband, passing out like that," I remonstrated scornfully. Martin snuffled. "Well then, bonkerhead—how do you like this?"

Martin gasped. He knew what was coming: his favorite horror—algebra!

"What's $6x^2 + 5xy^2 + y^2$?" I demanded.

Martin inhaled sharply and gave a small cry.

"C'mon capitalist scumbag! Do the problem!"

Martin exhaled his answer in a curt whisper. "Now this one: $X = 4x^2 \cdot 2x^3$!"

"Ach!" squealed Martin, not able to hold in his excitement. His cock sprung out harder and harder as he rubbed it against the rigid aluminum pole. "$8x^5$—ooh, ah, oh my god . . . !"

"Length of the hypotenuse if the legs of a right triangle are 3 and 4 respectively?"

"Um . . . uh . . . five . . . five . . . aieee!" He exploded like a balloon flubbing backwards, spitting air. Then he sighed and slumped forward, exhausted. I unchained him and ordered him off to bed with a cookie and a kiss on the pate.

Of course, Wanda and I stayed up to explore other erotic delights in front of "Hawaii Five-O." Yes, it was a blissful summer, and it just keeps getting better with True Transgressive Romance! So remember, folks, fuck fiercely and fight the power!

From the Sidelines #1

by Robbi Sommers

Sports enthusiast? Me? Well . . . I suppose so. No. I don't play soccer. Baseball, volleyball, basketball? No. So what do I play? I play rough. I play hardball. I play with the best. Sports erotics, that's my game.

Oh yeah, act like you don't know what I'm talking about. Act like you go to those games to watch a ball be smacked by a stick or tossed over a net. Nothing like that kind of excitement? Yeah, right.

I tell the truth about athletic events. A sport is a sport, wherever it's played. Doesn't make much difference to me. Whether on a field or in a gym—tie a bandana around a woman's head, show off her thighs in a pair of shorts, tease me with her biceps in a short-sleeved shirt, and that's what I call a good game.

Take baseball. Tough faced, with a jock swagger that could knock me from the bleachers, the batter approaches the plate. Shoulders back, attitude seeping like thick honey, the woman means business. Damn. If she's got that much intensity on the field, imagine what she'd be like in bed.

I watch her tap the bat against her cleats. Her weight shifts from foot to foot and her hips rock slightly. Nice ass, great ass, she bends slightly and does a warm-up swing. She's serious, all right. It's written all over her face. I like a woman with a one-track mind; a woman who can focus on the subject at hand.

I visualize myself across from her with a pitcher's mitt. High heels, garter belt, a bright red baseball hat—sure, I know about uniforms. She looks me straight in the eye with fierce, butch concentration. I toss her a pouty little smile. *You ready for a curve ball?*

Her eyes drop from mine and skim my tight, thin tank top. Strike one. I'm looking good, I'm looking fine.

Nervous, caught off-guard, she shoots me a lucky-break smirk. I spread my legs slightly. My high heels pierce the dirt, the tank top rides high on my midriff. Strike two.

Yeah baby, oh baby. I'm hot now. A harsh edge replaces the batter's smirk. She doesn't like my sassy attitude? I don't care. Let her come to the pitcher's mound if she's got a problem with me. Let her come right up and show me what she wants, show me exactly how she'd like me to do it for her.

Last inning, last chance. The score is tied. A tense silence blankets the crowd. Women in the stands, women on the sidelines—they all have their eyes on me. Can I do it again? Can I bring her to her knees?

The sweet scent of desire swirls from the batter and surrounds me in a sudden heat. Unbridled power spills from her strong arms, her thick hands, her muscular thighs. Our eyes lock. She's ready for it. She's hungry for it.

I caress the baseball against my smooth fin-

210

gers and consider her firm breasts. An immediate compulsion to drop the ball, rush to home plate, and press my desperate hands against her overwhelms me.

Breaking rules, playing dirty, she looks at me with fire in her eyes. It's clear she could take me. It's clear she could suck me dry. Dizzy, disoriented, I hold the ball close to my face. I focus, zero in on the imaginary line between us. Sparks dart from her eyes, her mouth, her fingertips.

She has me. She has me good. I throw the ball. It slices the air and the crowd begins to roar. Let her run. Let her go wherever she wants. I drop the mitt, I head toward first base. If she slides, let her ram into me. I can take it hard. I can take it as hard as she can give it.

The ball soars against the field and she leaps, as though in slow motion, to first base, second, then third. Her thighs are tight with power, her arms grab through the hot, summer air.

C'mon, C'mon, C'mon.

An explosion of pleasure races through me. Her ass is taut. Her eyes, determined. Into home she slides. I want her more than anything. I'd do anything now to have her. I snap from my fantasy and hurry toward the field.

Yes! Yes! Yes! That's it, baby. That's it!

Dust on her shirt, sweat on her face, she sees me, dressed to kill, on the sidelines.

"Need something cool?" I ask sweetly as I offer her a soft drink.

She nods her head and smiles.

Home run, for both of us.

And therein lies the concept of sports erotics. From start to finish, you'll find me at all the games. After all, I play hardball. I play with the best. I play to win.

A Dildo's Only as Good as the Woman You Use It With

by Anna Livia writing as Jiffy Lube

The time had come, we both agreed, to go and buy a dildo. We had each performed this act many times in other relationships, but now we felt we needed one that was wholly ours, not a relic of past excitement with previous loves, drenched in the body fluids of six-year-old orgasms. Actually, Spritz, my girlfriend, was so mad at her ex for leaving that she had thrown away her entire collection of dildos, harnesses, silk scarves, blinds, buckling bonds, and flagells in a fit of rage and humiliation.

"Where," I asked "did you throw them?"

How do you dispose of more than three hundred dollars worth of sex toys? Ceremoniously hurl them in the ocean, only to have them come bobbing past in a salt-drenched flotilla next time you're skinny-dipping at Baker's Beach? Or unceremoniously seal them in plastic bags and dump them in the trash—to the surprize of any wandering street person, no doubt, who opens the bag hoping for warm boots to protect her from the cold winter sidewalk.

"I buried them," Spritz said with an air of finality.

"And how come you had so many?"

"Oh," she said, "all my girlfriends buy me dildos. Or we buy them together and I end up with them."

A brief visualization of my best green Gap socks, my black muscle shirt from Crossroads, and the two Pendleton shirts which had all mysteriously become Spritz's property was enough to vouch for the fact that Spritz, through no apparent fault of her own, did "end up" with a remarkable amount of other people's property.

When Spritz and I played with sex toys, we used mine, which I had bought during a period of nonconsensual celibacy before I met her, and which were therefore untainted with the smell of fluids past. I had got my first harness and dildo from a catalog. The descriptions had intrigued and alarmed me. "If you'd like your rubber dildo to soften in a hurry, leave it lying in the sun," they advised, but they neglected to mention what to say to your neighbor when his dog mistakes your dildo for a bone. This time Spritz and I went to Good Vibrations which, since we live in the Castro, is within walking distance, so we didn't have to face the embarrassment of parking the car and having it recognized within a hundred yards of a sex-shop.

"What," all you girljocks are asking indignantly, "is your problem? You shouldn't be embarrassed about buying a dildo, or any other sex toy for that matter. You just go up to the counter, state your sexual needs clearly and forthrightly, and take your time picking out the products best suited to your mood, your orientation, and your, or your partner's, threshold of pain."

I have two words to say to you.

"Yeah. Right."

I suppose you grew up confident from the big butch bulge in your big butch diapers of the big butch bulldagger you would grow up to be. Well, let me tell you, dildos embarrass me, sex toys embarrass me, and realistic dildos with veins up the side and great hairy balls embarrass the hell out of me. I am not a bold, bulging girljock like you; I am a shy, sensitive butch with nice table manners, still sitting in the sand where Charles Atlas kicked me. While you all are watching *Monday Night Football*, I'm glued to reruns of *Murder She Wrote*. I'm a nerd, okay?

So where was I? Oh yeah, in Good Vibrations buying dildos. Before we set out, Spritz and me, we made a list, like a grocery list. At least, we tried to disguise it as a grocery list, only some of the items you couldn't buy at Safeway:

It was in code. We were only going to buy every second item. Sneaky, huh?

Toothpaste	Olive Oil
Dental dams	Lubricant
Light bulbs	Saran Wrap
Butt plug	Cling Film
Cheerios	Condoms
Dildo	

There was a little interlude before we actually got inside the door of Good Vibrations. Spritz said she recognized a guy from her differential calculus class slinking into the store, so we had to go and have a glass of Calistoga at the café opposite. You can't buy dildos in front of someone you do calculus with, I can see that. But it was getting on six, when the store closes, so finally we just had to put a brave face on it and go in there, come what may.

Well, we picked out a bottle of Astroglide and another of Probe, a dozen maximum strength condoms, an Eve dildo, a triple ripple butt plug, two new cock rings, and a pack of multicolored gloves—Spritz reckoned they'd be sexy if we were playing "Pap-smear." I thought we were doing pretty well, and having spent the last half hour talking about whether the butt plug could be used with a harness, and what size cock ring we needed for Eve, I'd even gained a certain self-assured swagger.

I gather up our booty and I'm striding over to join the line when I notice that Miss Spritz has disappeared. I look around to find out where she's got to when, lo and behold, who should I see standing in line right behind me, but Rapier Steele, God's gift to the sadomasochist community, the ultimate in bold, bulging girljocks.

Now, I am what is known as preternaturally polite. I come from a community which is oceanically, cosmically polite. We know more about politeness, and its evil twin, rudeness, than any other people on this planet. You know that Lea Delaria joke that goes "How do you know when you're dating a WASP? She gets out of the shower to pee?" I get out of the shower to pee. Because it's polite. No, really. So here is Rapier Steele standing behind me in line to buy dildos and Lord knows what else, and I can't just disappear like my brave femme girlfriend, so I do what I have to do, the only thing I can do under the circumstances, I say hello to her.

"Hey, Rapier. How's it hanging?"

She looks right through me, to the wall behind my head, her face expressionless, and then she curls the corner of her lip and nods ever so slightly. Recognition.

But now it's my turn at the counter. I line up the bottles of lube, the condoms, and the gloves.

"I'd like an Eve, please, and a triple ripple," I say, as calmly as if I was ordering ice cream at a Dairy Queen. The assistant goes to the drawer and brings out all the colors they have left: pale purple and baby blue. Meanwhile, another assistant is helping Rapier. She gets out one of the biggest dildos I have ever seen in my life and puts it on the counter next to mine. It's dark brown, I can't help noticing, with big hairy balls. Rapier glances briefly, dismissively, at my dildo. Her dick is bigger than my dick.

"You don't have to buy a pastel-colored dildo," she informs me, seizing control of the situation.

"This is all they have left," I attempt to explain, staring down at my limp pastel dick.

Rapier snorts but lets this pass. "You know what's really good?" she asks authoritatively. She is, after all, one of an elite group of San Francisco sexperts. "You put one condom on your dick, then fill another with lube and tie that on top. Slips around like hot wet honey."

"Is that right?" says the assistant, enthralled. "That's a great tip. We should start a suggestions board here in the store."

I smile pleasantly—well, actually, it's that pouty-lipped kind of smile where instead of your lips curling up at the edges, they puff out in the middle—thinking that the first suggestion I would make would be that customers

keep their opinions about the purchases of others to themselves. This message would, of course, be worded extremely politely. No brash, bullish "Butt out, Asshole!" for me. I picked the dildo that seemed the right length and width for my girlfriend, and between all you girljocks and me, when she and I get down, we don't need any extra lube. It's like the Mississippi bayous are on fire.

By now several other customers are gazing at Rapier's and my goods. Is it just my imagination or do they nod their heads meaningfully, as if to say, "Yuuup. It figures. She looks like a pastel-dick kinda gal."

"Double-bagging," one guy offers, "That's what it's called. That condom trick. Double-bagging." His admiring wife giggles admiringly. At least, I assume she's his wife. And that the sound that comes out of her mouth is a giggle and that it expresses admiration. Could be she's his long-suffering probation officer trying to repress a snort of contempt.

"Well, hallo, Mr. Edwards," says a nice young woman in beige pleats, who's standing in line waiting to buy a set of nipple clamps, no doubt. "Mother and I haven't seen you since Thanksgiving."

While they settle into a cozy chat about funds for the new dungeon in Walnut Creek, or whatever it is they have in common, I overhear another woman whispering indignantly to her friend, "Now how would he know about double-bagging? If he tried to tie a condom on his precious member, he'd asphyxiate himself."

"Lurking on the Internet," says the other. "I hate how those guys log on to women's bulletin boards to learn all our little secrets. It just don't seem natural."

"Like some guy dropping into a women's beauty parlor for a shave," her friend agrees.

I look around and notice something my search for the perfect dildo had previously blocked from my mind. The store is full of straight people with suburban clothes and bad hair. Including at least two Nan Parks looka-likes. Is Good Vibrations offering day passes to condo owners in San Rafael? Now I'm not usually so down on heterosexual couples, I mean, queers don't have the monopoly on sexual curiosity and desire for enhanced potency, we know that. But this was 'spose to be me and Spritz's dirty afternoon ogling sex toys so we could go home afterwards and fuck our brains out, and here I am surrounded by respectable mothers and daughters discussing what kind of butt plug Daddy would like for Christmas. Sex was meant to be dark, dirty, and shameful, my mother always says, other-wise where's the fun?

I wonder what Rapier Steele makes of this invasion of decency. She's standing by the pleasure swing, a kind of hammock slung from the ceiling near the window, totally in her ele-ment, giving an impromptu demonstration of the uses of the stirrups attached to the front end of the swing. The nice young woman in beige pleats is taking notes, as though she were planning to report back to an ad hoc commit-tee, while the double-bagging man and his wife–probation officer are testing the strength of the straps.

How did sex get to be so respectable? I don't know where to look. Am I the only per-son left alive who gets a thrill out of furtive fumblings and stuck zippers? Over in the far corner a door opens, revealing a soft velvety interior and framed pictures of women clad only in dildo harnesses. Thank heavens for the bathroom, last bastion of smut and secrecy. From behind the door, Spritz emerges. Tall, slim, with the sexiest look in her eyes. She glides over to the hammock and as she crosses the room, everyone in the place, male or female, queer or straight, draws breath, their hearts beating that little bit faster, their breath-ing heavier.

"Hi, Rapier," Spritz says.

And Rapier's craggy face begins to smile. If you've ever seen a rapier smile, you'll know how scary that can be.

"Hi, Spritz," she says, and her face actually softens. The hard-edged, razor-cheeked sharp-ness becomes more rounded, she looks younger and hungrier. She gazes at Spritz with an intensity I'm more used to seeing in pup-pies ogling a bone their master is holding way up in the air above their heads. The other cus-tomers gaze from Spritz to Rapier.

But Spritz turns to me, her flicking eye-lashes already dismissing Rapier. "Are you ready, sweetheart?" she asks, looping her arm through mine. And I forgive her disappear-ance, her desertion in the line of fire, the momentary weakness which left me to face Rapier Steele and the ultra-sophisticated Good Vibrations assistants all by myself. She's the one I get to go home with. After all, a dildo's only as good as the woman you use it with.

Dear Sports Slut

by Alison Gaitant

Dear Sports Slut,

    I have been playing basketball now for six years. My older sister told me that girls who play basketball will lactate suddenly and unexpectedly and, quite to my horror, the milk will be foamy because of all the up and down motion. Tell me, Sports Slut, is this true?

        Cappuccino Tits in Des Moines, Iowa

Dear Cappuccino Tits,

    Your sister is spending too much time with cows, apparently. Playing basketball is good for you, for any woman, despite all the 1950s propaganda suggesting otherwise. Just wear a good sports bra so your rack feels comfortable.

Dear Sports Slut,

    I was masturbating recently when I realized that all my masturbatory fantasies are the same: I am chasing Martina Navratilova through a poppy field. Then she trips and falls and I fall on top of her. We wrestle around for a while, giggling, and then she starts to get a little nasty. She pins me down and says menacingly, "I give to you spanking." Well, then, as you can imagine, I come. Here's the problem: I hate violence and never feel comfortable with any kind of SM play. I think SM play reinforces male-constructed notions about sex, power relations, domination, and control. Am I sick?

        Conflicted in Duluth

Dear Conflicted,

    Anything goes in fantasies. The fact that it goes against your political instincts, your mores, or whatever you wanna call it, is probably why it works for you. Don't police your own fantasies, for god's sake. The only problem I have with your fantasies is the way you mimic Martina. I think her English is a little bit better than that.

Dear Sports Slut,

    I am tried of being called a dumb jock, in fact, I'm tired of the whole myth of the dumb jock. I'm not dumb. Really. I am not dumb. I mean it. And I've got a lot to say.

        Not Dumb in Oregon

Dear Not Dumb,

    Thank you for sharing.

Dear Sports Slut,

    What is a good breakfast on the morning of a major tournament? I play rugby and occasionally we play in these all-day tournaments, and I never know what to eat on a day that I anticipate extreme physical exertion.

        tournament girl

Dear Tournament Girl,

    This column is devoted to serious inquiry from our Girljock readers relating to either sports or sex. We do not want to take up space with irrelevant, silly questions. Save your blathering whininess for somebody else.

Dear Sports Slut,

I am an office girljock surrounded on all sides by avowed homosexuals. They are nice and everything and I'm itching to tell them about my problem. Should I tell them that my girlfriend and I broke up since I am not a lesbian and she is?

Clueless with Chlamydia

Dear Clueless,

Well, you've raised a couple of issues with this question, 'mydia. First of all, yes, you should tell them that you broke up, as Sports Slut is a strong proponent of self-disclosure. People tend to give self-disclosing a bad rap, but I find that self-disclosure is an important means of gaining insight. We can only find ourselves by exposing ourselves. Talk to as many people as often as you can about yourself and your personal problems. You may even discover new problems this way. Secondly, let's dispel a little myth. I am glad that you are able to recognize that just because you have a girlfriend doesn't mean you are a lesbian. Why do people rush to categorize? Just because you're a woman who never sleeps with men and who licks another woman's clitoris on a regular basis doesn't mean you're a lesbian. Of course you're not a lesbian and it's fine your ex-girlfriend is.

Dear Sports Slut,

I am a junior in high school and I want to join the swim team. My only fear is that, you know, like every month I get my friend and I've always heard

that you can't swim when you've got this condition. Is this true, Sports Slut?

Testing the Water in Minneapolis

Dear Testing,

Not to worry. Sports Slut is an avid swimmer and she bleeds once a month too. Just do what I do during a heavy flow: I put in one tampon and then I duct tape my lips closed. Over that I put on a pair of Depends, a box of which you can find in any grocery or pharmacy. Then, over that, I find a black girdle in case there is any leakage and slip into that. Then, voilà, I put on my swimsuit and I'm ready to go!! No fuss!!

Dear Sports Slut,

I am starting a woman's boxing league. Now I just saw that movie Rocky, *and Burgess Meredith's character told Rocky that women are bad for the legs. Now I've got a girlfriend and I'm worried that this might be true. What's the deal, Sports Slut?*

Down for the C(o)unt

Dear Down,

It is actually true that women are bad for the legs. Lesbians are bad for the ankles down. Bisexual women are bad for the knees down. And straight women are actually bad for the femur. Blondes are bad for various muscle groups, such as the quads and the hamstrings. And brunettes are bad for the kneecaps. And finally, redheads are hell on the tibia. If you can avoid women while training, that would be best.

Dear Sports Slut,

I'm a thirty-eight-year-old woman and no one has taught me how to kiss. I'm a committed jock and have been all my life, which has afforded me precious little time for amorous pursuits. When I'm not playing ball, I'm watching it on TV. But now, I've met the girl of my dreams and I'm afraid to be alone with her cause I know she is gonna want to kiss and make out. What should I do, Sports Slut?

Timid in Tallahassee

Dear Timid,

Not to worry. Kissing is overrated and dedicated girljocks don't have time to learn the finer points of sexual technique. The idea is to get down her pants as quickly as possible

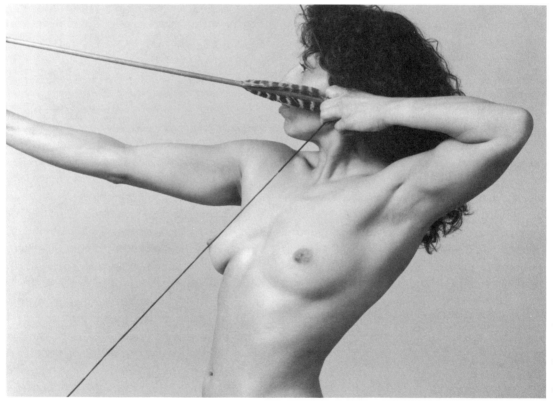

Photo © David Weisman

218

The Sauna

by Carol Queen

I caught her scent before I saw her. As soon as I stepped into the sauna I smelled the musk of her body rising into the hot air. When I drew my first long breath the cedar scent of the sauna mingled with her sweat and her sex to fill my lungs.

I spread my towel and lay down where I could look at her out of the corner of my eye. I'd never seen her at the gym before; never smelled anything like her either. She was long and muscled and looked powerful, lying motionless, one leg drawn up. Her eyes were closed, so I could look at her without being seen. While I took her in with my eyes and my breath I began to imagine my hands slipping across the sheen of sweat on her skin, imagined the salt of it on my tongue. I wanted to lie with my nose in the pit of her arm and drink her in. I wanted to lean across her and bury my nose between her thighs, right where the cleft of cunt and crack of ass come together, and root for her perfume like a pig for truffles.

The sear of hot cedared air, the scent of sex. A glisten of sweat began to form on *my* body; I began to smell my own paler scents. I wanted to run my hands across my breasts, my belly, between my cunt lips, freeing the moist smells there to compete with hers. In my mind I was having her, intoxicated and wild.

I was far too hot in every way to stay long in the sauna. Dizzily I sat up. As I felt my way out to the cool air I stole one last look behind me. She was looking at me with full-open, expressionless eyes.

In the shower I cranked the faucet, needing the rush of water to begin to bring my temperature down. I leaned on the cold pink tile, fighting the impulse to spring back from the chill, until the tile began to warm to my skin. The water licked like a cool tongue down my back, between my ass-cheeks; I spread wider to it and writhed, thinking of the woman in the sauna. A little moan escaped me, hidden from the hearing of others in the showers by the noise of the water. I wouldn't have cared if anyone *had* heard. I was far too hot to be cooled down by just the cool shower spray, and I wasn't thinking about propriety.

If the bus isn't crowded, I was thinking, I can start masturbating before I get home, coat over my lap, fingers slipping surreptitiously down into my unbuttoned jeans. I know I'll be at it all afternoon.

The shower curtain was yanked open so fast that I didn't realize my privacy was gone until I saw the heads of the other women in the locker room turn to look at me. A woman I didn't know had me by the arm and I had no time to shut the water off or even to protest— she was pulling me back toward the sauna!

I'd heard the Berkeley gym was a good

place to meet hot women, but I'd never imagined anything like *this*. She pulled the sauna door open, propelled me inside with a shove. "Here," she said, "I think you ought to get to know my friend." The door closed on me with a slam.

The woman and I were alone in the sauna and her musk scented the air even more strongly than before. This must be how animals in heat respond to each other, I thought—I could think of nothing but having her. Could it be that she had sent her friend out to bring me back? I was terrified.

"Don't worry," the woman said, looking at me now. "She'll watch the door. We'll be alone."

"That's not what I'm afraid of," I said, but she didn't wait for me to say anything more.

"Girl," she said, a command. "Get over here." Ordered to do exactly what I desired! An even stronger rush of feeling as I obeyed.

When I was near enough, she reached for me. I was off my balance for an instant, afraid I might fall but knowing she had me. I got my equilibrium back, kneeling on the cedar bench below the one she lay on, lost it again the instant our mouths came together in a long, hot soul kiss, my hand finally sliding across the sweat-slippery skin. I could feel my pulse in every near and far part of my body. She had me by the hair and did not let me up for a long time; when she did I saw that she had squeezed rivulets of water from my still-wet hair and they had pooled between her breasts and in the hollow of her throat. I bent down to lap up the water, finally taste the salt of her skin.

"You were watching me before, weren't you?" When I didn't answer instantly she gave my hair a sharp tug, pulling my face into her armpit where it had wanted to be all along. Such a tough thing. I drew in a deep, flavored breath, answered, "Yes, I was watching you; I couldn't help it, I was drunk on your smells."

I couldn't see her face but I heard the change in her voice. "You want me then?" She loosened her grip on my hair and I raised up from where I was nuzzling and sniffing to look into her eyes, glinting with desire at least as hot and pulsing as mine. Mesmerized, I could say only "Ohhhhh . . ." before falling into another kiss.

A wild kiss, and I bit and sucked at her full lips; she held my face too securely for me to pull away, and my cunt ached for her to push into me the way her tongue was parting my lips. I moaned into her. I wanted her to know she had me, that all my fear was gone, that there in the sex-and-cedar-scented sauna I would do what she said, be who she wanted.

She let me up. I bit her lip one last time. I began to lick the sweat off her torso. She moved into me when I began licking her breasts, her body telling me to bite, to suck; I began to tongue her belly and her breath escaped her in a long sigh. "Girl," she said, in a wholly different, voluptuous voice, "ohhh, girl." I moved over her then, straddling her, my face in her cunt and hers in mine, and I could feel her inhale me as I began, nose resting on her clit, to drink in the heady odors, wanting for a moment nothing but that. Her arms circled my back lightly. I could feel the power in them, wanted her to squeeze, pull me down onto her mouth, ease that ache.

But she was going to make me wait. Instead

I started to move my head from side to side, brushing my lips against the soft, tight kinks of her pubic hair, hot from the heat of the sauna. With each move of my head my nose tweaked her clit; she moaned and moved into me. I thought she was lost to the rhythm until I edged my body further down hers, ready to plunge my tongue into her cunt's recesses and found myself unable to do it, for she had hold of my hair again, wouldn't let my tongue down to its target, the wet folds of vulva, the musky nectar I could smell but not taste.

I squirmed against her, but her hold was too firm to break. "Wait, honey," she said. "You're going to have to wait." I could get no closer than her clit. But I could lap her scent if not her taste, and I closed my teeth around the swollen pearl, flicking my tongue against its hardness until I knew I had her rhythm again. Finally her fingertips began licking up and down the length of my vulva and it was all I could do as my orgasm reached its flashpoint to concentrate on hers; I rode her like a pony 'til it was done, her cries and sighs abating, marveling that she had not for an instant let go

of my hair, let my face come one bit closer to her cunt.

She pulled harder, in fact, as her fingers moved faster, arching me back, seeming as sure of when to let go and let my body take its own natural arc of orgasm as if she'd fucked me many times before. I clutched her for stability, riding wave upon wave, calling out in the secret language of climax, gasping for breath in the dry, super-heated air.

I made another move for her cunt and she had me by the hair again, quick as a flash. "What a pushy thing you are," she said, "so hungry for it you can't wait, can you?" I shook my head against her tug on my hair.

"Well, you're gonna have to. You're coming home with me, girl. We're gonna take our time." She pulled me up to my knees, let go my hair, sat up herself so her arms circled me from behind. "We're not done, honey; we've hardly started."

She led me out of the sauna, past her grinning friend. Captured, and even outside I could smell nothing but hot cedar and her scent on the air.

From the Sidelines #2

by Robbi Sommers

Sure, I go to the gym.

Ace works Thursday evenings at the Gym. She trains the novices. Yeah, me, I'm a beginner—looking for a sweaty workout. I sign up at Ace's desk for my first "consultation." My hot pink spandex outfit clings to my full womanly curves and I can see a glimmer of approval in Ace's eyes. Sure . . . we all wear spandex for maximum workout ease. Yeah, right.

Thinking of workout ease, I strut to the barbells. Ace, most probably thinking how easy of a workout I'll be, is there in less than a spandex-snap second.

"So, how much experience you got?" she says, her voice sultry as the summer night.

What do you say when a rock-hard butch asks a question like that? I glance at her bulging biceps, her thick thighs, her firm hands. Plenty, baby.

"Not much," I answer coyly.

She looks me up and down. "You looking to tighten up or build?"

I focus on her bodybuilding fingers and murmur, "I guess I want to be tight."

"Gettin' women tight, that's my specialty," Ace says, attitude seeping from every pore.

That's when I start wondering why I wasted so much time hanging around the baseball field the last month or so. When it comes to athletics, a smart sports enthusiast has to have her priorities straight.

"Got to warm you up first." Ace points to an exercycle. "Ten minutes."

I climb on the bike and start to pedal. Ace loses no time picking up a barbell and doing some reps. Standing before the full-length mirror, her muscles are firm, her stance steady, she looks good.

Beads of sweat tickle on my brow. One minute on the bike and I'm already sweating.

Ace tosses me a quick look. "You gettin' warm?"

"Yeah," I pant. I try to look nonchalant, like this goddamn bike is no big deal. Perspiration on my brand new outfit, son of a bitch.

"This is a leg press," Ace says as she straddles a machine bench.

She's face-up, legs bent in the air. From where I sit, I can almost see up her baggy gym shorts . . . and I thought spandex was the only way to go!

I'm drenched. Was this bike set on uphill, or what? I push harder on the pedals while Ace lies, legs up and out, across from me.

"Works the thighs," she grunts as she extends her legs.

My view up her shorts suddenly disappears. I lean forward and pedal faster, as if somehow, if I hurry, I'd get a better peek.

Ace's legs move back to their original, spread-eagled position. Me? I'm whirling on the bike, racing, wishing I could get closer.

Yeah, if I look at the right angle, I'll see up her shorts—those deliciously loose shorts.

My feet fly on the pedals. Ace's legs are spread again so wide, I can almost see everything she has to offer. Her nipples stand erect beneath her thin, white T-shirt. Her dark hair is plush under her panty-free gym shorts.

I make a sudden commitment to work out three, no four, no five times a week. Ace spreads her legs wider and I, leaning over the handlebars, ride to heaven. Oh shit, I can see everything. Faster, faster, I race alongside her.

C'mon, Ace. Keep them spread, Ace.

I grip the handle bars. I'll shoot through space if I let go.

Yeah, Ace. Yeah, Ace. Let me see it all.

I'm sliding back and forth on the thick bicycle seat. I'll work out everyday, two times a day, three times a day—just don't move your legs, Ace.

Out of nowhere a tiny bell rings. Ace climbs from the leg press and clicks off the exercycle timer.

"Good warm up, huh?" She runs her fingertip across the sweat on my face, and hands me a towel.

Yeah, I think I'm going to like getting pumped.

Resource List for Girljocks

by Roxxie

Here is *Girljock* magazine's basic list of organizations and resources so you can more easily navigate your way through the sporting universe. Or you can easily take off on the sports tangent of your choice. Bon voyage!

Center for Research on Girls and Women in Sports

Address:
College of Education
University of Minnesota
203 Cooke Hall
1900 University Ave. SE
Minneapolis, MN 55455
Phone: (612) 625-7327

Federation of the Gay Games

This is the group that has created and maintained the Gay Games (formerly called the Gay Olympics until the Olympic Committee sued the Gay Olympics and forced them to quit using the word Olympics even though lots of other organizations get to use the word), and oversees the continuation of the games from location to location. You can get on their e-mail news mailing list or sign up for their paper mailing list. They also provide links to information on the upcoming Gay Games.

Address:
Federation of the Gay Games
584 Castro Street, Suite 343
San Francisco, CA 94114, USA
Fax Phone: (415) 695-9222
Web: http://www.gaygames.org/

GAYSPORT. ORG

This is the index to an international collection of lesbian and gay sports information, the European Gay & Lesbian Sport Federation, the annual EuroGames (European Championships), and much more.

Web: http:/www.gaysport.org/
International lists of organizations and web pages.
Web: http:/www.gaysport.org/e-index.htm

GAYELLOW Pages

The GAYELLOW pages is an excellent guide to lesbian, gay, bixexual, and other friendly clubs and sports organizations all over the known universe.

Address:
Renaissance House
P.O. Box 533 Village Station
New York, NY 10014

Phone: (212) 674-0120

Web: http://badpuppy.com/gayellow

Girljock ONLINE

Here's some cool articles, a photo and graphics library, and a super bulletin board for Girljocks! Find new friends or teams or tournaments, help on your pitching, and more.

AOL: Just dial into AOL and use the keyword: Girljock

Web: cruise on into http://www.girljock.com

Go Girl! Magazine

An excellent women's online magazine that is a sports resource site with all kinds of useful training tips and reports in it.

Web: http://www.gogirlmag.com

Internet Metasearches

You would sidestep a big dogpile, were it on the sidewalk. But on the internet, dogpile is a metasearch engine and searches all the big search engines at once, so if you are going to look up lesbian jocks anywhere, anytime, any sport, this dogpile will help take you to the right parts of the web.

Web: http://www.dogpile.com

LGB Sports: Website and e-mail list

This website is Mark Mutrie and Lindsay Patten's excellent list of lesbian, gay, bisexual, and others sport organizations, resources, and sites on the net.

Web: http://www.kwic.net/lgb-sports

This site has evolved from Canadian Queer sportswriter Joe Clarke's e-mail list group where you can hear all the latest news and speculation on lesbian, gay, bisexual, and more . . . sports. To sign up for the mailing list:

To Subscribe: Send "subscribe lgb-sports" to majordomo@seta.fi

Contributions: Mail once only to lgb-sports@seta.fi.

To Unsubscribe: Send "unsubscribe lgb-sports" (no quotes) to majordomo@seta.fi.

Magazines we all wish would have more articles on Lesbian Issues in sports:

Condé Nast Sports for Women

Address:

Conde Nast Building

350 Madison Avenue

New York, NY 10017

Phone: (212) 880-8800

Women's Sports and Fitness

Only occasionally does *Women's Sports and Fitness* address lesbian issues.

Address:

Women's Sports & Fitness

P.O. Box 472

Mt. Morris, IL 61054 U.S.A.

Web:http://www.women.com/body/wsf/interview.html

Museum of Menstruation

If you need any information about that time of the month, this is the one and only Museum of Menstruation. I will admit that when first I received the e-mail post on the famous e-mail newsgroup called "sappho" from Sappho's administratrix Zonker, I had my doubts, but it is there, live in cyberspace, and there is a physical site as well. And the quote on the front page?

"It's fabulous that somebody out there is willing to . . . pull back the curtain."

—Mona Miller, Planned Parenthood Federation of America

Address:

Museum of Menstruation (MUM)

P.O. Box 2398 Landover Hills Branch

Hyattsville, MD 20784-2398 U.S.A.

Phone: (301) 459-4450

Fax (USA): (301) 577-2913

Web: http://www.mum.org

National Association for Girls and Women in Sports

A very cool women's sports organization.

"Since 1899, the National Association for Girls and Women in Sports has championed equal funding, quality, and respect for women's sports programs. Our efforts have lead to national championship programs in collegiate women's sports . . . and to the passage of Title IX legislation," the organization announces in its website.

Address:

National Association for Girls and Women in Sports

1900 Association Drive

Reston, VA 20191-1599

Phone: (703) 476-3452

Web: http://www.aahperd.org/nagws

E-mail: nagws@aahperd.org

National Council for Research on Women

Address:

530 Broadway, 10th Floor

New York, NY 10012

Phone: (212) 274-0730

Out for a Change: Addressing Homophobia in Women's Sports

This twenty-seven minute video is Dee Mosbacher's documentary on the negative effects of homophobia in women's sports, showing the problems lesbians in sports face and some excellent solutions, like bringing Pat Griffin's work to light. (Griffin is professor of the year at the University of Massachusetts—Amherst in the Social Justice Education program. She has developed and led workshops that educate sports teams to the symptoms and problems of homophobia.) The video includes interviews with both college athletes and administrators, and NCAA officers, as well as Martina Navratilova.

As Chris Evert says: "Homophobia is an important issue that affects all women athletes regardless of sexual orientation."

Address:

Woman Vision

3145 Geary Blvd. Box 421

San Francisco, CA 94118

Phone: (415) 346-2336

Fax: (415) 346-1047

The Queer Resources Directory

They have tons of links to lesbian and gay information sites, and you can do a search here using sports or whatever keyword you'd like.

"The QRD is an electronic research library specifically dedicated to sexual minorities—groups which have traditionally been labeled as 'queer' and systematically discriminated against."

Web: http://www.qrd.org

E-mail: ftpmail@qrd.org

More information: http://www.qrd.org/qrd/www/faq.html#What

SportsBridge: The Center for Girls and Women in Sports

SportsBridge, a nonprofit organization creates and provides free athletics programs and events, including an athletic mentorship program where grown women work with girls.

Address:

965 Mission Street, Suite 220

San Francisco, CA 94103

Phone: (415) 778-8390

Fax: (415) 778-8393

Title IX

The fabulous legislation that paved the way for increasing women's sports in educational institutions is located on the Web at http://www.mcs.net/~sluggers/titleix-page.html

(This site includes FAQ, text and regulations, and a study of the Brown University litigation.)

WISHPERD LIST: Women in Sports, Health, Physical Education, Recreation, and Dance

A very cool e-mail discussion list of great interest to girljocks. This list is very strong on academic issues. The WISHPERD web page is located at http:/www.sjsu.edu/faculty/christen/wishperd.html

To Subscribe: send the following e-mail note to listproc@listproc.sjsu.edu

SUBSCRIBE WISHPERD <yourfirstname> <yourlastname>

You will be asked to confirm your subscription request. If you fail to reply within 48 hours your request will lapse. You will receive confirmation and welcome messages.

Women's Sports Foundation

"The Women's Sports Foundation is a national member-based nonprofit educational organization that promotes the lifelong participation of all girls and women in sports and fitness. Established in 1974 by Billie Jean King, its founder; Donna de Varona, a founding member and its first president; and many other champion female athletes, the Foundation seeks to create an educated public that encourages females' participation and supports gender equality in sport. Join Us!"

Address:

Women's Sports Foundation

Eisenhower Park

East Meadow, NY 11554

Phone: (800) 227-3988 (9 A.M.–5 P.M.EST) or (516) 542-4700

E-mail: wosport@AOL.com

Web: http://www.lifetimetv.com/WoSport

AOL: Women's Sports Foundation does *Women's Sports World* on AOL.

Keyword: Women's Sports Foundation. Lots of great resources are listed here, plus educational materials.

Women's Sports Page by Amy Lewis

Incredible list of links to women's sports pages around the World Wide Web. More complete and detailed links to women's sports organizations all over the universe than in any other site I have ever found. Arranged by subject, including the big foundations and organizations and stuff. Great place to look up specific sport sites for women.

Web:http://fiat.gslis.utexas.edu/~lewisa/womsport.html

The Task Force on Women and Girls in Sports

(sponsored by the Feminist Majority Foundation)

They provide excellent resources including professional organizations plus publish print information. An excellent essay entitled "Barriers to Women in Athletics Careers" is live on the web at http://www.feminist.org/research/sports4.html

Address:

The Feminist Majority Foundation

1600 Wilson Boulevard

Suite 801

Arlington, Virginia 22209

Phone: (703) 522-2214

Web: http://www.feminist.org/research/sports2.html

Contributors

Alex Alexander: "Although my days of competitive bodybuilding are gone, I still lift weights regularly to keep in shape and do my job: I'm a firefighter—which I love. Plus, to play my favorite sports, soccer and softball, it never hurts to be strong! I can often be found clubbing (I totally love dancing!), eating out everywhere, or driving a fire engine. As we say in the fire biz, 'find 'em hot and leave 'em wet.'"

Chloe Atkins is a Bay Area photographer whose book *Girls' Night Out* will be published by St. Martin's Press in 1998. She is also featured in Susie Bright and Jill Posener's book *Nothing But the Girl*, and was in *The Official 1995 Drag King Calendar*.

Lucy Jane Bledsoe is the author of the novel *Working Parts* (Seal Press, 1997); *Sweat: Stories and a Novella* (Seal Press, 1995), a Lambda Literary Award Finalist; and of two novels for young people, *Tracks in the Snow* (Holiday House, 1997) and *The Big Bike Race* (Holiday House, 1995); a finalist for the Great Stone Face Children's Book Award as well as for the South Carolina Children's Book Award. Her stories have been published in *New York Newsday*, *Fiction International*, *WIG Magazine*, and in many anthologies.

Angela Bocage is the creator and editrix of *Real Girl*, "the sex comic for all genders and orientations by artists who are good in bed." She cartooned the AIDS epidemic for years in her strip "Sex, Religion, and Politics," with *Diseased Pariah News'* late editor, Michael Botkin. Just out of law school, she fights for tenants, community gardens, squatters, and other activists, and against police brutality in New York City, where she's an officer of the city chapter of the National Lawyer's Guild. Her works are also in *Lesbian Contradictions, Dyke Strippers, Weird Smut, Young Lust, Frighten the Horses, Slippery When Wet,* . . . you get the idea . . . and her Pirate comix appears in *The Shadow*.

The original suburban Tomboy Poet, **Nancy Boutilier** currently teaches high school English and coaches basketball in San Francisco. Her collection of poems and stories, *According to Her Contours* (Black Sparrow Press, 1992) was a Lambda Literary Award finalist.

Paisley Braddock is a Bay Area writer in hair transition.

Amy Cheney: "In High School, Femme Jock was the only girl on the boy's baseball team—for a week. Unfortunately, she attempted to catch a fly ball without a glove and ended up breaking her wrist. She then took up jogging—five miles a day in the morning, after her first cigarette of the pack of Marlboros she'd finish by 5:00 P.M. She found her true calling in the diving team as it allowed her to plumb the depths while scantily attired, being cheered on by other girls."

Phyllis Christopher watched as the brassiere fell like an avalanche off the two snowy mountains. The shutter clicked. The young nubile woman she was photographing moaned in involuntary ecstasy. It was another day in San Francisco for Phyllis Christopher, lesbian erotic photographer. You can find Phyllis's work in Susie Bright and Jill Posener's book: *Nothing But the Girl* (Freedoms Editions 1996) and *I Am My Lover* (Down There Press, 1997).

Rachel Corner just graduated from art school in Amsterdam. She is working as a newspaper reportage photo-journalist.

Diane DiMassa has no formal education in anything and does too many things at once. And on top of it, all she has to show for that is *Hothead Paisan, Homicidal Lesbian Terrorist.* She is currently living in Massachusetts, where she sits on Main Street rolling her eyes. Presently, she is illustrating Kate Bornstein's forthcoming *Gender Workbook*, and production on an animated Hothead short will follow.

Tara Eglin is a Northern California graphic designer and photographer.

While **Leisa Fearing**'s passions have turned from rugby jockdom to computer geekdom, she still enjoys an occasional tumble in the mud and participating in other girljock activities. Leisa now spends most of her time developing web applications for major corporations but continues to champion the cause of women's sports. Recently, her company, Elf Systems Corporation, developed one of the first women's pro basketball websites for her local team, the San Jose Lasers.

Heather Findlay is the editor-in-chief of *Girlfriends* magazine. Her work has been widely published in the gay popular and academic press. Her latest book-length publication is *A Movement of Eros: 20 Years of Lesbian Erotica* (Kasak) 1996.

Stacey Foss: "Working with *Girljock* for the past five years as a contributing writer and assistant editor I have been lucky to come into contact with some amazing writers, athletes, and artists. After taking a break from working on magazines and newspapers to write a futuristic, erotic novel (my first novel . . . you novel writers can empathize with my suffering), I am looking forward to writing short stuff, poetry, etc. Now with the book in the final editing process, I will soon be free to do other publishing projects. Other interests beyond publishing include surfing and

dancing. I have recently been certified in Shiatsu Massage and am looking for victims."

Leanne Franson is a completely nonjudgmental bi-girl cartoonist and illustrator who lives with her cat, St. Bernard dog, and hopefully soon, a baby, in Montreal. She has published over thirty comic zines and one book: *Assume Nothing* [1997]. All available at PO Box 274, Succ. Place Du Parc, Montreal, Quebec, CANADA H2W 2N8.

Mimi-Freed was a terrible girljock, but she loves her smelly sisters and agrees that sweat can be considered a marinade.

Nigel French is the head design divinity and consultant for *Girljock* magazine. He owns the San Francisco company Small World Productions, and is the author of *The Pagemaker for Windows Bible.*

Alison Gallant's writing career high point came at age 8, when she learned to print her name unassisted. It's been an uphill struggle ever since. Ms. Gallant is no longer as enamored of Ultimate Frisbee as she once was, as she recently sacrificed a ligament to the sport. Ms. Gallant currently resides in Los Angeles, where she is doing everything she can to contribute to the decline of Western Civilization. She was last seen working on a sitcom, "The Naked Truth," on NBC. She is currently working on a screenplay.

Joan Hilty is a cartoonist and illustrator living in New York. Her work has appeared in the *Village Voice, Gay Comix, Real Girl, OH, Girljock,* and *The Advocate,* to name a few. She pays her rent editing mainstream comics, and has had a pleasantly checkered career as a crew, soccer, and volleyball girljock.

Romy Kozak is currently completing a Ph.D. dissertation in the Modern Thought and Literature program at Stanford University, writing on intersections between music, sexuality, and nineteenth- and twentieth-century

American fiction. She lives in San Francisco and is an active soccer player and state-level referee. She would like to thank Nancy Peck for her letter, published in Girljock 15, offering the information that the concept of the jogbra was originally developed by Hilda Schreiber-Miller and Lisa Lindahl in Burlington, Vermont, and subsequently sold to Champion.

Anna Livia is the author of four novels and two collections of short stories including *Minimax* and *Incidents Involving Mirth*. She has articles and stories in over a hundred publications. Currently she has a day job as professor of French Linguistics at the University of Illinois. "A Dildo is Only as Good …" is the opening chapter of her novel *Slippery When Wet*.

Marguerite Lutton is a Bay Area designer.

Evelyn McDonnell is co-author of *The Official History of the Musical Rant* and is co-editor of the anthology *Rock She Wrote: Women Write About Rock, Punk, and Rap*. She writes for a gang of publications and lives in New York.

Sara Miles lives in San Francisco. She is a contributing writer for *Out* magazine, and writes for other magazines including *HotWired, The New Yorker, and Focus*.

Laura Miller is a senior editor at the Internet magazine *Salon* (www.salonmagazine.com).

Ming Nagel: "I am currently in a transitional state but still writing, still traveling, and still playing rugby."

Helen Privett won gold medals in women's volleyball at the Gay Games in 1990 and 1994. A former rock 'n' roller who celebrated the birth of punk rock during her high school days in London, Helen is an avid traveler, women's sports fan, and high tech guru.

Carol Queen's erotic fiction has appeared in many anthologies, including *Best American Erotica 1993 &*

1994, Best Gay Erotica 1996 & Best Lesbian Erotica 1997. She is the author of *Real Live Nude Girl: Chronicles of Sex & Culture* (Cleis Press), *Exhibitionism for the Shy* (Down There Press), and is co-editor of *Switch Hitters; Lesbians Write Gay Male Erotica And Gay Men Write Lesbian Erotica* (Cleis), *Pomosexuals* and *Against Essentialist Ideas About Gender & Sexual Orientation* (Cleis; both co-edited with Lawrence Schimel), and *Sex Spoken Here: Tales From The Good Vibrations Erotic Reading Circle* (Down There Press, co-edited with Jack Davis).

Trina Robbins is the paperdoll and thrift shop queen of San Francisco. She has too many cats, and she never learned to put things away. She is also a cartoonist and an author.

Susan Fox Rogers has edited a lot of anthologies, but her first was *Sportsdykes: Stories from On and Off the Field* [St. Martin's Press]. She is working toward her MFA at the University of Arizona in Tucson.

Stephanie Rosenbaum is a freelance journalist whose work has been published in numerous Bay Area and national publications. Her fiction can be found in *Beyond Definition, Virgin Territory, Tangled Sheets*, and *Pillow Talk*. She is currently working on a mystery novel and a cookbook. Although she is not a jock, she is proud to be a former *Girljock* cover girl, perhaps the only woman ever to grace the pages of *Girljock* wearing high-heeled sneakers.

Your editor, **Roxxie**, is the founder and chief editrix of *Girljock* magazine. Although throughout her life she has been found on many of the playing fields of our sporting nation, she readily admits that in writing she hits her stride. She still polishes her cardiovascular routines though. Roxxie also was a co-editor of *Dagger: On Butch Women*, along with Lily Burana and Linnea Due (Cleis Press).

Winifred Simon, superfan, published seventeen issues of *The Fans of Women's Sports* newsletter from

1992–1996. She still collects sports information, memorabilia, and memories.

Robbi Sommers is the best-selling author of *Pleasures, Players, Uncertain Companions, Kiss and Tell, Behind Closed Doors, Personal Ads, Getting There,* and her most recent book, *In The Mood*—all published by Naiad Press. Her work, both fiction and nonfiction has appeared in many anthologies and magazines including *Penthouse, Redbook,* and *Reader's Digest.*

Cherie Turner: "Raised in Santa Barbara, California, I attended UCSB and earned a B.A. in Religious Studies. During my late teens and early twenties I raced bicycles professionally throughout the U.S. and Canada. After retiring I picked up inline skating and was a member of the first ever all-women's relay skate from San Francisco to San Diego (650 Miles). Subjects of writing I focus on are women in sports and women's issues."

Sharon Urquhart lives in Sonoma County, California. She is the author of *Mock Rock: A Guide to Indoor Climbing* and *Placing Elvis: A Tour Guide to the Kingdom.*

Dafna Van Delft: "My sports are wrestling, kick-boxing, and partner-acrobatics. I work in a bike shop and I love my cat."

Monique Vanhyfte lives in Amsterdam. She went to photography college in The Hague and Utrecht, did various apprenticeships, and worked for a photo-agency and press office. Currently, she is working freelance and doing computer image manipulation.

Maria Vetrano is one of the founding members of the Boston Beehives, a women's ice hockey team. When not dreaming of becoming a cabaret singer, she plays sports and spends quality time with her partner Helen and two cats.

David Weisman:"Rocky Romero taught me to genuflect when I was ten, so we could rob the poor box. Of course,

I had my Bar Mitzvah at age thirteen. And at seventeen, while 'exercising the Pentagon' in Washington, I got stoned the first time. Nowadays I rock climb, ski, photograph, and design in the San Francisco Bay Area."

Jackie Weltman: "Believe it or not, my primary writing expresses itself in poetry and nonfiction. You can find my work in journals of experimental and women's poetry: *Six, Exposures, Luk, Texture, Rooms* . . . For almost a decade, San Francisco has given me a lot of material to satirize; now you'll find me in the East coast studying theology at Harvard. After that I have no idea where I'll be. Maybe I'll see you there?"

Pollyanna Whittier is a Bay Area photographer and frequent *Girljock* contributor.

Chela Zabin was born in Chicago, where she spent as many days as possible neck-deep in Lake Michigan. Later, she got a clue and moved to California, where she learned to surf and scuba dive. Formerly a girl reporter, she used to fill her cravings by leaving for "interviews" when the surf was good, or even when it wasn't. She is now attempting to legitimize her ocean addiction by working on a doctorate in waveology at Surf City University. She lives with her longboard companion, a cat, two boats and eight surfboards.

Richard Zoller is a Northern California photographer.

Permissions

All Dinah Shore Golf Action, © Roxxie, first appeared in the *Village Voice,* 1993, and a revised version of that appeared in *Girljock #10, The Can't Take My Eyes Off of You Issue,* Fall 1993. *Tara Vanderveers's All-Female Basketball Fantasy Camp,* © Roxxie, article originally appeared in the *San Francisco Bay Guardian,* and a revised version was published in *Girljock #10, The Can't Take My Eyes Off of You Issue,* Fall 1993. *Baseball's New Open Season for Women,* © Roxxie, originally appeared in *LA Weekly,* and a revised version was published in *Girljock #12,* Spring 1994. *Long-Haired Lesbians,* © Roxxie, was first published in *Girljock #4, The Long-Haired Lesbians Issue,* Summer 1991. *The Big-Monster Cycles of Life and Georgette's Confession,* © Roxxie, originally appeared in *Girljock #13,* Fall 1994. *Notes for the Newly Single,* © Roxxie, originally appeared in *Girljock #14,* Summer 1995. *Susie Bright on Girljocks* © Roxxie, originally appeared in *Girljock #5,* Fall 1991. *Bodybuilding's Secret Workout* © Roxxie, originally appeared in *Girljock #6, The Flowers and Showers Issue,* Spring 1992. *To the Beach and Back* © Roxxie, originally appeared in *Girljock #8, The Gettin' Kinda Chilly Issue,* Winter 1992. *Bees on Ice* © Roxxie, first appeared in *Girljock #8, The Gettin' Kinda Chilly Issue,* Winter 1992. All reprinted with permission of the author.

Am I Stuck-Up? The Test, How to Be Friendly, and *Nike's "W" Soccer League,* © Roxxie and *Girljock* magazine, first published in *Girljock* 15, 1997.

The Cunnilympics: What Sport Means to Me and How I Won My Gold Medal, © Diane DiMassa, first published in *Girljock #7,* Late Summer Issue 1992. Reprinted with the author's permission.

A Dildo's Only as Good as the Woman You Use It With, © Anna Livia writing as Jiffy Lube, first published in *Girljock #14,* Summer 1995. Reprinted with permission of the author.

Everything You Always Wanted to Know About Trading Cards, © Winifred Simon, first published in Fans of Women's Sports, and published in *Girljock #14,* Summer 1995. Reprinted with permission of the author.

Femme Jock Corner © Amy Cheney, first published in various issues of *Girljock* since issue number two, 1991.

From the Sidelines #1 and *From the Sidelines #2,* © Robbi Sommers, first published in *Girljock #9, The Thaw Out Now Issue,* Late Spring 1993. Reprinted with permission of the author.

Gay Gaming, © Nancy Boutilier, first published in *Girljock #13,*

The Jogbra Nation Issue, Fall 1994. *How Girljock Are You?* and *Take Back Tonight,* both © Nancy Boutilier, first published in *Girljock #10, The Can't Take My Eyes Off of You Issue,* Fall 1993. All reprinted with permission of the author. Nancy's photographs also appear with her permission.

Girl Sloth, © Laura Miller, first published in *Girljock #6, The Flowers and Showers Issue,* Spring 1992. *Looking for Ms. Goodbar,* © Laura Miller, first published in *Girljock #10, The Can't Take My Eyes Off of You Issue,* Fall 1993. *All Workout Video Action* © Laura Miller, part one, first published in *Girljock #8, The Gettin' Kinda Chilly Issue,* Winter 1992, and part two first published in *Girljock #9, The Thaw Out Now Issue,* Late Spring 1993. All reprinted with the author's permission.

Girljock Paper Dolls, © Trina Robbins, first published in *Girljock #14,* Summer 1995. Reprinted with permission of the creator.

The Grudge Match, © Joan Hilty, originally published in *Girljock #6, The Flowers and Showers Issue,* Spring 1992. *Zlata Holčička,* © Joan Hilty, first published in *Girljock #14,* Summer 1995. *Grand Island Assist,* © Joan Hilty, first published in *Girljock #10, The Can't Take My Eyes Off of You Issue,* Fall 1993. *Girljock Eats Food,* © Joan Hilty, first published in *Girljock #2,* Winter 1990. *First and Worst,* © Joan Hilty, first published in *Girljock #3,* Spring 1990. *The Mag that Made a Jock Out of Mackie! (AD),* © Joan Hilty, first published in *Girljock #11, The Anti-Freeze Issue,* Winter 1994. All reprinted with the author's permission.

Handbuilt Custom Bikes: A Joy to Put Between Your Leg, © Sharon Urquhart, first published in *Girljock #12,* Spring 1994. *Hot Rock Babes Scale Largest Plastic Peak in North America!,* © Sharon Urquhart, first published in *Girljock #11, The Anti-Freeze Issue,* Winter 1993. All reprinted with the author's permission.

How to Pick Up a Cyclist, © Lucy Jane Bledsoe, first published in *Girljock #8, The Gettin' Kinda Chilly Issue,* Winter 1992. Reprinted with the author's permission.

In Search of the Rugby Goddess © Maria Vetrano first published in *Girljock #12,* Spring 1994. *Women Swimmin'* © Maria Vetrano first published in *Girljock #15,* Summer 1995. *The Queens of the Court,* © Maria Vetrano originally published in *Girljock #11, The Anti-Freeze Issue,* Winter 1993. All reprinted with the author's permission.

Is Writing a Sport?, © Sara Miles writing as Laz-Y-Girl, first published in *Girljock #7,* Late Summer Issue 1992. Reprinted with the author's permission.

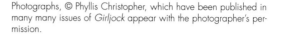
The Joy of In-line Skating, © Cherie Turner, 1996, first print publication, *Girljock* #16, the sweet sixteenth issue, 1998. Published with the author's permission.

Learning to Brace Yourself Against the Tackles and the Non-believers: © Ming Nagel, first published in *Girljock* #14, Summer 1995. Reprinted with the author's permission.

Love, Ace, Match, © Heather Findlay, originally published in the Jan/Feb 1995 issue of *Girlfriends* magazine. Reprinted with the author's permission.

Loving and Leaving Your Jogbras, © Stacey Foss, first published in *Girljock* #13, The Jogbra Nation Issue, Fall 1994. Reprinted with the author's permission.

Major Fun: Unrepentant Confessions of a Baton Twirler, © Angela Bocage, first published in *Girljock* #5, The Freezin' Season Issue, Fall 1991. Reprinted with the author's permission.

Memories of a Grade-School Girl Jock, © Leanne Franson, first published in *Girljock* #11, The Anti-Freeze Issue, Winter 1993. Reprinted with the author's permission.

Mimi Meets Martina, © Mimi-Freed, first published in *Girljock* #10, The Can't Take My Eyes Off of You Issue, Fall 1993. Reprinted with the author's permission.

Nation of Jogbras, © Romy Kozak, first published in *Girljock* #13, The Jogbra Nation Issue, Fall 1994. Reprinted with the author's permission.

No Fear of Flying, © Evelyn McDonnell, was originally published in the *Village Voice,* 1993, and reprinted in *Girljock* #10, The Can't Take My Eyes Off of You Issue, Fall 1993. Reprinted with the author's permission.

Photographs, © Chloe Atkins, first published in *Girljock* #9, The Thaw Out Now Issue, Late Spring 1993. Reprinted with the photographer's permission.

Photograph © David Weisman, first published in *Girljock* #9, The Thaw Out Now Issue, Late Spring 1993. Reprinted with the photographer's permission.

Photographs from the Alex Alexander Archives, first published in *Girljock* #6, The Flowers and Showers Issue, Spring 1992. Reprinted with the owner's permission.

Photographs, © Helen Privett were originally published in *Girljock* #11. Reprinted with the photographer's permission.

Photographs © Leisa Fearing, published in various issues of *Girljock* magazine, reprinted with permission from the photographer.

Photographs, © Marguerite Lutton, first published in *Girljock* #7, Late Summer Issue 1992. Reprinted with the photographer's permission.

Photographs, © Phyllis Christopher, which have been published in many many issues of *Girljock* appear with the photographer's permission.

Photographs by Pollyanna Whittier, published in many of the issues of *Girljock* magazine, reprinted with P. Whittier's permission.

Photographs © Rachel Corner, first published in *Girljock* #14, 1996. Reprinted with the photographer's permission.

Photographs © Richard Zoller, first published in *Girljock* #8, The Gettin' Kinda Chilly Issue, Winter 1992. Reprinted with the photographer's permission.

Photographs © Tara Eglin, first published in *Girljock* #4, The Long-Haired Lesbians issue, reprinted with the photographer's permission.

Putting on the Gloves, © Stephanie Rosenbaum, first published in *Girljock* #13, The Jogbra Nation Issue, Fall 1994, a revised edition of an earlier article in the Bay Area Reporter, 1993. Reprinted with the author's permission.

The Sauna, © Carol Queen, first published in *Girljock* #7, Late Summer Issue 1992. Reprinted with the author's permission.

Search and Destroy, © Dafna Van Delft, first published in *Girljock's* Sweet Sixteenth Issue, 1998

Shaved Glory, © Paisley Braddock, first published in *Girljock* #9, The Thaw Out Now Issue, Late Spring 1993. Reprinted with the author's permission.

Sunde White, Skateboarder, © Pollyanna Whittier, was published with the author's permission. Photographs printed with P. Whittier's permission as well.

Taking My Girlfriend Rockclimbing, © Susan Fox Rogers, first published in *Girljock* #11, The Anti-Freeze Issue, Winter 1993. Reprinted with the author's permission.

True Transgressive Romances, No. 25, © Jackie Weltman, first published in *Girljock* #7, Late Summer Issue 1992. *The Top 13 Most Unlikely Matchbook Covers,* first published in *Girljock* #13, The Jogbra Nation Issue, Fall 1994. All reprinted with the author's permission.

Ultimate Thrills, © Alison Gallant, first published in *Girljock* #12 Spring 1994, and *Dear Sports Slut,* © Alison Gallant, first published in *Girljock* #13, Fall 1994, and #14, Summer 1995. All reprinted with the author's permission.

Wave Obsession & Surfgirl Revelations, © Chela Zabin, was first published in *Girljock* #8, The Gettin' Kinda Chilly Issue, Winter 1992. Reprinted with the author's permission.

Wrestling New York, © Marianne Ijnsen and Dafna Van Delft, first published in *Girljock* #14, Summer 1995. Reprinted with the author's permission.

Essential
Girljock Stuff

t Girljock

to The Gay Games or Not To
e Myth of "Dumb Jocks" finally
ned, and lots more in the classic
sue.
sized for only $5.00

ond Girljock

ck's Answerwoman Femme Jock
rs for the first time in the
, award-winning second issue
jock. Bandanna color confusion,
ovick cartoons, and more!
sized for only $5.00

rd Girljock

ll musings, the Gay Games at
, Sunah Cherwin dishes night
ptain Condom becomes female,
ilty's unforgettable "First &
Girlfriend" Comic, and more!
sized for only $5.00

rth Girljock

rst large Girljock is devoted to the
and tribulations of the modern
ck. Long-haired lesbians speak, a
's true confessions, Femme Jock
eady to shave her .... and more
s to keep you up all night.
c Limited Edition Big Girljock:

h Girljock

Bright reveals the real reasons
he left *ON OUR BACKS*
zine. Angela Bocage on Baton

Twirling, Jackie Weltman's
"True Transgressive
Romance," Kris Kovick's
unforgettable golfing story,
and the "Age Police" attack
Roxxie. And more funny stuff.
**Classic Limited Edition Girljock
Five: $6.00**

Girljock Six

Bodybuilding secrets of Alex
Alexander, Festival of the Babes
report by Nancy Boutilier,
Alaskan Women's ice hockey, more
Joan Hilty Cartoons, Laura Miller's
great "Girl Sloth" article and others.
Classic Limited Edition Girljock Six: $6.00

Girljock Seven

Madonna's Batting Report and more
from *A League of their Own*. Martina
Navratilova's ex-lover Nancy Lieberman
Cline makes startling confessions,
Robbi Sommers gets steamy, Carol
Queen's unforgettable SAUNA is a true
roast, Diane Dimassa tells how she won
gold and more wild and funny stuff.
Classic Limited Edition Girljock Seven: $6.00

Girljock Eight

Surfing tell-all! And lots more than
wave catching: Joan Hilty's Olympic
Musings, pickup game advice, the real
scoop on exercise videos, and a new
view of Slam Dancing by Terry Sapp,
and more stuff in this classic spashy

surfin' Girljock.
Classic Limited Edition Girljock Eight: $6.00

Girljock Nine

Ice Hockey Revolution! We talk to
Maria Vetrano and the Boston
Beehives about their passion for the
ice, the need for a "jill strap" and more.
Girljock Astrology, Manon Rheaume's
Hockey Card, workout videos and
wintry cartoons by Julie Franki.
Classic Limited Edition Girljock Nine: $6.00

Girljock Ten

Jam packed super-Girljock: Cirque du
Soleil's Trapeze Twins, Amy Wallace's
Behind the Golden Door, Tara
Vanderveer's Fantasy Camp, Advice
from Nancy Boutilier for softball wives,
Laura Miller rates energy bars, and
Roxxie scoops the Golf and the Scene at

the Dinah Shore Palm Springs LPGA Tournament.
Classic LImited Edition Girljock Ten: $6.00

Girljock Eleven

Rock Climbing Special – we interview climber Diane Russell, Susan Fox Rogers takes her girlfriend outdoor climbing, Sharon Urquhart writes on indoor climbing, Maria Vetrano checks out Women's Pro Beach Volleyball, incredible Joan Hilty cartoons, and more!
Classic Girljock Eleven: $6.00

Girljock Twelve

Roxxie tries out for the Silver Bullets, Maria Vetrano goes out for Beantown's Rugby team, Leanne Franson's "Confessions of a Rugby Wife" and more fun!
Classic Girljock Twelve: $6.00

Girljock Thirteen

The Jogbra Nation Issue: Romy Kozak explores Jogbras! Barbie's little sister Stacy goes out for Sports (really she does!), Nancy Boutilier writes about the Gay Games and Mariah Burton Nelson's new book, World Rugby, and more!
Classic LImited Edition Girljock Thirteen: $6.00

Girljock Fourteen

Ace cartoonist Trina Robbins designed Girljock paper dolls for this issue. Winifred Simon writes about women's sports cards, Mariah Burton Nelson's article on the theoretical Tampax Tour, Notes for the Newly Single, New Zealand women's rugby, Women wrestling at the New York Gay Games, and a special story about going to a sex toy store, from Anna Livia writing as Jiffy Lube. More goodies in this collecter's special.
Classic LImited Edition Girljock Fourteen: $6.00

Girljock Fifteen

Tracey Ullman is the cover girl and we rock with her as she takes on the LPGA. Cures for sports burnout, Pickup Lines and Anti-Pickup Lines, Am I stuck up: the test, How to be friendly, Solo Backpacking, Women's Marathon Swimming, and a report on the Nike women's soccer league. Plus lots more in this almost sold-out beauty of an issue of Girljock. *"This was your best issue of Girljock yet,"* said girljock supporter Zane Tlapek.
Classic LImited Edition Girljock Fifteen: $6.00

Girljock's Sweet Sixteen

A groundbreaking look at kickboxing: an in-depth feature interview with kickboxer Michelle A'Boro. Advice for softball players and for beginning inline skaters, plus many more cool articles on team behavior and other women's sporting dilemmas. A peek into the territory of Mind Games by Rachel Coulombe. The insert magazine is Snax, and is all about our love/ mixed feelings about food. Special Snax stories by Mikel Wadewitz, Barbie Brennan, Nicole Franz, Roxxie and more!
Classic LImited Edition Girljock Sixteen: $6.00

Are you Girljock Enough?

*Get the
Girljock T-shirt,
a classic
just like you*